AF531602

Rural Women

Maternal, Child Health and Family Planning Services

By

K. P. Neeraja
Principal
Navodaya College of Nursing
RAICHUR
(Karnataka)

DISCOVERY PUBLISHING HOUSE
NEW DELHI-110002

ISBN: 978-81-7141-626-4

Rural Women

Maternal, Child Health and Family Planning Services

Published by:
DISCOVERY PUBLISHING HOUSE PVT. LTD.
4383/4B, Ansari Road, Darya Ganj
New Delhi-110 002 (India)
Phone: +91-11-23279245, 43596064-65
Fax: +91-11-23253475
E-mail: discoverypublishinghouse@gmail.com
sales@discoverypublishinggroup.com
web: www.discoverypublishinggroup.com

Printed at:
Infinity Imaging Systems
Delhi

Contents

Contents

Preface

The global concern about the health of the women and children of the developing countries have drawn greater attention during the recent past. The Cairo international conference on 'Population and Development (1994)' formalized a growing international consensus for improving reproductive health, including family planning for human welfare and development.

In India, promotion of reproductive and child health has been considered as one of the most important objectives of the Family Welfare programmes. However, the Government of India took steps to strengthen maternal and child health services as early as the first and second five year plans. During the fifth five year plan as part of the minimum needs programme maternal health, child health and nutrition services were integrated with family planning services. In 1992-93, the child survival and safe motherhood programme continueded the process of integration by bringing together several key child survival intervention with safe motherhood and child health services were incorporated into the reproductive and child health programme. The new programme seeks to integrate maternal health, child health and fertility regulation interventions with reproductive health programmes for both women and children.

In rural areas, the government delivers reproductive and other health services through its network of Primary Health Centres (PHC's) sub-centres and other government and health facilities. In addition, pregnant women and children can obtain services from private maternity homes, hospitals, private practitioners and in some cases, non-governmental organizations.

The National Population Policy adopted by the Government of India in 2000 reiterate the governments commitment to the safe motherhood programmes within wider content of reproductive health. Moreover empowering women for improved health and nutrition is another strategic themes identified in the policy.

Although the preceding progressive health service goals to mother and children are laudable at the implementation level. In peripheral areas, these programme could not succeeded to the expectation of both the Central and State Governments. For instance the extent of utilization of PHC service for all the programmes did not cross the single digit level in several states in Central and northern region of India. Nevertheless and overwhelming proportion of mothers used to utilize such services in an exceptional state like Kerala. No doubt in other South Indian States and Western Indian States reported moderate level of utilization.

However micro level information of such utilization of MCH services across different regions and within the State are very negligible. Under these consideration the present study is a welcome one and very timely too.

The main focus of this research stems out of the prevailing inadequate utilization of health services among the rural women of Andhra Pradesh. Since maternal and child health services are provided as a package to women/clients. There are several factors that individually affect the utilization also. Incidentally the maternal and child health services are not uniformly progressed in several districts of this state. Since district wise variations are there in development, such differential development *per se* also may contribute to differential utilization of services. This assumption forms a major focus of the present study. Very rightly the present study was carried out in two contrasting developed districts from two regions of Andhra Pradesh Viz; Mahaboobnagar district from Telangana region and Kurnool district from Rayalaseema region.

As expected significant region-wise differentials in utilization of MCH services were observed between these districts. For instance, while 55 per cent of respondents as a whole utilized antenatal services, however in Kurnool district better level of utilization was seen (60%) as against Mahaboobnagar district (49%). The over all findings of the study revealed that women belong to higher socio-economic status and had better interpersonal communication would tend to utilize the maternal, child health and Family Planning services to a large extent. Type of services extended by Multi-purpose Health Assistant (M.P.H.A.) Female is emerged as one of the major variables which has shown as significant influence on the Family Planning adoption.

The study concludes with the following recommendations:

1. Efficient administration and monitoring and evaluation system may generate the necessary momentum for successful implementation of safe motherhood programme at grass root level and to improve the qualitative services;

2. Intensive efforts particularly through personal contacts by the health providers has to be strengthened to modify the behaviour of mothers;

3. Stay of multipurpose health assistants (f) at the sub-centres may ensume better services of antenatal checkup, immunization, treatment of common ailments etc. This will also increase the credibility of multipurpose health assistants, as well as to promote greater utilization of services.

K. P. NEERAJA

whole utilized antenatal services, however in Kurnool district better level of utilization was seen (61%) as against Mahaboobnagar district (49%). The over all findings of the study revealed that women belong to higher socio-economic status and had better interpersonal communication would tend to utilize the maternal, child health and Family Planning services to a large extent. Type of services rendered by Multi-purpose Health Assistant (M.P.H.A.) Female is emerged as one of the major variables which has shown a significant influence on the Family Planning adoption.

The study concludes with the following recommendations:

1. Efficient administration and monitoring and evaluation system may generate the necessary momentum for successful implementation of safe motherhood programme at grass root level, and to improve the qualitative services.

2. Intensive efforts particularly through personal contacts by the health providers has to be strengthened to modify the behaviour of mothers.

3. Stay of multipurpose health assistant(f) at the sub-centres may ensure better services of antenatal checkup, immunisation, treatment of common ailments etc. This will also increase the credibility of multipurpose health assistants, as well as to promote greater utilization of services.

K.P. NEERAJA

Acknowledgements

It is my duty and pleasure to place on record my gratitude to all those who have helped me in completing this research work.

My deep sense of gratitude to Prof. K.A. Parvathy, Head of the Department of Women's Studies, for permitting me to enroll as a part time research scholar.

I am immensely thankful to Dr. R. Jayasree, Reader, Department of Women's Studies. Sri Padmavathi Mahila Viswavidyalayam, Tirupathi for guiding and encouraging me in completing the research work in time.

I am immensely indebted to my beloved teacher, Dr. K. Sreenivasa Reddy, Social Scientist, R.H.F.W.T.C., Kurnool for his austitute guidance, encouragement, inspirative force, motivation, unstinted support for completing this research work in a more enthusiastic way.

Many persons have directly or indirectly helped me to complete the study. It would be impossible to acknowledge them all individually. I express my sincere thanks to all of them.

K. P. NEERAJA

Chapter—1
Introduction

BACKGROUND OF THE STUDY

In India women in reproductive age (15-44 yeas) and children below 5 years of age comprise 62 per cent of the total population. They are the most vulnerable group in the society. Naturally they need better health care and attention. Hence the health services directed to the women and children are given priority by the Government of India.

There is an English proverb which states that, "the song of the mother to the baby at the cradle rings down to the body in the coffin". This aptly describes the extent to which the mental health of the child is dependent on its mother from womb to tomb. So, the health of children is largely dependent on that of the mother. Longevity of the newborn has a definite impact on the fertility of women and the size of the family. For better survival of the children, health and welfare of the mother through her reproductive period are essential components. Thus a large number of women and children in India demand greater care and attention in the matters of health.

Inspite of the wide spread infrastructural facilities and service interventions in the rural areas, the morbidity and mortality among the women and children continue to be a major cause of concern to the planning commissions. The focus seems to be the quality and level of utilisation of services which are linked to the knowledge and availability of these services to the target population. It is quite apt to quote an anecdote here:

A young Ethiopian girl was asked, "What do you want to be when you grow up?", "Alive", she replied (Benakappa, 1988). The situation in India is also the same. Although this country has achieved the highest technology, the achievements are not commensurate with them in the prevention of maternal and childhood morbidity and mortality. This clearly emphasises the need to develop a positive attitude towards health among the population, especially the rural poor.

The present health scenario in India depicts the enormous efforts made by its Government with the assistance of international agencies, in promoting the health of its population and in particular women and children. Various programme interventions in the form of maternal and child health services through the years, have come to stay, to protect the health of mother and child.

In the post independent period, the policy makers have taken care of the health of its population by incorporating the recommendations of Bhore Committee (1946) and Mudaliyar Committee (1959) into the five year plans.

The primary health care approach was adopted long back as a measure, for rural health care and its delivery system. Later on, India, being a signatory to the Alma-Ata Declaration (1978) has restructured and strengthened the primary health care delivery system. In fact the goals of "Health for all by the year 2000 A.D." Through the National Health Policy which was unanimously endorsed by the nation in 1983. The National Health Policy accords high priority to maternal and child health programmes. The health interventions are significant not only in preserving the health of the mother and children, but also the socio-cultural factors. These determine the judicious use of the services under health interventions. India is the first country to officially launch the Family Planning Programme in 1952. However the programme could make some strides during sixties after the clinic approach was replaced by extension approach. Upto 1976, the family limitation through male sterilization was more acceptable among the Indian couples. The emergency excesses during 1976 had a far reaching effect on family planning programme. Subsequently gender bias crept into the acceptance of family limitation. So family planning has come to stay as a female oriented programme of contraception. As a result, the women are subjected to hardships of contraception and family limitation, besides child bearing. This again underlines the need for enlightening and motivating the men for accepting contraception and vasectomy. The National Population Policy of 1976 which highlighted the need for raising the age at marriage and other interventions were revised in 1986. The emphasis was on two child norm without gender discrimination and interventions like oral rehydration therapy, care of the children in preventing and treating acute respiratory tract infections in order to ensure the survival of the newborn children. The Revised National Population Policy has defined a midterm goal of reaching a birth rate of 21 and infant mortality rate to below 60 by 2000 A.D. Further it has clearly indicated the long term goal of zero population growth by 2050 A.D. Thus the success of population policy lies on utilisation of maternal, child health services and Family Planning Services.

Since the enactment of National Health Policy in India, there has been a concerned effort to attain these goals of "Health for all by the year 2000 A.D." With the assistance of International agencies. Special campaigns and programmes are directed towards the health of mothers and children. The goals related to maternal and child health are:

- To reduce the net reproduction rate to one;
- To reduce maternal mortality to two;
- To reduce the infant mortality to sixty;
- To promote small family norm;
- To conduct 100 per cent deliveries by trained personnel;
- To increase the female literacy;
- To increase the demand for contraception to achieve a couple protection rate of 60 per cent;
- To enhance child survival through universal immunisation programme, oral rehydration programme, to control acute respiratory tract infections and to conduct the well baby clinics;

- To secure the maximum involvement of non-governmental agencies, voluntary organisations at national and international level.

These goals are obviously related to the greater utilisation of maternal and child health services. The enormous efforts made by Government of India, by launching various programme interventions, show its commitment to the health of mothers and children. These efforts have helped to improve the health of mothers and children. However the attainments are still far from the reach of the goals.

Various programmes launched by the Government of India, to benefit the health of the community, particularly mother and children include:

- Community Development Programme (1952);
- Family Planning Programme (1952);
- Sharada Act (1952);
- Applied Nutrition Programme (1961);
- Midday Meal Programme (1962) later revised as, School Health Programme;
- Iron and Folic Acid Supplementation Programme (1970);
- Vitamin 'A' Prophylaxis Programme (1970);
- Special Nutrition Programme (1970);
- Balwadi Nutrition Programme (1970).

Later on Special Nutrition Programme and Balwadi Nutrition Programme were merged into Integrated Child Development Services Scheme (1975).

- Medical Termination of Pregnancy Act (1971)
- Water Supply and Sanitation Programme (1972)
- Minimum Needs Programme (1974-78)
- Family Welfare Programme (1977)
- Rural Health Scheme (1977)

- Diarrhoeal Diseases Control Programme (1974-78)
- Dai's Training Programme (1971)
- Expanded Programme of Immunisation (1978) later revised as Universal Immunisation Programme (1985)
- Integrated Rural Development Programme (1978)
- Child Marriage Restraint Act (1978)
- National Health Policy (1983)
- Revised National Population Policy (1986)
- Child Survival and Safe Motherhood Programme (1992)
- Acute Respiratory Tract Infections Control Programme (1992)
- Pulse Polio Programme (1995)
- Prevention of Deaths from Hunger and Malnutrition Programme (1996) and
- Reproductive and Child Health Programme (1996)

The global concern about the health of the women and children of the developing countries have drawn greater attention during the recent past. The Cairo International Conference on "Population and Development (1994)" formalized a growing international consensus for improving reproductive health, including family planning for human welfare and development. This consensus provides a new vision of population policy which recognises a crucial distinction between the overall goals of population policy and the Reproductive and Child Health Programme. The goal of this programme is to reduce unwanted fertility safely and to provide high quality health services, thereby responding to the needs of individual, as well as, to stabilise the population growth. The Reproductive and Child Health approach is adopted to strengthen the existing infrastructural interventions in order to promote the health of the women and children. This is an effort to build the nation. The adoption of Reproductive and Child Health approach by the government in 1996, is a right step and right direction to ensure greater health care of mothers and children.

It has been rightly pointed out, that every effort by the government to provide services is, not only to be appreciated, but also should be rightly and judiciously utilised through effective community participation. Still much needs to be done to ensure safe motherhood and child survival.

Thus the history of development of maternal and child health service interventions show the enormous inputs to ensure the health of mothers and children. However the infant mortality rate (74) and the maternal mortality rate (3.6) besides morbidity are still high. The low utilisation of related services interfere with the health of mother and children.

Significant gaps in health care infrastructure, health personnel and health services, have been observed when there was a maximum need in a country where more than one third of population is below poverty line. These gaps are bound to widen, if appropriate steps are not initiated to bridge them.

Numerous studies have revealed that, the rural people are frustrated with the health services provided, due to non-availability of health providers in institutions, non-availability of medicines or quality services, inaccessibility of primary health centres and sub-centres, inadequate facilities to check health of pregnant women and the health of the child. The claims of the Government in terms of reduction in infant mortality rate and maternal mortality rate are heartening, but the felt needs as visualised by the people are different and much needs to be done to reach the goals of "Health for all by the year, 2000 A.D."

There is an imminent need to identify the factors that interfere with the utilisation of maternal and child health services in order to develop appropriate strategies to overcome the hurdles and enhance their utilisation.

Need for the Study

The main focus of this research, stems out of the prevailing inadequate utilisation of maternal, child health and family planning services in the state of Andhra Pradesh. This research identifies the gap in the existing literature and to assess the pattern of utilisation of maternal, child health and family planning services by the beneficiaries. Since maternal, child health and family planning services are provided as a package to women/clients, it was decided to make this problem jointly, instead of separately, in view of the overlapping factors that influence their performances. Of course, there are several factors that individually affected the performance also. Incidentally the maternal, child health and family planning services are not uniformly progressed in several districts of this state. So there was a need to study it on a contrasting basis by taking differentially progressed districts on these aspects from Andhra Pradesh state. On the basis of these assumptions the present study was conceptualised. It also attempts to investigate the utilisation of maternal, child health and family planning services by the rural women in Kurnool and Mahaboobnagar districts of Andhra Pradesh. Comparative studies with a district as a unit are very negligible today. Since the district constitutes the major administrative unit and major viable geographical area for future planning and development, comparative studies at the district level have great relevance for the future socio-economic development of the country. Hence the present study is undertaken to assess the influence of some of the hindering (intervening) variables in the utilisation of maternal, child health and family planning services by the rural women in the study area, in order to develop appropriate strategies to overcome the hurdles and to enhance the higher utilisation of services.

General Objective of the Study

To study the level and determinants of utilisation of maternal, child health and family planning services on comparative basis in two differentially developed districts of Andhra Pradesh *viz.*, Kurnool and Mahaboobnagar districts. (The specific objectives are printed in the Methodology chapter).

Organisation of Thesis

This thesis consists of VII chapters which have been organised on the following lines:

Chapter—I has introduction covering background of the study, and need for the study;

Chapter—II Comprises exhaustive review of literature, focusing on studies related to utilisation of maternal, child health and family planning services and its determinants, the reasons for non-utilisation of maternal (antenatal, natal, postnatal services), child health and family planning services and its determinants;

Chapter—III Deals with Methodology covering specific objectives of the study, hypotheses, conceptual frame work, operational definitions, sample frame and size, pilot study, data gathering technique, data collection procedure and data analysis;

Chapter—IV Describes results and discussion. This chapter deals with two subsections, it begins with the discussion on Socio-economic, Socio-cultural and Demographic profile of the respondents, besides infrastructural facilities and quality of services rendered by health functionaries. The second sub section deals with the utilisation of maternal and child health services namely antenatal, natal, postnatal, child health and family planning services (dependent variables) were cross tabulated with the selected independent variables such as socio-economic, socio-cultural, demographic and infrastructural facilities;

Chapter—V Explains multiple determinants of utilisation of maternal, child health and family planning services by Logistic Regression Analysis;

Chapter—VI Few case studies focusing on the central theme of the study were presented as an off-shoot of the study;

Chapter—VII Focuses on a summary of the study and suitable implications for policy planning.

Chapter—2

Review of Related Literature

A large number of studies have been conducted on maternal, child health care, family planning and family welfare services in India and abroad during the last one decade. It is of great significance to scan abundant literature available in order to develop greater insight into the maternal, child health care, family planning and the utilisation of services. The review may facilitate a broader view of the policies and the programme interventions developed by the different governments throughout the world and particularly in India. It helped the investigator to develop deeper insight into the problem and gain information on what has already been done on the subject, and the existing gaps to be filled.

The review of literature has been organised into various subsections:

- The Utilisation of
  - Antenatal Services
  - Natal Services
  - Postnatal Services
  - Child Health Services and
  - Family Planning Services

  } are jointly called as Maternal Health Services
- Determinants in utilisation of maternal, child health and family planning services.

Utilisation of Maternal Health Services

Meera Shekar *et al* (1984) studied the health practices in relation to child birth and infant care in Ranjit Nagar of New Delhi and found that, 50 per cent of the sample visited an antenatal clinic for check up during third trimester of pregnancy, only 35 per cent of them had received Tetanus Toxoid.

Nearly 40 per cent of the pregnant women preferred to have home delivery and 60 per cent of lactating mothers delivered at home, 56 per cent of deliveries were conducted by untrained personnel, mostly elders within the family.

Talwar and Bhatia (1985) observed that in rural Rajasthan only 6 per cent got registered for antenatal care. Only 41 per cent of women visited by health personnel at home and only 8 per cent received Iron and Folic acid supplementation of which only 2 per cent consumed them.

Srinivas, M.N. (1986) revealed that, in Bihar only 25 per cent of 496 pregnant women got registered, and only 16 per cent of them registered in the first trimester followed by 21 per cent in the second trimester and 33 per cent in the third trimester. Only 6 per cent of women were visited at home by the health workers.

96 per cent of deliveries took place at home in rural area and 68 per cent in urban area. Only 8 per cent births in rural area and 28 per cent in urban area were attended by trained personnel.

Chuttani and Naik (1986) in their study found, 17 per cent of the births were attended by the health centre staff and 83 per cent by untrained dais. Only 2 deliveries were conducted at primary health centres. Among the deliveries conducted at home by staff, only 5 out of 136 were attended by doctor, one by lady health visitor, 40 by MPHA (F) and 90 by trained dai.

About 20 per cent of mothers received postnatal care by the health centre staff. Among them 71 per cent were seen by MPHA (F) followed by lady health visitor (33%) and none by the doctor. 43 per cent were visited only once. 156 of the neonates (20%) were visited by health personnel. Among them 28 per cent were visited once, 27 per cent twice and 45 per cent thrice during the first week of birth. The quality of care provided in all areas was poor. Physical examination was not done, the services were deficient in utilisation and quality coverage.

Hema Nalini, B.E., (1989) found in Andhra Pradesh that 94 per cent of pregnant women were immunised for Tetanus with 2 doses. It was also observed that Information, Education and Communication activities related to health of pregnant women were organised to increase their awareness.

Two thirds of the sample was visited by health personnel in their postnatal period, among them 30 per cent mother's had one visit by the health personnel and received IFA supplementation indicating that there should be greater awareness among mothers for maximum utilisation of health services during postnatal period. Majority (96%) of postnatal mothers had no health problem, 70 per cent newborns weight has been checked. 57 per cent mothers were doing normal household work after one week and 20 per cent did household work after 4 days. 43 per cent were going for work after one month; nobody was aware of postnatal exercises. 44 per cent of mothers took rest during postnatal period. 27 per cent wanted to be hale and healthy. 17 per cent wanted their babies to be taken care of. About 33 per cent took bath after 3 days, followed by 20 per cent after 9 days and 3 per cent on the same day. These aspects indicate lack of knowledge on the importance of hygiene.

Ratna Dhar (1989) in Delhi assessed the antenatal services provided in two hospitals: In one hospital out of 144 women, 61 per cent women made 1-3 visits, in another hospital 135 women interviewed, 35 per cent made 3-7 visits. In both the hospitals general examination was done for all cases. Urine examination was carried out for all cases and blood examination for 91 per cent cases. 7.7 per cent cases in first hospital, 10 per cent cases in second hospital got registered in the first trimester and a majority of the cases got registered in the second trimester. About 55 per cent in first hospital and 27 per cent in second hospital did not receive Tetanus Toxoid.

Talwar *et al* in Madhya Pradesh (1990) assessed the antenatal services utilisation among rural women. Only 7 per cent mothers reported registration and received Iron and Folic acid tables and Tetanus Toxoid. About 4 per cent women were visited by health staff during pregnancy.

About 3.5 per cent women had delivery in the institution and only 5 per cent deliveries were attended by trained staff and the remaining 95 per were carried by untrained dai.

Usha *et al* (1990) in rural area of Pune identified the absence of antenatal care. Self delivery was associated with high rates of mortality both among mothers and babies.

Satish Kumar *et al* (1990) in Varanasi noted that 21 per cent of cases were registered in the second of third trimester. Registration during first trimester was poor. A low level of deterioration of maternal and child health services were observed over a period time.

Okafor, C.B. (1991) in his study noted that, 38 per cent of the respondents delivered in a supervised service, 30 per cent delivered at maternity centre, 30 per cent at home, 2 per cent at prayer house. The traditional birth attendants were therefore the most utilised service for delivery. Reasons given for use of home delivery were: lack of transport to the maternity centre, cost of service, maternal education, previous physician contact, Maternal occupation and distance from service centre etc., necessitate an increased service to the pregnant women.

National Family Health Survey in India (1992-93) found that antenatal care was provided at home by a health worker for only 21 per cent of births during the last 4 years. However, in the case of 40 per cent of births, the mother went outside her home and received antenatal care from an allopathic doctor. Antenatal care was provided by nurse/midwives, ayurvedic or homeopathic doctors for 9 per cent of births. Antenatal care through home visits is much more common in rural areas (covering 25% of births) than in urban areas (covering 10% of births). Urban women receive antenatal care more (70%) from allopathic doctor than rural women (31%). Utilisation of antenatal services is nearly universal in Kerala (97%), Goa (95%), Tamilnadu (94%). On the contrary only 31 per cent of births in Rajasthan received antenatal care from an allopathic doctor.

61 per cent of mothers received atleast one dose of Tetanus Toxoid vaccine. Over half of births (51%), mothers received Iron and Folic acid tablets. Institutional deliveries were conducted for 26 per cent of mothers. Women in southern states of India had utilised maternal and child health services comparatively at higher side than those women residing in central and northern parts of India.

Only 26 per cent of births during the last four years were delivered in health institutions and 74 per cent delivered at home. However, 34 per cent of deliveries were attended by trained personnel. In Tamil Nadu (71%), Andhra Pradesh (50%) and Uttar Pradesh (17%) deliveries were conducted at health facility centres, 74 per cent of deliveries are carried at natal home. Home deliveries are performed in other states as under: in Karnataka (28%), Maharastra (20%), Tamilnadu (11%), Haryana (9%), Uttar Pradesh (7%) and in Goa (3%).

Shah and Shah, (1992) in Calcutta found that mothers who failed to avail the antenatal care, delivered low weight babies as compared to those who had more antenatal care.

Neeraja, K.P. (1992) observed, 36 per cent of respondents received antenatal services, of which only 19 per cent received these services from government agency and the remaining 17 per cent obtained from private agency, only 15 per cent were examined by health personnel for lab investigations like urine for albumin, sugar and haemoglobin. Only 9 per cent received health education regarding diet, child care and immunisation. About 36 per cent received Tetanus vaccination and Iron and Folic acid tablets but only 18 per cent consumed Iron and Folic acid tablets.

25 per cent of deliveries were conducted at home by untrained personnel, 50 per cent were by trained dai and the remaining deliveries were conducted at institutions.

About 11 per cent of mothers obtained postnatal services by the health personnel. The practices of mothers during postnatal period were also observed, 94 per cent of mothers had taken bath on the third day of delivery, the remaining 6 per cent took on 7th day. 26 per cent of sample took perennial care,

29 per cent of mothers modified their diet during postnatal period to improve their health status and to increase the production of the breast milk. 49 per cent of mothers performed normal activities after 15 days of delivery, nearly two thirds of mothers (61%) had resumed outside work after 3 months.

Sudha, C. Patel (1993) in Gujarat found that, 70 per cent of mothers did not utilise postnatal services but only births were registered by health personnel. The level of satisfaction among mother's seemed to be low.

Ramanarao, G.V. and Ch. Sitarama Rao, (1994) narrated in their study that, 77 per cent of deliveries have home deliveries. Out of them 69 per cent were conducted by untrained dai. Again out of 71 institutional deliveries, 52 per cent, were private hospital deliveries.

Ashokkumar (1994) in Lucknow found, 90 per cent of deliveries took place at home, 8 per cent in hospital and only 18 per cent were handled by trained personnel. Out of them nearly half were by trained dais. Among the deliveries conducted by untrained dais 61 per cent were performed by elderly women of the family. These are more acceptable to muslim families. The reason given for delivery at home were: convenience (66%), earlier bad experience at hospital (16%), inaccessibility of health facilities (18%) and fear of hospital (3%).

Jayalakshmi (1996), in her empirical analysis to assess the reproductive health status of rural women found that, 48 per cent of women received antenatal services, 28 per cent are visited by health personnel. Among them ANM visited 18 per cent cases in home, whereas 10 per cent of women are visited by trained dais.

Radhakumari, I, (1997) found that, 79 per cent of pregnant women received tetanus vaccine. Only 6 per cent of women reported that they received Iron and Folic acid tablets total cycles. About 29 per cent of women modified their diet in pregnancy.

Half of the respondents were visited by health personnel in their postnatal period, 10 received medical care, health personnel given nutritional education, information regarding hygienic care for 30 per cent of mothers. 50 per cent of mothers expressed dissatisfaction towards health personnel in provision of services.

National Tuberculosis survey (1994) found that, two thirds of the deliveries were conducted at home, out of all the institutional deliveries 27 per cent were attended by trained dais, 27 per cent by doctor and just 4 per cent by multipurpose health assistants (Female) only.

Raju, K.N.M. (1994) in his study in rural Karnataka found that 58 per cent of pregnant women had been examined by health professionals and 69 per cent of women were protected against Tetanus.

Sharma, *et al* (1995) in a semi-urban community of Pondicherry observed the trend of mothers in utilisation of maternal care services. His findings revealed that 26 per cent of women sought antenatal care in the first trimester and 40 per cent did so during their subsequent pregnancies. Primipara had the highest average clinic visits.

Sreenivasa Reddy, K. (1997) observed that, the registration of antenatal mothers has increased to 100 per cent during the Reproductive and Child Health project period from the previous 70 per cent. The mothers receiving Tetanus Toxoid almost reached 100 per cent in 55 per cent registered antenatal cases. The early registration of antenatal cases were possible due to accessibility, availability of MPHA (F) in the village, regular home visits and the quality of antenatal services available.

The maternal, infant morbidity and mortality depends on the availability and utilisation of the nature of natal services. About 17 per cent of deliveries conducted were institutional. It is interesting to note that MPHA (F) conducted only 18 per cent deliveries followed by 52 per cent by trained birth attendants and the remaining 30 per cent by untrained personnel. However the situation has changed remarkably during the implementation of Reproductive Child Health Project where 81 per cent of deliveries were conducted by MPHA (F) alone and the remaining 19 per cent by trained birth attendant. This signifies a change in the attitude and behaviour of mothers. There was no occasion for untrained dais to attend the deliveries. This was possible because of MPHA (F) stay at headquarters, treatment of minor ailments, involvement of women groups and taking the assistance of trained dais during delivery. The trained dais who assisted the MPHA (F) were given a honoroium of Rs. 100/- per month which facilitated active involvement of trained dai in mobilising the community, resulting in greater utilisation of natal services and a related decline in morbidity and mortality of mothers and infants.

Audinarayana, N. and Jayasheela (1998) observed that, in Andhra Pradesh, 87 per cent of antenatal mothers received health care during pregnancy, 33 per cent delivered in institutions and 50 per sought assistance of health professionals.

DETERMINANTS OF MATERNAL CARE SERVICES

(i) Education and Utilisation of Maternal Care Services

Many studies have confirmed inverse relationship between education and fertility and positive relationship between education and utilisation of health services. Vilasini, 1985; Levine *et al*, 1991; Obermeyer and Joseph Potter, 1991; Kavita and Audinarayana, 1997; NFHS (1992-93), Jeresa Castro Margin, 1995; Audinarayana, and Sheela, 1998.

The NFHS survey in India (1992-93) brought out that, mothers in lower age groups and higher order births and higher educational levels utilised the health facility during prenatal and delivery time more than the mothers who were in higher age groups and had higher order births and lower educational levels. This survey also showed that an increase in the level of education of respondents and receipt of antenatal checkup, resulted in more institutional deliveries. This is found to be statistically significant. The utilisation of antenatal care services, Tetanus immunisation and the receipt of Iron and Folic acid tablets are negatively related to mothers' age at first birth, birth order of the child, but positively related with womens' education.

In Morocco study, Obermeyer (1993) revealed that, urban women of lower age groups, higher age at life events, higher educational attainment and small household size utilised the antenatal services and natal services more than women living in rural areas lower age at life events, lower educational levels and large family size.

Becker *et al* (1993) in Metro Cebu study found that the differentials in prenatal care vary considerably by child's age, maternal age, education of couple, economic status, place of residence and possession of radio or T.V. when all the other variables were held constant, the receiving of prenatal care was observed to be large and statistically significant with maternal education and place of residence.

Rajeswari and Hasalkar (1994) in Karnataka observed that religion, caste, age, literacy and occupation had received a strong effect on number of prenatal medical checkups and receiving of Iron and Folic acid tablets. Tetanus immunisation is negatively related with the parity, income and literacy of wife. These were partially related to the utilisation of T.T. vaccine.

Bhatia and Cleland (1995) highlighted that place of residence, high educational level and economic status and hygiene consciousness, had exerted a strong net influence on natal care, and positively associated with postnatal checkups.

Audinarayana and Sheela, (1998) in their analysis of NFHS data observed that, women educated upto high school or more had utilised the maternal care services significantly at a higher level than the illiterate women.

All the above studies suggested that higher level of education enhances the women's knowledge of modern health care facilities, modifies their beliefs about pregnancy and child care practices. It also enhances their status within the family and role in decision-making, improves their ability to communicate with modern health care providers and utilizes the health care services to obtain optimum health and prevent/reduce morbidity and mortality levels.

(ii) Occupation and Utilisation of Maternal Care Services

Hema Nalini (1989) narrated that, in rural areas, except those from aristocratic family, most of the women go out to work along with men in order to supplement the family income. Lack of time for the rural women working in field denies them a chance to get the services from health worker. Because these rural women attend both household work and occupational activities. They get hardly 4-5 hours rest period. Due to poverty, economic assistance, ignorance, customs and increased working hours and due to low utilisation of maternal health services, women tend to suffer with higher morbidity and mortality.

Women who were interviewed were conscious that heavy physical work had an adverse effect on the foetus. It may lead to premature labour and miscarriage. Heavy work was restricted until the 4th month of pregnancy and again after 8th month of pregnancy since the probability of having an abortion during the former period and still birth during the later period are high.

Some women believed that hard physical labour leads to an easier delivery. Sex was avoided during the first and last trimester as it causes malformations and miscarriages. Some women avoided heavy lifting during antenatal and postnatal period as it may cause prolapse of the uterus.

Swarnalatha (1992) in Andhra Pradesh found that, agricultural labourers tend to utilise services at low level compared to non-working women due to non-availability of time and economic necessity. She suggested that work opportunities have to be utilised to improve women's status and create the motivation for better utilisation.

Work status of respondents has shown a negative effect on antenatal checkup (*i.e.,* non-working women being received more antenatal care). It is significant at 0.01 level, as the women who were mostly engaged in labour to earn some income for living. Such expectant mothers will loose the wages if they go for antenatal checkup to the government or private hospitals which are mostly situated in nearby towns and therefore they may neglect regular antenatal services (Kavita and Audinarayana, 1997).

(iii) Income and Utilisation of Maternal Care Services

Sreevastava, J.N. and D.N. Saxena (1990) observed that, working women had low utilisation than non-working women. The female participation in work to improve their family income had a negative effect on fertility, positive effect over their utilisation levels.

Yesudian (1991) in Bombay found a wide gap in income, education, occupation and economic status between social classes. Low class people had lower knowledge of disease and health services. Their perception of health services was lower than that of middle and high class people. High class people preferred utilisation of private health services, while low class people utilised freely available government health services.

Many studies revealed positive relationship between income levels and utilisation of maternal and child health services. (Heer Bhosale, 1975; Mahadevan, 1979; Rele and Kanitkar, 1980; Ray *et al,* 1988; Kanitkar and Sinha, 1989; Obermeyer and Potter, 1991; Levine *et al,* 1991; NFHS, 1992-93; Elo 1992; Obermeyer, 1993; Almazrou *et al,* 1993; Becker *et al,* 1993; Rajeswari and Hasalkar, 1994; Pebleu, 1994; Bhatia and Cleland, 1995; Kavita and Audinarayana, 1998).

Majority of the middle socio-economic group women went to hospitals/maternity homes for their deliveries while in low socio-economic group the majority stayed at home under the care of trained personnel.

Institutional care during delivery was positively associated with education and income, whereas it was negatively associated with parity of women (Rajeswari and Hasalkar—1994), wage earners (women) had utilised institutional facility more than those engaged in salaried employment.

Women who belong to high socio-economic strata seem to go for institutional delivery to a large extent, but statistically not significant. Monthly family income is positively associated with medical examination during pregnancy. *eg:* the proportion of respondents who had received antenatal checkups and higher among those whose family income is Rs. 2,000/- and above than those whose monthly family income is Rs. 1,000/- or less (Kavita and Audinarayana, 1997).

(iv) Religion and Caste

The NFHS in India (1992-93) observed that, institutional deliveries were less common among scheduled caste/scheduled tribe women than in non-scheduled caste/ scheduled tribe women.

Rajeswari and Hasalkar (1994) noticed that, religion and caste were significantly associated with 2 doses of Tetanus immunisation during antenatal period and institutional deliveries.

Bhatia and Cleland (1995) identified that Muslims do not go for deliveries in a hospital to the extent Hindus go. Kavita and Audinarayana (1998) observed that the women belong to non scheduled caste community and of lower parity utilised the postnatal check up than those women of scheduled caste and higher parity.

(v) Age and Maternal Care Services Utilisation

NFHS survey in India and Andhra Pradesh (1992-93) found that, the active reproductive age group of mothers (20-29 years) utilised antenatal services more when compared to natal and other health services.

(vi) Parity and Utilisation of Maternal Health Services

Parity was found to be significant at 0.05 level. Women with lesser number of partly utilised antenatal and natal services more than women with higher parity (Okafor, 1991).

Women with higher order of births had utilised maternal care services to a lesser extent than primi order of birth. Thus it shows a negative association with all the maternal care indicators. This is possible because such women might not have experienced any problems during earlier pregnancies or might be aware of appropriate care to be taken during pregnancy and delivery besides resource constraints (Audinarayana and J. Sheela, 1997).

(vii) Infrastructural Facilities and Utilisation of Maternal Care Services

The Director of Family Welfare, Government of Andhra Pradesh (1989) assessed the coverage of maternal and child health services and reported that, a better utilisation was observed in coastal Andhra region, where the female literacy, socio-economic status was higher when compared to backward regions like Telangana and less developed Rayalaseema region. The identified reasons for low utilisation were: lack of awareness about health care services, non-availability of health personnel, inaccessibility of health centres, lack of transportation facilities and migration of population.

Swain *et al*, (1992) studied some aspects of referral system in maternal and child health care in rural Varanasi. 45 per cent were detected to be high risk cases, 49 per cent referred to primary health centres, 34 per cent to district hospital. However only 9 per cent of cases availed the referral services.

Rupert and others (1992) observed that, major percentage of women use institutions for antenatal checkup, regarding delivery services 47 per cent prefer to use the services of traditional birth attendant the services of trained dais were preferred by 14 per cent, MPHA (F) by 17 per cent and the health institutions by 23 per cent. 77 per cent of the households did not receive any services from the health workers at their door steps. Only 5 per cent of the total persons residing in the households received one or more services. 31 per cent of respondents utilised maternal, child health and family planning services. 22 per cent obtained curative services.

Almazrou (1993) found distance did not exhibit any association with persons attended to postnatal checkups.

Vijayalakshmi Groover (1994) in her study observed that 80 per cent of the mothers never visited a maternal and child health centre during the antenatal period. 10 per cent had visited regularly and 10 per cent visited when they had some problem.

Rajeswari and Hasalkar (1994) stated that, the number of antenatal visits and place of antenatal care are important for the health of the mothers and outcome of the pregnancy. 32 per cent received no antenatal care outside or at home at their pregnancies. 31 per cent had such check ups more times. 45 per cent received the services from private institutions and the rest from government hospital (16%) and subcentre (7%).

Studies have shown that the utilisation of primary health centre is less than 8.3 per cent signifying the declining credibility of the service both personnel and organisational (Sujatha Rao, 1997).

The pilot project or Reproductive and Child Health care in Alur Mandal of Andhra Pradesh established credibility with the maternal and child health and other health services, since the MPHA (F) were attending outpatient cases. Antenatal clinics were conducted including laboratory *eg:* haemoglobin estimation, urine analysis services, deliveries conducted in homes or institutions by the MPHA (F) or trained persons. At first referral unit services were provided. The results are encouraging which show substantial reduction in infant and maternal deaths with 99 per cent antenatal registration, 100 per cent immunisation of children, 100 per cent Tetanus coverage to antenatal mothers, 100 per cent deliveries by trained personnel, 100 per cent follow-up of postnatal cases, improvement of family planning performance, decrease of maternal deaths to only one, reduction to infant deaths (IMR=48) and decline in reproductive health problems. Thus an effort was made through an innovative approach to deliver quality maternal and child health services. There was a marked improvement in acceptance of immunisation and other services beside a decline in maternal and infant morbidity and mortality pattern (Sreenivasa Reddy, K. 1997).

UTILISATION OF CHILD HEALTH SERVICES

India's abiding interest in the welfare of children is an expression of the country's commitment enshrined in articles 24, 39 and 45 of India's constitution under the different five year plans to meet the special requirements of child (Ministry of Health and Family Welfare, 1981). These specific programmes were largely aimed at providing maternity services, child care services like supplementary nutrition, immunization, preschool education and other welfare measures. In 1974, National Policy for children was formed by the social welfare department. It has been explained in the policy that to provide adequate services to children both before and after birth and through the period of growth, to ensure their total physical, mental and social development, subsequently this was strengthened through the programme interventions like National Health Policy (1983), Revised National Population Policy (1986) and Child Survival and Safe Motherhood Programme (1992) to give a thrust to the health care of mothers and children. Thus child survival is an essential factor and an indicator for a welfare society.

DETERMINANTS OF CHILD HEALTH SERVICES

(i) Education and Utilisation of Child Health Services

Female literacy has a great significance in Indian context, as child survival used to be influenced by the literacy level of women. Maternal education may help the entire family including their children and their health care. It is still more significant, as mother will be the principal agent of socialization of the children who spends most of her time with the children at home. Educated women unlike illiterates may follow appropriate methods of child rearing practices and avoid the risk of child morbidity and mortality. Thus maternal education paves way for better utilisation of child health services and ensures greater child survival. Hence the mother's education is considered as a variable in the study.

The health and survival status of children was found to be better in case of women with higher education (Kucera, 1985; Kaushral Kishore Siddu, 1986; Davanzo, 1986; Rajinder Singh and Chowdary, 1986; Gurumurthy and Prabhakar, 1987; Schaefer and Hughes, 1988; Irma, Elo, 1992).

The NFHS conducted at national and state levels (1992-93) also found the same result. Child mortality is high (19.3%) among illiterate women but it is least among educated women. Child mortality is slightly higher in Andhra Pradesh (23.2%) than in Uttar Pradesh (16.7%) among illiterate and also educated mothers.

Viswanathan (1991) conducted a study on the effect of maternal knowledge and attitudes on utilisation of child health services in his interview of 624 mothers in rural areas of Andhra Pradesh and found that, mothers who were better educated and higher social class and were willing to actively seek child care services and their children were fully immunized.

Gandhigaram researchers (1991) interviewed 210 mothers in Tamilnadu and found high awareness about child care services among literate mothers than illiterate mothers of rural areas. They also observed 1.9 per cent of children did not receive even a single dose of any vaccine. 26.2 per cent children were fully immunised. 68.1 per cent children did not receive Measles vaccine. The utilisation of child care services is more prevalent among higher income group than the low or middle income groups. 25 per cent of children went to private practitioners for vaccination, the rest had chosen government facilities.

Rajguru (1991) studied 1000 families in Ahmadabad rural areas and Mosley (1993) conducted a nutrition survey in Kenya revealed that the mother's education has a positive effect on the child's nutritional status and is marginally greater between those children with uneducated mothers and those with primary education; 36 per cent decline in child mortality with primary school education and 83 per cent decline with secondary school education, below the level for uneducated women.

Neeraja, (1992) conducted a study in tribal area of Anantapur district and observed that the mothers with middle school education showed higher awareness against the illiterate mothers, the latter showed low awareness about child rearing practices and child health services. With an increase in educational level, there was an increase in the level of awareness, indicating a positive association between education and awareness. The mean awareness score of illiterate mothers was significantly lower than the mean awareness scores of the mothers with primary school education.

Taluja (1995) in a study on immunisation status of children in Jabalpur cantonment area, found parental awareness for immunisation and utilisation of the services was found significant high in high socio-economic status, maternal literacy and nuclear family. This results were also confirmed by other studies like Dhilon and Menon (1995) in Punjab state and Sahu and others (1989).

Rajender Singh and others (1996) reported about utilisation of child health services by parents belonging to various educational groups. The study showed that the percentage of utilisation was higher in medically educated group than non-medically educated group. Positive correlation was found between the educational status of parents and utilisation of child health services. This indicates the highly favourable influence of health knowledge on health practices. In every economic setting, the children of literate women have a better chance of survival than those born to illiterate women. Women with schooling tend to marry later, delay child bearing practice, family limitation, reject harmful traditional practices related to child birth, adopt healthy habits, go for immunisation, keep domestic hygiene and use available health services in childs' sickness.

(ii) Occupation and Utilisation of Child Health Services

Synthia (1991) noticed that, women's participation in economic activities increases the arrival of additional children and low utilisation of child health services. Female employment is acting against breast feeding and health care of children resulting in an increase in child morbidity.

Neeraja (1992) in her study found that, Housewives had high awareness compared to labourers and factory workers. Average awareness was high in factory workers (81%) than in labourers (70%).

Rajeswari and Hasalkar (1994) noticed that, mothers's education and occupation had executed a positive influence and had a negative influence over utilisation of child health services.

Higher survival status among children was observed in the Housewives category, because the women usually stay at home, most of them had higher education and belong to higher economic group and better social status. Therefore Housewives bestow their greater attention for child care (Bhatia and Cleland, 1995).

However non-utilisation of child health services was more in Housewives followed by labour group. Participation of women in the labour force has generally been found to be negatively associated with utilisation of services for children. The children are more neglected due to the labour force. The involvement of women in employment away from the home tends to promote the use of home remedies and traditional methods for treatment of sick children, which in turn worsen the health condition of the child (Bhosale, *et al* (1995).

(iii) Income and Utilisation of Child Health Services

Bhatia and Cleland (1995) found, the effects of economic status and autonomy were in the positive direction on child care, but observed to be very week and statistically insignificant. While children from higher income groups are maintaining good health than the children from poor families who present a declining health. Radhakumari (1997) in her study found that, 80 per cent of children had very poor health and 64 per cent had poor health from lower income families.

Viswanathan, (1997) conducted a study on the effect of maternal knowledge and attitudes on child health services. He interviewed 1624 mothers and found that, mothers of fully immunised children were better educated, of a higher income and willing to seek child health services. The source of information regarding immunisation was generally a healthy trend.

(iv) Caste and Utilisation of Child Health Services

Higher caste women possess the children with sound health and against the children from lower social status who suffered with nutritional deficiency disorders and infections.

The child survival status is high in higher caste whereas the morbidity and mortality levels are high in children belonging to lower caste (Radhakumari, 1997).

(v) Family Type and Utilisation of Child Health Services

Neeraja (1992) in her study found, among the mothers in the nuclear families 71.62 per cent had average awareness and two per cent had high awareness about child health services and good child rearing practices. Among the mothers belonging to joint families, 62.50 per cent had average awareness and 5 per cent had high awareness. The range of awareness score was higher for nuclear families as against to joint families.

On the contrary the children from nuclear families are likely to marry at a later age because they have economic independence to provide care for themselves and to their children, whereas children in joint and extended families tend to marry at young. age because the young couple is not economically and socially independent to provide care for themselves or their children (Audinarayana and Rajashree, 1995).

Bhosale, (1995) in his study found that, 79 per cent of poor utilisation and 69 per cent of fair utilisation of child health services in joint families.

Radhakumari, (1997) in her study found, better health status among the children of nuclear families. 11 per cent of children with very good health, 76 per of those with good health and 65 per cent of children with average health are from nuclear families. Positive relationship was found between health status and nuclear family status.

(vi) Sex Preference and Utilisation of Child Health Services

In different cultures throughout the world "sex preference", particularly the desire for a son still holds the couples from utilising the health care delivery system or to limit their families. Sex preference is attributed to a variety of social, economic and cultural factors. Sex composition of living children was systematically related to fertility behaviour. In rural areas, having more sons raises the status of women in the family. The couple had sex preference utilised child health services more than the couple who does not have sex preference (Dyson and Moore, 1983; Choudhary *et al*, 1993; Nag, 1991).

The NFHS survey (1992-93) conducted in India shows, that women in every state wanted more sons. Particularly this idea is strong in Punjab, Rajasthan, Uttara Pradesh, Bihar and Gujarat and is weak in Kerala, Delhi, Assam, Goa, Karnataka and Tamilnadu. No significant difference in utilisation pattern of health services was observed based on sex preference.

(vii) Infrastructural Variables and Utilisation of Child Health Services

The quality services definitely enhance the utilisation of maternal, child health and family planning services. The role of health provides in ensuring the qualitative services is crucial for the better health of mother and children.

Benjamin and Zachariah (1991) in Ludhiana identified the reasons for low utilisation of child health services. They are: long waiting time, acute illness of the child, social causes and lack of motivation on the part of health professionals.

Azuh (1992) narrated in his study, for the population as a whole it is gratifying to note that respondents who received information on one or the other aspects of health care, and information on various aspects from the peripheral workers, have very high chances of child survival (86%) compared to those who have no access to health information (83%). This implies that frequent visits of peripheral workers would have inclined these respondents towards effective utilisation of medical services. Only 18 per cent had received the services of the health workers and 16.9 per cent respondents who did not obtain health services experienced child mortality. Poor transportation facilities, non-availability of health personnel, dissatisfaction towards functioning system of health services *eg;* waiting for long hours, style of functioning of the doctors and peripheral staff etc., contribute under utilisation of health services.

Balachandra Kurup (1992) in his study in Andhra Pradesh found that 9 per cent of women who stay within 6-10 kms of a district hospital and 13 per cent within 1-5 kms have utilised the health services. In Kerala, 73.4 per cent sample of women are staying within 6-10 kms and 19.9 per cent are 1-5 kms distance. In Andhra Pradesh child survival was noticed in nearly 81 per cent for those within 6-10 kms distance and 84 per cent in the next higher group. In Kerala the 6-10 km distance group reported 94 per cent survival and 96 per cent survival observed in other group. For mild morbidities, they seek primary health centres and private hospitals. For high morbidity, they seek services from district hospitals. Thus proximity of health facilities and utilisation of child health services are positively related.

Indu (1993), in her study on utilisation of child health service in Nepal observed that, 60 per cent of mothers obtained health information from their neighbours, 22 per cent through radio and 18 per cent from health personnel.

Damodar Bachni *et al* (1993) conducted a study on utilisation of preventive services at the under five clinic. They found that distance of the clinic and lack of facilities mainly affected the utilisation.

Singh and others (1994) noticed that health workers were the major source of information (78%) and 76 per cent knew the use of health services for the maintenance of child health. It was also observed that the respondents received health information about child survival from various resources *viz.*, health personnel (78%) relatives (9%), mass-media (7%) and from neighbours (6%).

Shafiqul Islam and others (1996) found in their study that accessibility of health care services, frequency of health visits are associated with child survival, childhood morbidity, and mortality. Visits by health personnel are likely to enhance awareness among mothers regarding various child and maternal problems. Thus a negative association was found between the number of visits by health personnel and child mortality.

Viswanathan (1997) identified the health facility is the main source of information, hence he suggested that a strategy of out reach services would benefit the poor and ill-informed mothers to fully utilise the child care services.

Radhakumari, (1997) in her study found that mass-media exposure exercised greater influence on awareness of child health. About 72 per cent of respondents received the information through the radio and 17 per cent from printed material. It was also observed that majority of the respondents (65%) were exposed to health education information, which overcome the barriers of ignorance, prejudice, fears, phobias and misconceptions regarding child rearing practice.

Varshney, (1997) in his working paper stated that the health status of the population is determined by the availability of health care delivery system and its accessibility. Utilisation of health facilities is considered as a positive illness control behaviour and one of the proximate determinants of child survival. About 44 per cent of respondents in the rural India gave inaccessibility of the primary health centre as the reason for not availing of health services.

The Reasons for Non-utilisation/Low Utilisation of Maternal and Child Health Services

Cultural factors, poor quality care, inadequate awareness and baseless fears were described as reasons for non-utilisation by population action (1987). Sahu *et al* (1989) in their study identified inadequate facilities, negligence, illiteracy, superstitions, combined family, elders' pressure, engagement in field activities, ignorance, non-availability of facilities, spousal indifference, ill-health and poor educational status are reported as the reasons for non-utilisation.

Bhandari, *et al* (1989) in their study "Maternal, child health services and infant mortality rate" listed, the reasons for non-utilisation of maternal child health services. They are: time lag (51.6%), inadequate treatment (32.2%), terminal stage of illness (29%) indigenous line of treatment due to ignorance, financial hardship, apathy, fatalistic attitude of parents, lack of faith in health department and logistics.

Mayachansuria (1989) observed, different reasons for not utilising maternal, child health services. They found that majority of the respondents did not utilise the services due to economic conditions, others due to good health and very few feeling it as a waste of time.

Interestingly Satish Kumar (1990) touched upon the infrastructural aspects in relation to non-utilisation of maternal and child health services. They include: poor supervision and guidance of MPHA (F) non-availability of equipment for carrying out lab investigations and women not feeling a need for routine maternal and child health care.

Kaul (1991) identified the reasons for preference of local traditional dai for conducting the delivery. The reasons for treating minor ailments by the mothers themselves, are: Common practice (77%), family preference (65%), lack of privacy (61%), less expensive (54%), non-availability of trained health personnel (24%) and lack of awareness (14%) etc.

Devi (1992) identified the reasons for low utilisation of maternal, child health services such as, lack of interest, fear of medical services, non-availability of infrastructural facilities and beneficiaries at home.

Taluja (1992) in this study listed the reasons for low utilisation. They are non-availability of facilities at centre, lack of knowledge, absence of visits by health team, non-availability of beneficiaries at home and inconvenient time for the visits.

Singh and others (1994) in their study identified the reasons for partial utilisation of maternal and child health services, which include lack of information (60.3%), lack of motivation (8.62%), busy family life (12.5%) and non-availability of health facilities (13.79%).

In Mexico study (1995), the reasons reported for non-utilisation of maternal and child health are, that 66 per cent of mothers felt that it unnecessary, others for lack of knowledge (8%), some for financial cost (7%) and in many cases elders do not permit the mothers to go to health centres (95%).

Maya Natu *et al* (1995) also in their study observed the reason for non-utilisation such as domestic difficulty, lack of knowledge and neglect of maternal care.

However Jaimala Hitesh (1996) observed in her study of "factors influencing the non-utilisation of maternal and child health services" are: lack of transportation facilities (43%), non-availability of health personnel 45 per cent unsympathetic attitude (40%), economic constraints (40%), and absence of follow-up services (60%).

Radhakumari, (1997) in her study reported that the women were not aware of maternal care facility and non-availability of health personnel is the reason for low utilisation of maternal and child health services.

FAMILY PLANNING SERVICES

Studies Focusing Knowledge of Family Planning Methods

NFHS survey (1992-93) conducted in India found that, the knowledge of a method of family planning, is almost universal in India. 96 per cent of currently married women know atleast one contraceptive method, and 89 per cent know where to obtain a modern method. However, this widespread knowledge about family planning is only limited to female sterilisation. But only half of the women know about spacing methods. However all the awareness does not result in acceptance due to various reasons.

Women who know about modern spacing methods such as the pill, IUD and Condom are few; 76 per cent know about atleast one modern spacing methods. The most well known method of spacing is pill (66 per cent) followed by IUD (61 per cent) and Condoms (58 per cent). Thus the knowledge of family planning methods is lower in rural areas—(64 per cent), than in urban areas (82 per cent).

The NFHS survey conducted in Andhra Pradesh (92-93) found the knowledge of family planning is nearly universal (rural 99 per cent and urban 96 per cent). The spontaneous response regarding atleast one modern spacing method is 90 per cent in urban and 91 per cent in rural areas. The most well known among the spacing methods is the pill (54 per cent) followed by IUD (44 per cent) and Condom (42 per cent).

The Studies Related to Contraceptive Adoption

About current contraceptive prevalence in Andhra Pradesh, (NFHS 92-93) found that 47 per cent of couples are using modern methods and one per cent adopted terminal method. 38 per cent of currently married women are sterilised. Among them female sterilisation accounts for 81 per cent of current contraceptive prevalence, 7 per cent adopted Vasectomy.

The NFHS survey in India (1992) reported the interstate differences in family planning adoption. The highest use of contraception was in Kerala, Himachal Pradesh, Maharashtra, Punjab and Mizoram and New Delhi. At the other extreme, current use rates are less than 25 per cent in Uttar Pradesh and Bihar as well as Assam and many other morth-eastern states.

Gupta and others (1996), in Bombay conducted a study and found 24 per cent of family planning adopters, adopted sterilisation as a method of contraception and 20 per cent of couples adopted Vasectomy.

Sreenivasa Reddy, K. (1997) in his study, quoted that, developed Guntur district has highest acceptance of contraception (60.4 per cent) where 36.9 per cent of couples adopted it in less developed Kurnool district.

The studies related to family planning adoption when reviewed found that, higher percentage of adoption was mainly tubectomy followed by modern contraceptive methods, whereas the adoption of male methods was low because of popularity of female sterilisation.

The Reasons for Non-utilisation of Family Planning Services

Chipoma, (1986) in his study found in rural areas, that fatalistic attitude was strong among educated and illiterates, which made them for low adoption of family planning methods (30 per cent). They stated that God would decide their family size. 41.5 per cent of urban dwellers said that using birth control methods was against the will of God. 36 per cent of mothers expressed fear of surgery. 4 per cent did not utilise family planning as elders came in the way. 14.5 per cent felt sterlisation as an interference in Godly affair. 93.7 per cent waited for male child.

Husbands disapproval, lack of interest, the religious outlook, low socio-economic status, high fertility, less modernity were quoted as reasons for non-adoption of family planning by Shivaraju (1987).

ICMR Bulletin (1990) describes the following reasons for discontinuation of IUD in the nation. They are: partial expulsion of Copper T, bleeding P/V, pain in the abdomen, Menorrhagia, follow-up failure, change of residence, objection from husband and need of more children.

Rao, (1992), identified the major reasons for not accepting family planning which include: fear of operation (27 per cent), opposition from elders in family (26 per cent), post operative problems in work (24.5 per cent), after effects (24 per cent), poor health (18 per cent), religious dogmas (25.7 per cent), desire for more children (5 per cent), non-availability of suitable services (13 per cent) and ignorance of contraceptive methods (9 per cent).

DETERMINANTS OF UTILISATION OF FAMILY PLANNING SERVICES

(a) Education and Family Planning Adoption

A positive relationship, between contraception and lavel of education of couples were observed by may studies (Nagmoni 1980; Yadav and others 1984; Jolley 1986' Hema Nalini, 1989; Rao, 1992; Somayajulu, 1992; NFHS survey 1992-93; Chakravarthy, 1993; Saisujatha and Murthy, 1993; Rao, *et al*, 1995; Gupta 1995; Bhuyan, 1996; Caldwell, 1996; and Reddy, 1997.

The NFHS survey conducted in India (1992-93) had discovered that the adoptation of family planning is higher among literates (55 per cent) than illiterate women (34 per cent) but the same literacy is not strongly related to the adoption of family planning in Himachal Pradesh, Maharashtra, Goa, Kerala and Tamilnadu though these states have relatively high average levels of education. The curvilinear relationship tends to weaken the otherwise strong positive relationship between education and the levels of current use is seen for spacing methods both in modern and traditional methods.

Education and gainful employment are regarded as more susceptible to improvement through policy intervention than are deeply rooted cultural conventions, hence, their appeal as vehicle for woman empowerment and as agents of social change is very effective (Dasgupta, 1995).

Castro (1995), found that between educated women want smaller families than the illiterates. It suggest that education is linked to shift in women's attitudes towards child bearing and their perception in the cost of child rearing. Lack of education hinders reproductive choice.

Sundari, (1996) observed that it is not female literacy alone, but the level of female education that affects the use of contraception. 25 per cent of illiterate women adopted contraception with primary level of education (37 per cent) and secondary level of education (45 per cent). Education affects contraceptive behaviour only after five years of schooling.

(b) Occupation and Family Planning Adoption

Female occupation is another important factor which determines family size. Women who work outside the home are less likely to expose themselves to the risk of repeated pregnancies. Hence, changes in occupational pattern and family planning acceptance are positively related.

Rao *et al*, (1985) found, persons engaged in non-agricultural activities are likely to realize the benefits of family planning. Women generally, go out to work, tends to accept contraception immediately.

The study by Ramana Rao, (1994) revealed that the acceptance of contraception was lowest among semi-skilled persons compared to highest among professionals. However when education was controlled, effect of occupation was not significant.

Castro (1995) in his study revealed that the industrial workers and non-agricultural workers are conscious about their health and that of their children and so they readily accept contraception.

Shafiqual Islam and others (1996) conducted study in Bangladesh and found that women who work outside the home may take less care of their children and of their own health during pregnancy. One might expect a positive relationship between women's work status and utilisation of family planning services.

Reddy, (1997) conducted study in Andhra Pradesh found that the housewives showed higher family planning acceptance than the agricultural labourers, because of higher education, economic status and exposure to information.

Decision Making

The lower status of women in society influences the decision making role of women in the affairs of the family particularly the family size. In male dominated societies, the status of woman elevates with the number of children, particularly sons she produces. Child bearing often continuous during the entire fecund period, even at the cost of her health.

Several studies quoted that men's views are more influential than women's vies in making family decisions. Husbands alone should make decision about family size and the practice of birth control (Amna Swar-Eldohab, 1993; Rose Barzelatt, 1984; Mahadevan, 1984; Sandhya Rao and Patel, 1994: Michael and Donald, 1991).

Vinit Sharma and Anuragini Sharma, (1993) indicated that women had to depend on their husband or mother-in-law for the decisions, related to family planning adoption and health care matters.

(c) Religion, Caste and Family Planning Adoption

The NFHS survey in A.P. (1992-93) discovered highest adoption of family planning among Christians (50%) followed by Hindus (47%) and Muslims (45%), interestingly the use of modern spacing method is higher among Muslims than Hindus and Christians. The percentage of family planning adoption is much higher among non S.C/S.T women (50%) than S.C/S.T. women (36%).

Religion has become an important factor in the cultural life of Indians. It prescribes a code of life, refers to a system of beliefs, attitudes and practices which individuals share in groups. This affects their fertility behaviour and contraceptive adoption (Reddy, 1997).

Interspouse Communication and Family Planning Adoption

Shiva Raju (1987) in his study of coastal and Rayalaseema regions of Andhra Pradesh that interspousal communication on family planning was greater among adopters and than non-adopters of contraception.

Charles Warren *et al* (1990) found that 41 per cent couples have not discussed the family size issue together while 75 per cent of husbands, think that God decides couples' family size and not the inter spousal communication, in Jordan.

The NFHS survey in Andhra Pradesh (1992-93) showed that a majority of women who have never used a family planning method have discussed the topic with their husbands (72%).

Among the non-adopters, two fifths of the respondents have discussed the issue on family size limitation with their husbands in the past years.

Husband-wife communication is one of the significant factors which influence the fertility behaviour of couple. Improved communication between the spouses is a predictor of the closeness of the conjugal relationship and has been known to affect fertility and contraceptive behaviour. (Sujatha and Murthy, 1993).

Amna Swar-Eldahab (1993) in his study found that 75 per cent of men discussed of family planning and its concepts with their wives. Greater awareness about family planning methods (90%) did not translate into actual practice.

Mahadevan (1979), Shivaraju (1987) and Sujatha and Murthy, (1993) reported that "Positive relationship between husband and wife communication and use of family planning methods and a concomitant negative relationship between interspousal communication and desired fertility and contraceptive behaviour.

(d) Infrastructural Facilities and Family Planning Adoption Status

The NFHS survey in Andhra Pradesh (1992-93) found that health functionaries constitute a major percentage (78%) of resources for the current adopters. 2 per cent of users obtain their methods from other sources such as shops, friends and relatives. Government, Municipal hospital supplied 60 per cent of current users compared with 18 per cent from private sectors. 66 per cent of users obtained condoms from shops 86 per cent of modern methods in rural areas are supplied by public sectors. While in urban areas, the public sector supplies 62 per cent of methods, in all, one tenth of sterilisation are conducted in private sectors.

Only 31 per cent of users obtain birth control pills from government sources. The majority obtained pills from private medical sector (42%) or from shops, friends or relatives (27%). The private sector has an even greater role in the provision of condoms. The private medical sector supplied 20 per cent of condom and other private sector sources supply a further 65 per cent.

For many years, the family welfare programme is utilising the electronic mass-media to promote family planning messages through various mass-media. The respondents were asked whether they heard such messages on radio or television in the last few months. The effort to disseminate family planning information through the electronic mass-media has succeeded in reaching 58 per cent of married women in Andhra Pradesh. This suggests that the electronic media play only a limited profile in reaching potential users of family planning in nation. Health provider's availability, acceptability for information and services play a crucial role for family planning adoption.

The preceding review of literature highlights the piece-meal efforts made by several researchers who study one or the other variables which are influencing maternal, child health and family planning services utilisation. Hence, there is a dire necessity for a detailed study of the subject under research which was considered all the dimensions of maternal and child health and the influence of intervening factors over the different stages of maternity cycle.

Chapter—3
Methodology

The selection of research design is an important and essential step in research, as it is concerned with the overall framework for conducting the study by giving a plan, structure and strategy of investigation (Abdellah and Leveine, 1987). Therefore this chapter deals with the objectives, hypotheses, conceptual frame work, operational definitions, sample frame and size, area of the study, tool of data collection, plan of data analysis and limitations of the study.

OBJECTIVES OF THE STUDY

1. To study the extent of utilisation of maternal, child health and family planning services in the two contrastingly selected districts (Kurnool and Mahabubnagar) of Andhra Pradesh.
2. To study the socio-economic, socio-cultural and demographic profile of the respondent.
3. To study the health infrastructural factors and quality of services such as accessibility, availability of health services and their influence on the utilisation of maternal, child health and family planning services.
4. To study the socio-cultural practices of respondents associated with the different levels of maternal care.
5. To study the influence of selected socio-economic, socio-cultural and demographic variables that influence the

utilisation of maternal viz, antenatal, natal, postnatal, child health and family planning services.

6. To study the morbidity and mortality pattern among mothers and children in the study area.
7. To study atleast one representative case study focusing on the antenatal, natal, postnatal, child health and family planning services, problems faced by respondents and remedial measures taken to prevent them (The problems like risk cases in antenatal period, self delivery practices, parinatal morbidity and mortality).
8. To recommend the strategies for effective utilisation of health interventions for optimum level of health functioning.

HYPOTHESES

On the basis of the objectives and the review of related literature, the following hypotheses have been formulated:

1. a. The level of female education is positively associated with the utilisation of maternal and child health services;

   b. Higher the level of female education, higher will be the contraceptive adoption;
2. Higher the level of annual family income, higher will be the utilisation of maternal, child health and family planning services;
3. a. The forward caste women may utilise better maternal, child health and family planning services than the lower caste women because of their better socio-economic status;
4. Greater the infrastructural facilities (*viz.*, accessibility and availability of health facilities) better will be the utilisation of maternal, child health services and adoption of family planning;
5. a. Better the quality of service, (*eg:* availability of health personnel and their approach to community

in providing health services to the needy population) higher will be the utilisation of maternal and child health services;

b. Better quality of services facilitates higher contraceptive adoption;

6. a. Increased interspouse communication may have a greater influence on the utilisation of maternal and child health services;

   b. Increased interspouse communication may have better influence over the family planning adoption;

7. Women in younger age groups are likely to make use of the utilisation of maternal and child health services to a greater extent, as compared to women of higher age groups. It is because younger women are more innovative by virtue of better education and exposure to modern life;

8. Age at marriage will have a positive association with the adoption of family planning methods because of several reasons such as greater awareness and exposure to information, education of communication activities;

9. a. Decision-making by the women, jointly with their husbands will lead to greater utilisation of maternal and child health services than decisions taken by husband alone;

   b. Joint decisions by the couple may lead to higher acceptance of family planning adoption because the decision by the couple is an improvement over the traditional decisions of the husbands alone.

Operational Definitions

(i) Utilisation of Health Services

The maternal, child health and family planning services provided by government and other agencies that are adopted and practised by the rural women and children for their well being.

(ii) Maternal Health

The total health of the mother during the total maternity cycle *i.e.* conception, antenatal, intranatal, postnatal and interconceptional period.

(iii) Child Health

The total health of the child from birth to under five years of age.

(iv) Family Planning Services

The services that are provided to the couple:

- to control the time at which births occur in relation to the age of mother;
- to determine the number of children within the family;
- to avoid unwanted pregnancies;
- to help the country in controlling population explosion.

(v) Maternal, Child Health Services

The health services provided to mother and child in relation to prevention of diseases, promotion of health, curative and restorative in nature.

(vi) Respondents

Currently married women, who are in reproductive period (after puberty till menopause *i.e.*, 13-45 years) and are having atleast one under five living child.

(vii) Rural Area

A permanent small settlement area having katcha, pucca and thatched housing systems, consisting of different castes and agricultural communities, relevant for conducive living in order to meet the minimum basic needs of the community.

Conceptual Framework

Review of literature in the preceding chapter highlighted the influence of many independent variables on the utilisation of maternal, child health and family planning services. Therefore a conceptual model (*i.e.* the theoretical basis) is required to identify and explain in linkages between the different independent variables, with utilisation pattern (dependent variable). A model for explaining the utilisation pattern in the less developed and backward regions has been developed, using variables generally found to be determining utilisation pattern. This model was tested, with the help of data collected from the two differentially developed districts, and to gain an insight into differences between these two districts.

Some of the following important studies have been considered as the basis for the development of the present conceptual model. (Mahadevan. 1989; Kanitkar *et al* 1989; Srivastava and Saxena, 1988; Ray *et al*, 1988; National Family Health Survey, 1992; Yagob *et al*, 1993; Rajeswari and Hasalkour, 1994; World Bank and Cairo reports, 1994; Bhatia and Cleland, 1995; and Reproductive and Child Healthcare Studies Models, 1996 etc).

Maternal and child health services through various programmes are initiated by Government of India to benefit the large number of beneficiaries who are at risk. The preventive, promotive and curative services under these programmes were delivered to the beneficiaries through the infrastructure network which primarily consist of primary health centres, sub-centres and other agencies. Since a large number of beneficiaries are in rural areas, various factors intervene in the delivery and utilisation of maternal, child health and supportive family planning services. The goal of reducing the morbidity and mortality among mothers and children could not be realised because of various reasons.

The conceptual model explains the influence of the factors that intervene in the utilisation of maternal, child health and family planning services. The important aspects are infrastructural facilities and quality of services that decide the accessibility, availability and acceptability of these services. Secondly the socio-economic, socio-cultural and demographic characteristics of the women respondents, influence the level of utilisation of maternal and child health services. However the extent of community participation in these programmes may also act as a catalyst for between utilisation of health services. Of course, the prevalence of morbidity and mortality among mothers and children, the level

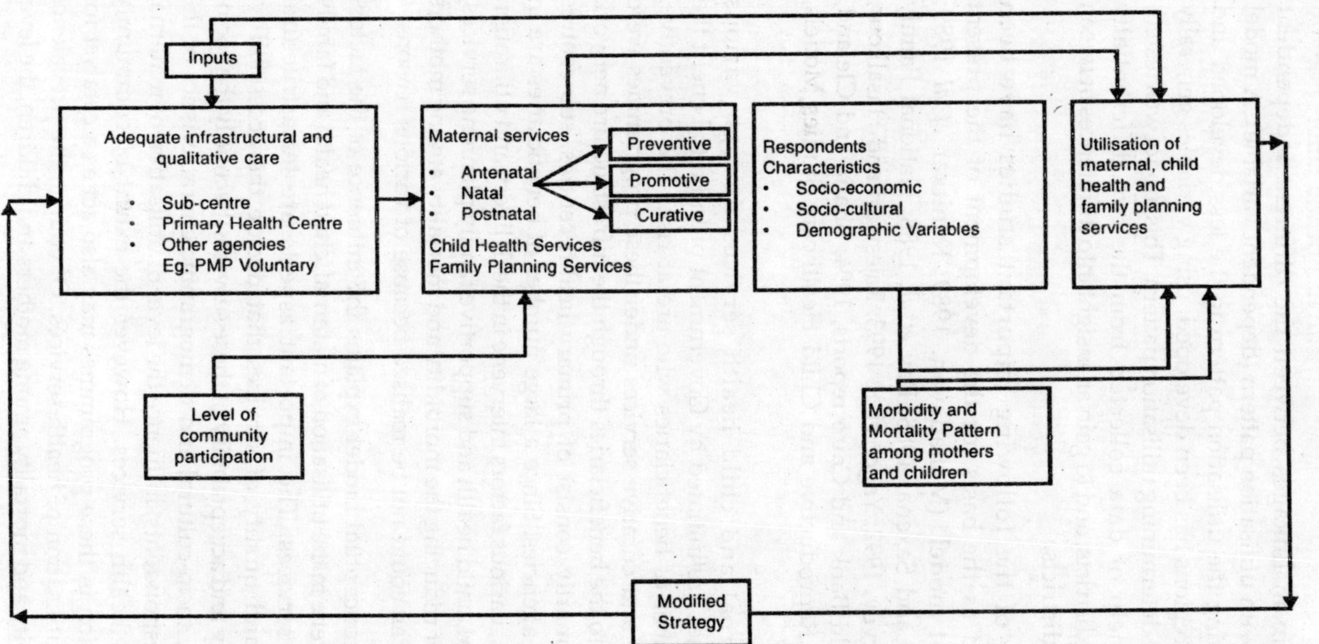

Schematic representation of utilisation of Maternal, Child Health and Family Planning Services

of awareness about the maternal, child health and family planning services may also contribute to restore and maintain the health of the mothers and children.

A simple schematic conceptual model on utilisation of maternal, child health and family planning services on the above discussion is presented here. *(See diagram on page 44)*

Sample Frame and Size

It is based on an empirical study, an integrated approach *i.e.*, both qualitative and quantitative methodology with random sampling technique has been adopted.

In the first stage of sampling two districts of Andhra Pradesh, the Mahabubnagar district from the most backward region of Telangana and the another moderately developed Kurnool district of Rayalaseema region have been selected randomly.

In the second stage of sampling, all the 137 primary health centres in the two study districts were listed out. Out of them, two primary health centres from each district were selected at random.

Subsequently in the third stage of sampling, 124 villages under the four primary health centres were listed out. From this list, one village with a sub-centre and the other which is an interior village were selected at random. Thus two villages from each primary health centre with a total of eight villages (that is 4 sub-centre villages and 4 interior villages from the selected primary health centres) were considered for the study.

A sample of 200 respondents from each primary health centre were selected at random. Thus 400 respondents from each study district and 800 respondents for the entire study area consist of the total sample. The respondents for the study were: currently married women in the reproductive age group (13-49 years) with atleast one under-five living child.

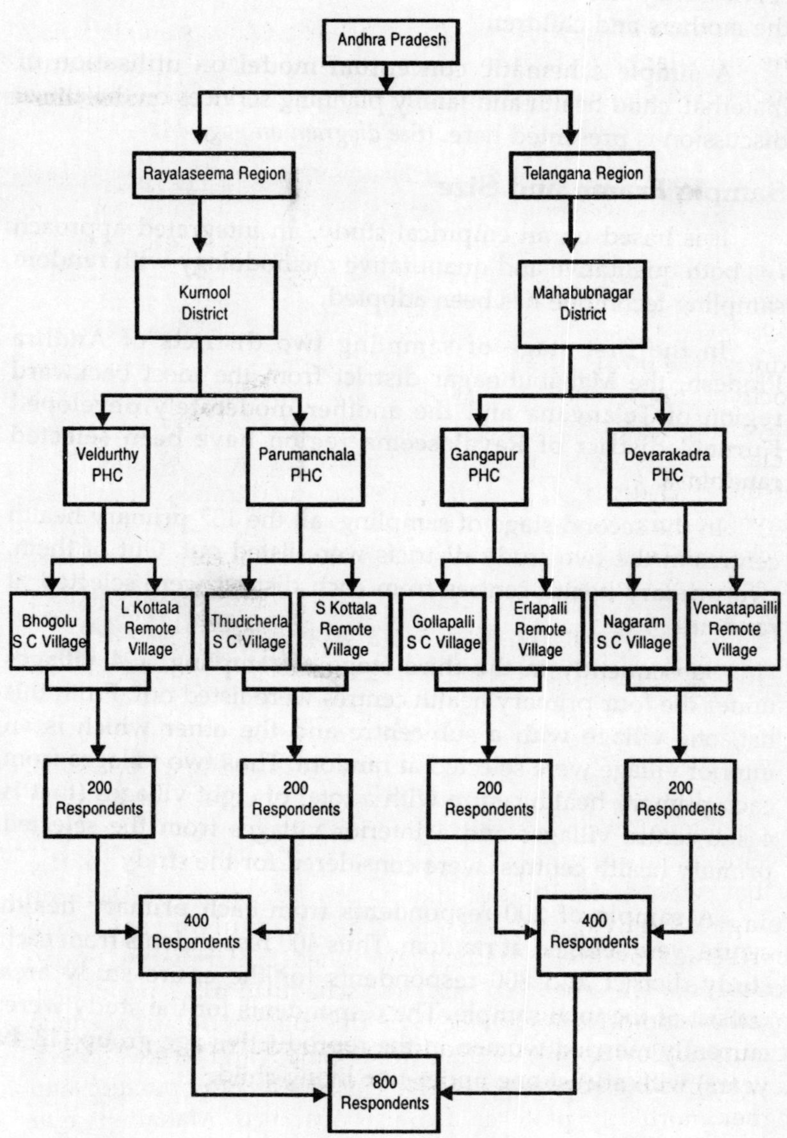

Schematic Representation of Sample Frame and Size

Area of the Study

Andhra Pradesh is not only a heterogeneous state, but also the fifth largest state in India, both in terms of area and population. It has an area of 275,068 sq. kms. and a population of 66,508,008 (1991 Census).

The state has three distinctly developed, geographical and ecological regions *viz.* Coastal Andhra, Telangana and Rayalaseema regions spreading over 23 districts. Coastal Andhra region has nine districts. Rayalaseema region four and Telangana region ten. Coastal Andhra covers 34 per cent of land area, Telangana 42 per cent and Rayalaseema 24 per cent in the state. Among the three regions, the Coastal Andhra is well developed socio-economically, compared to the other two regions. The Rayalaseema region is moderately developed and the largest Telangana region is the most backward region in the state. Out of these 23 districts, one district from moderately developed Rayalaseema region *i.e.,* Kurnool and another district from backward Telangana region that is, Mahabubnagar are randomly selected for the present study.

PROFILE OF THE DISTRICTS

Mahabubnagar District

The district is largely covered by forest and hilly areas, hence, the concentration of the population is mostly in the plains, leading to high density of population in plain areas. The district is considered backward in may aspects such as low per capita income, more percentage of seasonal migrants, a high percentage of backward communities like backward caste representing Telaga, Kuruva, Uppara etc. The scheduled castes are represented by Mala, Madiga and scheduled tribes by Sugali population. The scheduled caste and scheduled tribes population together comprise 25 per cent of the total population which account for low socio-economic development and backwardness. Low female literacy, high decadal growth rate of population and higher morbidity patterns are also observed. Mahabubnagar district has the mean age at marriage of 16.5 years, lower than state average, highest birth rate (30.3), with low couple protection rate (35.2). The total fertility rate in the district is highest (4.2) in the state.

The infant mortality rate (99) and maternal mortality rate (4.2) are also high. The utilisation of maternal, child health and family planning services are low viz, percentage of deliveries conducted by trained personnel (46.3 per cent). Institutional deliveries (20.5 per cent), protection to antenatal mothers from Tetanus (61.4 per cent), fully immunised children (12-24 months—44.3 per cent) etc.

In Mahabubnagar district, there are 67 primary health centres, out of which two primary health centres *viz.*, Gangapur and Devarakadra were randomly selected for the present study.

Gangapur primary health centre is located 26 kms east of the district headquarters, with a total population of 77,956 spread over 57 villages, covered by 12 sub-centres. Of the 12 sub-centres, Gollapalli, a sub centre village and Erlapalli, a remote village were randomly selected.

The other primary health centre, Devarakadra is located 26 kms. west of Mahabubnagar town with a total population of 25,575. The primary health centre is spread into five sub-centres covering 16 villages. Of these, Nagaram, a sub centre village and Venkataipalli, a remote village were randomly selected.

Kurnool District

In contrast, Kurnool district which is adjacent to Mahabubnagar district has higher birth rate (25.0) in Rayalaseema. It stands eighth in the state of Andhra Pradesh. The mean age at marriage is 17.64 years. The total fertility rate is 3.4. The female literacy rate is also low (22.2 per cent) and ranks 14th in the state. The maternal mortality rate (3.2) and infant mortality rate (70) are moderately high. The scheduled caste and scheduled tribe population comprise 17.42 per cent and 11.90 per cent of the total population, 85 per cent children are fully immunised. Through the district is less developed in many facets, it is picking up in health development because of the implementation of national health programmes such as Child Survival and Safe Motherhood Programme, Reproductive and Child Health Programme.

To cater the primary health care needs, the district has 70 primary health centres, of which 2 PHCs, *viz.*, Parumanchala and

Veldurthy primary health centres were randomly selected for the study.

Parumanchala primary health centre is located 34 kms. east of the district headquarters with a total population of 14,287 consisting of 3 subcentres with six villages. Among the 3 sub-centres. Thudicherla, a sub-centre village and Siddeswara Kottala, a remote village were randomly selected for the present study.

Thudicherla is located 10 kms. from the primary health centre, with a total population of 3,378. Siddeswaram Kottala is situated 14 kms. away from primary health centre, 6 kms, from sub-centre covering a total population of 3,209. No transportation facilities are available to this interior village.

The other primary health centre selected for the study, Veldurthy is situated 32 kms. away from the district head-quarters, with a total population of 49,823. The primary health centre has nine sub-centres covering 42 villages. Out of nine sub-centres, Bhogolu, a sub-centre village and L.Kottala, a remote village, were randomly selected for the study. Bhogolu covers a total population of 1483 and L. Kottala 737. The topographical, geographical and other salient features of the two districts on a comparative basis are given in Appendix—I.

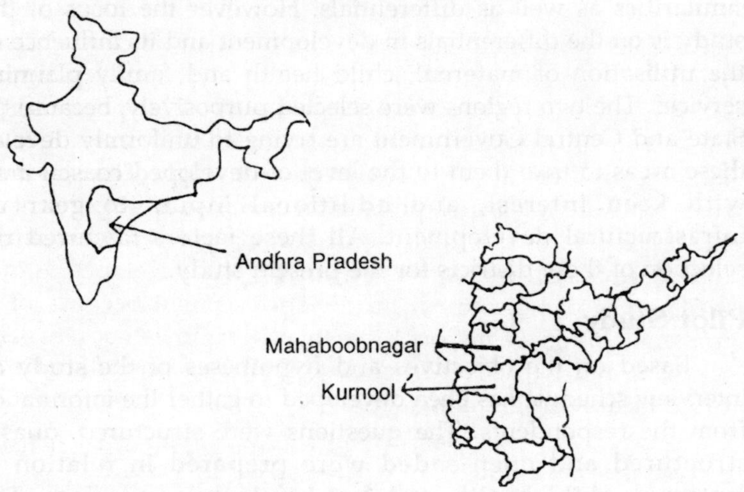

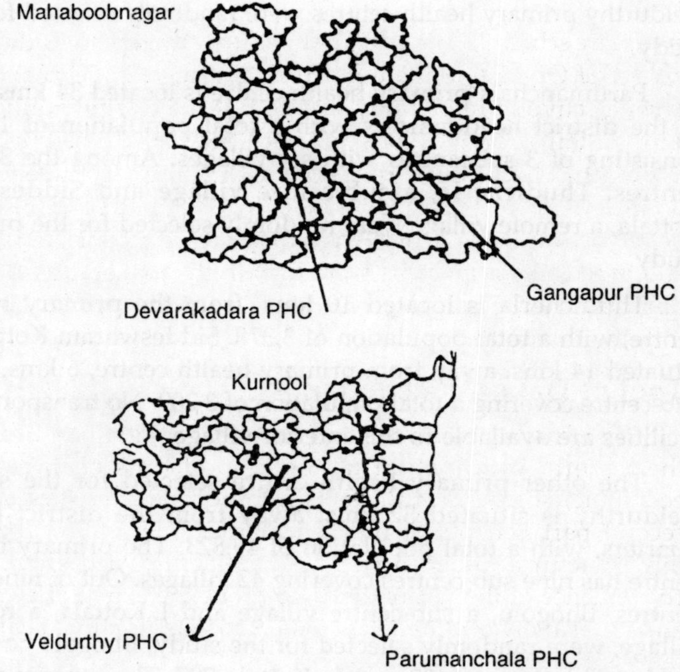

Map showing the area under the study

These two neighbouring districts represent certain cultural similarities as well as differentials. However the focus of this study is on the differentials in development and its influence on the utilisation of maternal, child health and family planning services. The two regions were selected purposively, because the State and Central Government are trying to uniformly develop these areas to take them to the level of developed coastal area, with keen interest, and additional inputs to gear up infrastructural development. All these factors favoured the selection of these districts for the present study.

Pilot Study

Based on the objectives and hypotheses of the study an interview schedule has been developed to gather the information from the respondents. The questions were structured, quasit-structured and open-ended were prepared in relation to maternal, child health and family planning services. The interview schedule was tried out on fifty mothers in Rudravaram village of Orvakal Mandal in Kurnool district in February, 1996. The objective of pilot study was to test the clarity, applicability and feasibility of questions. Pilot study was followed by survey approach. Some vague questions which the respondents were unable to respond were deleted in the final schedule. Only perfected questions, which were found to be reliable, meaningful and practically applicable were kept in the tool and used for the final study. The sample considered for pilot was not included for original study.

Tool of Data Collection

The final schedule has two sub section. First part deals with the general information of the respondents such as socio-economic, socio-cultural, demographic characteristics etc. The second part consists of the items about information regarding infrastructural facilities such as availability, accessibility and convenience of the respondents, to probe the extent of awareness and utilisation of antenatal, natal, postnatal, child health and family planning services.

The variables considered for this study include:

Dependent Variables

The utilisation of maternal, child health and family planning services have the following dimensions. All these five dimensions have separately analysed.

- **Antenatal Services**
  - Type of services obtained during antenatal period.
    - Lab investigation
    - Iron and folic acid tablets consumption
    - Immunization
    - Health education received
- **Natal Services**
  - Place of delivery
  - Person conducted delivery
  - Newborn care practices

❑ Postnatal services	• Postnatal visits • Postnatal services *eg:* Perinneal care, breast care, health education activities etc. • Treatment obtained during postnatal problems
❑ Child health services	• Feeding pattern • Immunisation services • Remedy services obtained during child morbidity
❑ Family Planning Services	• Preacceptance services • Adoptive Status • Follow-up services

Independent Variables

(a) Socio-economic Variables

- Education
- Occupation
- Annual family income

(b) Socio-cultural Variables

- Religion, Caste
- Type of family
- Consanguinity
- Sex-preference
- Interspouse communication
- Decision making

(c) Demographic Variables

- Current age of respondents
- Age at marriage of respondents
- Duration of married life

- Number of
  - — Conceptions
  - — abortions
  - — still births
  - — living children

(d) Infrastructural Variable

- accessibility
- availability of health providers
- qualitative care

(e) Cultural and hygienic practices related to maternal and child care.

(f) Awareness of respondents related to maternal, child health and family planning services.

Data Collection Procedure

Prior to the actual data collection, attempts were made to build rapport with the community and health care authorities, in order to win the confidence of the respondent and co-operation and to prove correct answer without any inhibitions. The survey approach was used for data collection. For the study, data were generated to establish the casual relationship between major independent and dependent variables. The mothers were interviewed either in the morning or in the evening, depending upon their availability at their residence from 7.00 a.m. to 5.00 p.m. for a period of six months. Responses were recorded simultaneously during interview. It look 15 minutes for introduction to gain the confidence of people and 45 minutes for actually interviewing each other.

Data Analysis

The data were scrutinised and edited before they were subjected to coding and verification. After that, computer facility was used for the entire analysis of data. The univariate, bivariate, multivariate tables and indexes have been prepared to identify the relationship among the variables, to explore the extent of utilisation of maternal, child health and family planning services. The data related to utilisation of services by the respondents were dichotomized into two categories *viz.* utilised and non-utilized category. If the respondents used either one or the other health services during maternity cycle they come under "utilised category" and if the mother does not avail single service, they come under, "non-utilised category's. Logistic regression analysis was used separately for all the dependent variables.

Limitations of the Study

- The study is confined to rural women, who are currently married and are having atleast one under five living child.
- The study is limited to the rural area of two districts of Andhra Pradesh (*i.e.,* Kurnool and Mahabuhnagar districts).
- Verbal statements of rural women regarding utilisation of maternal, child health and family planning services are considered for analysis.

Chapter—4

Results and Discussion of Findings

This chapter deals with two sub-sections. It begins with a discussion on socio-economic and socio-cultural profile of the respondents. The variables considered for the study are:

I. a. Socio-economic Variables *eg:* Education, occupation and income;

b. Socio-cultural Varibles *eg:* Religion, caste, consanguinity, interspousal communication and sex preference;

c. Ecological Variables *eg:* Housing conditions, environment;

d. Demographic characteristics of respondents *eg:* Current age of the respondent, age at marriage, age at conception and age at first birth etc;

e. Infrastructural facilities *eg:* Accessibility of services, availability and quality of services rendered by health functionaries.

The data were analysed and interpreted in aggregate for both the districts at the first instance and separately for each of the districts, wherever the findings vary significantly.

II. The second sub-section deals with the utilisation of maternal, child health and the family planning services throughout the maternity cycle of women *viz.*, antenatal,

natal, postnatal, child health and the family planning services. Each of the above services were considered as dependent variables and they are cross tabulated with the selected independent variables and they are cross tabulated with the selected independent variables such as socio-economic, socio-cultural, demographic and infrastructural facilities.

PROFILE OF THE RESPONDENTS

I. (a) Socio-economic Characteristics of the Respondents

This sub-section deals with the distribution of respondents according to their socio-economic characteristics in total and their distributions in each district (Kurnool and Mahabubnagar) and are represented in Table—4.1. The variables considered here includes education, occupation, annual family income and the number of hours spent by the respondent in relation to the household and income generating activities.

Table—4.1

The percentage distribution of respondents by socio-economic characteristics

Socio-economic characteristics	*Kurnool District*	*Mahabubnagar District*	*Total*
1	2	3	4
(i) Education			
Illiterate	78.50 (314)	87.00 (348)	82.75 (662)
Primary School	11.00 (44)	5.75 (23)	8.38 (67)
Middle School and above	10.50 (42)	7.25 (29)	8.88 (71)
(ii) Occupation			
Housewives	19.00 (76)	11.00 (44)	15.00 (120)
Cooly	59.50 (238)	73.25 (293)	66.38 (531)

(Contd . . .)

1	2	3	4
Cultivation	19.25 (77)	15.25 (61)	17.25 (138)
Petty business	2.25 (9)	0.50 (2)	1.38 (11)
(iii) Annual Family Income (Rs.)			
< 10,000/- (low)	17.25 (69)	23.75 (95)	20.50 (164)
10,001/- to 14,000/- (middle)	39.50 (158)	31.75 (127)	35.63 (285)
14,001/- to 18,000/- (middle)	27.25 (109)	29.75 (119)	28.50 (228)
18,001/- +(high)	16.00 (64)	14.75 (59)	15.38 (123)
Average	16,035/-	14,612/-	15,323/-
(iv) Utilisation of Time (hours/day)			
(i) Household activities			
< 7	16.50 (66)	20.00 (80)	18.25 (146)
8 – 9	44.00 (176)	48.25 (193)	46.13 (369)
10 +	39.50 (158)	31.75 (127)	35.63 (285)
Average	8.9725	8.5675	8.77
(ii) Income-generating activities			
< 7	25.75 (103)	18.50 (74)	22.13 (177)
8	61.25 (245)	66.25 (265)	63.75 (510)
9 +	13.00 (52)	15.25 (61)	14.13 (113)
Total	100.00 (400)	100.00 (400)	100.00 (800)

(Figure in the parenthesis represents absolute numbers)

(i) Education

The literacy rates in the nation and in the states show that about 50 per cent population are illiterates (India-51.6%; A.P.-45%). The female literacy rate is still very low in India (39.3%) and in Andhra Pradesh it is 33.7 per cent as per 1991 Census.

According to the present study, an overwhelming percentage of respondent (83%) are illiterates. Even among the literates (17%), 8 per cent were educated upto primary school level only. The remaining 9 per cent studied upto middle school and above. None of them crossed above high school level.

The districts-wise data shows a clear picture in consonance with the census data to education (Kurnool district—26.2% and Mahabuhnagar district 15.9%). (Hand Book of Statistics, 1993-94). Women in Mahabuhnagar district manifest lowest literacy *i.e.* 13 per cent against 22 per cent in Kurnool district. It is surprising to note that among the literates, 11 per cent of respondents in Kurnool and just 6 per cent in Mahabubnagar have studied upto primary school level only. Around 11 per cent in Kurnool district and 7 per cent of respondent in Mahabubnagar district studied upto middle school and above. The findings show that the education of the girls is given low priority in both the districts as is found in any rural India.

(ii) Occupation

Two thirds of the respondents (66%) are coolies including agricultural labourers. 17 per cent are engaged in cultivation and 15 per cent are Housewives followed by negligible percentage (1%) of respondents taking up petty business. The districts wise data shows similar trends. In Kurnool and Mahabubnagar districts, the highest percentage of respondents are engaged in coolly occupation (59%-Kurnool; 73%-Mahabubnagar) followed by cultivation (19% in Kurnool and 15% in Mahabubnagar). Low percentage of respondents are housewives (Kurnool-19%, Mahabubnagar-11%) Thus majority of respondents are dependent on agriculture and its related occupations only. As expected, none of the respondent had higher occupational status.

(iii) Annual Family Income

Income from ıll sources of family is considered as 'total family income'. The annual family income of the respondents are broadly divided into three categories, those with annual family income upto Rs. 10,000/- are considered as 'low' income group' and with Rs. 10,001/- to Rs. 18,000/- are considered as 'middle income group' and more than Rs. 18,000/- income are considered as 'high income group' Nearly two thirds of respondents (64%) in the study sample were belonging to middle income group and one fifth of the sample lies under low income group, whereas few percentage of (15%) respondents fall in high income group. Among the districts, the trend is more or less the same. However slightly higher percentage of respondents in Kurnool district are having income than in Mahabubnagar district. With regards to the average income, it is Rs. 15,323/- for total population, however it is Rs. 16,035/- for Kurnool district and Rs. 14,612/- for Mahabubnagar district respectively.

The respondents economic status in Mahabubnagar district is slightly lower than their counterparts in Kurnool district. The reasons attributed for high income in Kurnool district are: high per capita income, high literacy status, irrigation facilities, industrialisation, labour potential, mineral resources and less migration. Higher percentage of respondents fall in middle income group category in both the districts (Kurnool—67%; Mahabubnagar—62%), followed by low income group (Mahabubnagar—24%; Kurnool—17%) and high income group (Kurnool—16% Mahabubnagar—15%).

(iv) Activities of Respondents (Utilisation of Time)

The woman have a very important function of 'home-making' in which she has to perform many functions and play multiple roles at home to befitting her status in the family. Apart from the primary role of woman *i.e.* child bearing and rearing, home management, socialisation, she has additional responsibility of supplementing the family income by taking up certain income generating activities such as employment.

The time spent for activities at home and occupation in pursuit of income present in the Table—4.1. points to the drudgery that woman undergoes which affects her health. On an average, the women are spending about 16 hours per day (8.77 hours for household activities and 7.67 hours for income generating activities) in both the districts. Thus women share greater responsibility and shoulder greater burden at home than men, besides adding to the family income.

Nearly half of the respondents (46%) are spending 8-9 hours per day for household activities. Around 36 per cent of women are utilising more than 10 hours for household activities.

Nearly two thirds of women are sparing daily 8 hours for income generating activities (64%) and are assisting their spouses to meet the economic needs. It clearly depicts that women work outside the home in agricultural activities mostly to add income to the family. This is a common phenomenon observed in rural areas.

Table—4.2
The percentage distribution of respondents by socio-cultural characteristics

Socio-cultural characteristics	*Kurnool District*	*Mahabubnagar District*	*Total*
1	2	3	4
(i) Religion			
Hindu	92.75 (371)	93.75 (375)	93.25 (746)
Muslim	3.75 (15)	5.50 (22)	4.63 (37)
Christian	3.50 (14)	0.75 (3)	2.13 (17)
(a) Caste			
Forward	19.50 (78)	11.25 (45)	15.38 (123)
Backward	52.75 (211)	56.25 (225)	54.50 (436)
Scheduled Caste and Scheduled Tribe	25.75 (111)	32.50 (130)	30.13 (241)

(Contd . . .)

1	2	3	4
(ii) Type of Family			
Joint	29.25 (117)	33.75 (135)	31.50 (252)
Nuclear	70.75 (283)	66.25 (265)	68.50 (548)
(iii) Relationship with Husband before Marriage			
No relationship	50.75 (203)	45.25 (181)	48.00 (384)
Maternal uncle	32.25 (129)	36.75 (147)	34.50 (276)
Cousin	17.00 (68)	18.00 (72)	17.50 (140)
(iv) Interspouse Communication			
(i) On sexual matters			
No	70.25 (281)	87.00 (348)	78.63 (629)
Yes	29.75 (119)	13.00 (52)	21.38 (171)
(ii) On family size limitation			
No	47.75 (191)	69.00 (276)	58.38 (467)
Yes	52.25 (209)	311.00 (124)	41.63 (333)
(v) Sex Preference			
Yes	12.25 (49)	22.50 (90)	17.38 (139)
No	87.75 351)	77.50 (310)	82.63 (661)
Total	**100.00** **(400)**	**100.,00** **(400)**	**100.00** **(800)**

(b) Socio-cultural Characteristics of the Respondents

Human behaviour is complex and is influenced by a variety of cultural factors. The ideas, attitudes values of the people and the way of life, are greatly effected by the culture of their society. The traditional cultural practices still have their hold on health practices of people. The inbuilt system of cultural belies and values affects the desires of couples for a larger family. The religion, caste and higher preference for male child influence the acceptance of health care services and its utilisation. Thus the socio-cultural practices, either facilitates or hinders the utilisation of health services particularly related to mother and child care.

This sub-section deals with socio-cultural variables such as religion, caste, family type, consanguinity, sex preference and interspouse communication etc. are depicted in Table—4.2.

(i) Religion and Caste

Religion and Caste are the social stratification variables which are to be considered in studying the traditional and modern practice related to health behaviour.

In Andhra Pradesh, as per 1991 census the Hindus constitute the major community (89%) followed by Muslims (9%) and Christians (2%) who are negligible. The present study also observed the similar trend with all three religions. The sample shows an overwhelming per cent (93%) of respondents who belong to Hindu religion followed by 5 per cent Muslims and 2 per cent Christians. However, the distribution of respondents by caste rather than the religion is of great significant in analysing the extent of utilisation of maternal, child health and family planning services.

The study population is broadly classified into forward caste, backward case, scheduled caste and scheduled tribes. In the study area, backward castes constitute about 55 per cent (Telaga, Boya, Kuruba, Uppari, Sali, Balija etc) followed by 30 per cent scheduled castes (Mala, Madiga) and scheduled tribes, (Erukala and Sugali) and forward caste.

Only 15 per cent. (Kammas, Reddys, Kapus, Brahmins and Vysyas). The weaker section are largely represented in the sample, because in rural areas generally the representation of forward castes are limited.

With regards to the district data, the representation of backward caste is more or less the same (Kumool district—53%; Mahabubnagar district—56% respectively). However the forward caste are significantly higher in Kurnool district (20%) than in Mahabubnagar district (11%). The reverse trend is observed among scheduled castes and scheduled tribes (Mahabubnagar—33%, Kurnool—26%). The higher representation of scheduled caste in Mahabubnagar district reflects the socio-economic and socio-cultural backwardness of the district.

(ii) Family Structure

The type of family reflects, the nature of social environment, provided to the members and formation of their attitudes through socialisation process. In the present study, the respondents' families are dichotomised into nuclear and joint families/extended families. In the present study, joint and extended families are clubbed as single unit as extended families are limited in number.

More than two thirds of families were nuclear (68.5%), and the remaining 31.5 per cent were joint families. Almost similar trends were observed within the districts also. Major percentage of families are belonging to nuclear (Kurnool—71% and Mahabubnagar—66%) and the rest of families are joint families/ extended (Kurnool—29%, Mahabubnagar—34%). the transition of joint families into nuclear families were observed in the study area.

(iii) Relationship of Husband with the Respondent Before Marriage

The marriage between relatives is a customary practice, which is commonly observed in southern states especially in Tamilnadu and Andhra Pradesh. The people preferred consanguineous marriages because of traditional and cultural reasons such as, girls getting adjusted to relatives family, feeling a sense of security and comfort, strengthening family property and supporting the aged in the family. For these reasons the girls are well looked after by older generation. This maintains reciprocal kinship obligation traditionally followed by the society. It promotes better interpersonal relationships also.

In the study sample, more than half of the respondents (52%) married their relatives, among them 34.50 per cent married their maternal uncle, and the next preference being cousins (17.50%) the percentage of consanguineous marriages were high in Mahabubnagar district (55%) than in Kurnool district (49%) which indicates the prevalence of traditional, cultural practices within Mahabubnagar district. Consanguinity is said to affect the progeny, hence it needs more mother and child care from the eugenic point of view National Family Health Survey (1992-93) conducted in Andhra Pradesh also found that about 36 per cent of marriages are consanguineous only.

(iv) Interspouse Communication

The communication between the couples facilitates the decision-making process on health care matters. It brings change in the attitudes and behaviour towards healthy practices and life style modifications.

The present study made an attempt to gather the information regarding interspouse on sexual matters and family size limitation. Major percentage (78.63%) of respondents were found to be not discussing sexual matter with their husbands, perhaps they feel that interaction on sexual matters is a taboo and there is nothing to discuss among themselves. The prevalence of high percentage of reproductive tract infection among rural women is a fact that needs a mention here, because of the poor interspousal communication and ignorance, the poor women do not reveal her sexual problems. The trend is still more worse in Mahabubnagar district with 87 per cent of the women agreeing that they do not discuss sexual matters with their husbands. This might be due to deep rooted beliefs, lack of privacy, shyness coupled with ignorance and illiteracy.

The decision to limit family size with two children, promotes small family norm and regulate birth rates. Thus the intraspouse and interspouse communication on family size in time is crucial. The data shows 41.63 per cent of couples had a role in decision-making on family size. Even though the husbands play a decisive role in deciding the family size, wife and members too have an influence in this situation.

In Kurnool district, 52.25 per cent of the couple interacted among themselves on family size against only 31 per cent of them in Mahabubnagar district. The low rate of interspouse communication results in larger family size due to delayed and untimely decision by the couple or husband. Greater awareness on intraspouse and interspouse communication has to be promoted for small family norm, which is crucial for accepting cotraception.

(v) Sex Preference

In the study area, it is observed that major percentage of respondents (83%) did not have sex preference. Only 17 per cent of sample reported sex preference. However in Mahabubnagar district nearly one fourth of respondents (23%) had sex preference against Kurnool district (12%). This again reflects the low status of girls and women in Mahabubnagar district than in Kurnool district.

(c) Ecological Variables

The housing environment and its conditions reflect the socio-economic status, family, size, life style pattern, cultural practices, social participation, social support, health care practices, hygienic environment, susceptibility for morbidity and standard of living.

In this sub-section the variables such as housing conditions *eg:* type of house, number of rooms, ownership of house, and housing environment such as source of drinking water, ventilation, electrification of house, type of fuel used, toilet facilities, disposal of sullage, refuse, garbage sewage etc., have been considered and are shown in Table—4.3. *(See table on page 67)*

Based on the materials used for the construction of the walls, roof and floor, houses in the study area are trichotomised viz: katcha houses (made from mud and low cost materials);

Thatched houses (made from brick or stones, but roof is by leaves or sticks) and pucca houses (made from high quality materials including the roof, walls and floor). In the total sample population, around half of the respondents (49.75%) are residing in pucca houses, followed by katcha houses (36.75%) and thatched houses (13.50%) the districts also show similar trend. A major percentages of sample are residing in own houses (88.25%), only few percentage of sample are residing in rented houses (11.75%). 41 per cent of respondents had one living room, other than kitchen, 43 per cent of respondents did not have separate living room. They have one room in which all the needs like cooking, bathing, sleeping activities will be performed.

The housing environment is an important of the health status of the members in the family specifically the children. More than half of the sample 51.13 per cent get water from borewell, 22.63 per cent from public well and 26.25 per cent of them from public tap and other resources. 82 per cent of the sample reside in moderate ventilated houses. Nearly two thirds of people (60.88%) are still using non-electrified houses. Several types of fuels are used for cooking but, firewood (87.50%) is the most common fuel. 9 per cent of sample use kerosine stove. Only a small percentage (3.50%) use gas as fuel.

The availability of sanitary facilities is an important determinant factor for health status. The majority of families (87.13%) did not have toilet facilities within the house. They either utilise public toilet (5.25%) or go outside. Only 7.63 per cent of the sample had sanitary latrines within the houses.

80.38 per cent of respondents throw refuse and garbage by means of open dumping. Only 19.63 per cent dispose the refuse and garbage in manure pits. The closed drainage facilities are available for 15.25 per cent of respondents' houses. Only 7 per cent of residents are having soaked pits and the remaining household are with open draining facilities. 25.75% per cent of repondents had livestock in the form of pet animals; 15 per cent of them keep it within the residence and the other 10.75 per cent of them keep it away from the residence.

Table—4.3
The percentage distribution of respondents by ecological variables

Ecological Variables	*Kumool District*	*Mahabubnagar District*	*Total*
1	**2**	**3**	**4**
1. Housing Conditions			
(a) Type of house			
Katcha	35.25 (141)	38.25 (153)	36.75 (294)
Thatched	11.00 (44)	16.00 (64)	13.50 (108)
Pucca	53.75 (215)	45.75 (183)	49.75 (398)
(b) Ownership of the house			
Rented	12.50 (50)	11.00 (44)	11.75 (94)
Own	87.50 (350)	89.00 (356)	88.25 (706)
(c) Number of living rooms			
No separate room	39.25 (157)	42.25 (169)	40.75 (326)
One living room	45.25 (181)	41.25 (165)	43.25 (346)
Two living rooms	15.50 (62)	16.50 (66)	16.00 (128)
2. Housing Environment			
(a) Sources of drinking water			
Public well	30.50 (122)	14.75 (59)	22.63 (181)
Bore Well	51.25 (205)	51.00 (204)	51.13 (409)

(Contd . . .)

1	2	3	4
Public tap	17.25 (69)	31.75 127)	24.50 (196)
Own tap	1.00 (4)	2.50 (10)	1.75 (14)
(b) ***Ventilation***			
Poor	10.50 (42)	13.00 (52)	11.75 (94)
Moderate	80.75 (323)	83.25 (333)	82.00 (656)
Good	8.75 (35)	3.75 (15)	6.25 (50)
(c) ***Lighting of the house***			
Kerosine lamp	52.50 (210)	69.25 (277)	60.88 (487)
Electricity	47.50 (190)	30.75 (123)	39.13 (313)
(d) ***Type of fuel used***			
Firewood	85.25 (341)	89.75 (359)	87.50 (700)
Kerosine stove	10.25 (41)	7.75 (31)	9.00 (72)
Gas	4.50 (18)	2.50 (10)	3.50 (28)
(e) ***Toilet facilities***			
No toilet facilities (Open field defecation)	86.25 (345)	88.00 (352)	87.13 (697)
Within the Residence (RCA latrine)	6.75 (27)	8.50 (34)	7.63 (61)
Away from the residence (Public toilet)	7.00 (28)	3.50 (14)	5.25 (42)

(Contd . . .)

1	2	3	4
(e) Disposal of refuse and garbage			
Near the resident	33.00 (132)	31.25 (125)	32.13 257)
Open dumping	45.25 (181)	51.25 (205)	48.25 (386)
Manure pit	21.75 (87)	17.50 (70)	19.63 (157)
(f) Disposal of sullage			
Open into the streets	69.25 (277)	86.25 (345)	77.75 (622)
Drainage	39.75 (119)	0.75 (3)	15.25 (122)
Soakage pit	1.00 (4)	13.00 (52)	7.00 (56)
(g) Domestic animals and place of keeping them			
No pet animals	73.50 (294)	75.00 (300)	74.25 (594)
Within the residence	17.50 (70)	12.50 (50)	15.00 (120)
Away from the residence	9.00 (36)	12.50 (50)	10.75 (86)
Total	**100.00 (400)**	**100.00 (400)**	**100.00 (800)**

(d) Demographic Characteristics of Respondents

The demographic characteristics of respondents provide a basis for understanding the distribution of respondents by the different demographic variables.

In this sub-station, the variables in the reproductive life span are considered. The age of the respondent at the occurrence of a particular event in their life cycle may explain the health status behaviour of women. The variables such as the current age of the respondent, age at marriage, age at first birth, number of conceptions, living children, foetal wastage (abortion) and still birth are analysed in the present investigation as depicted in Table—4.6.

(a) Current Age of Respondents

Age is a demographic variable, which influences the utilisation of health services indirectly. The women in the younger age groups *i.e.*, <19 year and 20-24 year of age together constitute 58 per cent of the total sample. However the remaining 42 per cent of the women are distributed in the age groups of 25-29 years (29%) and 30 years and above (13%).

The district wise distribution of respondents shows that 56 per cent of the respondents are below 24 years of age in Kurnool district as against 60 per cent in Mahabubnagar district. The remaining higher age groups *i.e.*, 25 years and above are almost equally distributed. The mean age of respondents is 23.82 years in the total sample.

(b) Age at Marriage

Marriage is an important socio-cultural variable which is considered as the basis for family structure, relation and social life. It is the first step for family formation activity. It is also liked with the status of women. It is observed that, women are marrying at an early age and that in turn leads them an early child bearing period, higher levels of fertility, maternal and child morbidity and mortality.

Legislations are brought to prevent early marriages. The Child Marriage Restraint Act of 1978 or the earlier Sarada Act could not restrain the marriage of girls at an early age. Modernisation and attitudes related to socio-cultural changes have influenced the parents' ideas to same extent, as seen from the gradual raise in the age at marriage of girls in Andhra Pradesh is 18.1 years (1991 census). But still low age at marriage is prevalent in the study area *viz.*, the mean age at marriage in total population is 12.6 years. A significant difference has been observed between the districts, it is 14.4 years in Kurnool district and 13 years in Mahabubnagar district respectively.

It is also evident from the Table—4.4 that the child marriages *i.e.*, < 11 years of age (10%), adolescent marriages (12-13 years—37%, 14-17 years—48%) are highly prevalent in the study population. The data in the study area tells about higher prevalence of (95%) early marriages (before legal age at marriage which is 18 years).

Table—4.4
The percentage distribution of respondents by demographic characteristics

Demographic characteristics	*Kurnool District*	*Mahabubnagar District*	*Total*
1	**2**	**3**	**4**
A. Current Age (in years)			
< 19	13.00 (52)	19.75 (79)	16.38 (131)
20-24	43.25 (173)	40.25 (161)	41.75 (334)
25-29	30.50 (122)	28.25 (113)	29.38 (235)
30 +	13.25 ·(53)	11.75 (47)	12.50 (100)
Mean age	24.00	23.64	23.82
(B) Age at marriage (in years)			
< 9	0.50 (2)	2.25 (9)	1.38 (11)
10-11	4.00 (16)	13.50 (54)	8.75 (70)
12-13	25.25 (101)	48.75 (195)	47.00 (296)
14-15	43.00 (172)	29.25 (117)	36.13 (289)
16-17	20.00 (80)	4.00 (16)	12.00 96)
18 +	7.25 (29)	2.25 (9)	4.75 (38)
Mean age at marriage	14.43	12.98	12.62

(Contd . . .)

1	2	3	4
(C) Age at first birth (in years)			
< 13	3.50 (14)	7.75 (31)	5.63 (45)
14	12.50 (50)	24.00 (96)	18.25 (146)
15	19.25 (77)	26.25 (105)	22.75 (182)
16	23.50 (94)	18.75 (75)	21.13 (169)
17	16.75 (67)	13.75 55)	15.25 (122)
18	11.00 (44)	5.25 (21)	8.13 (65)
19 +	13.50 (54)	4.25 (17)	8.88 (71)
Mean age at first birth	16.36	15.43	15.90
(D) The duration of married life (in years)			
< 5	22.25 (89)	18.50 (74)	20.38 (163)
6-10	38.50 (154)	38.00 (152)	38.25 (306)
11-15	26.00 (104)	26.25 (105)	26.13 (209)
16 +	13.25 (53)	17.25 (69)	15.25 (122)
Mean duration of married life	9.57	10.67	10.12
Total	100.00 (400)	100.00 (400)	100.00 (800)

The data within the districts presents significant variation denoting cultural and traditional practices. However in both districts an overwhelming percentage of respondents got married very early before legal age at marriage *i.e.,* Kurnool district 93 per cent, Mahabubnagar district—98 per cent. Mahabubnagar it is observed that childhood marriages (16%) preadolescent marriages (49%) are high when compared to Kurnool district with 4.5 per cent—childhood, 25 per cent preadolescent marriages.

The data clearly focuses that the family building activity starts much earlier than 18 years *i.e.*, the stipulated age, because of the low literacy levels, poor economic status, anxiety of parents culture, fear of dowry, delayed marriages etc. To preserve the health of the mother and child, greater need of maternal, child health and family planning services are more essential.

(c) Age at First Birth

First birth signals the beginning of reproductive span in womens' life. The age at first birth depends upon the age at marriage, menarche and contraceptive adoption. In our culture a women's status in the family is high with an early delivery. Early motherhood maintains family lineage also. Interestingly 47 per cent had their first delivery by 15 years of age. However 83 per cent had their first baby by 17 years. Thus it is obvious that early age at marriage, early age ãt consummation, coupled with non-use of spacing methods have resulted in the first birth at a very low age.

The district-wise analysis show differentials in this regard. Kurnool district shows higher mean age at first birth *i.e.*, 16.36 years against 15.43 years in Mahabubnagar district.

First birth at the age of 15 years in Karnool seems to be lower *i.e.*, 35 per cent against 58 per cent in Mahabubnagar district and at 16 years, 59 per cent in Kurnool and 77 per cent in Mahabubnagar district. However about 14 per cent in Kurnool and just 4 per cent in Mahabubnagar have their first baby after 19 years. This shows the impact of differential development in these districts.

(d) The Duration of Married Life

The duration of marriage has its effect on the number of conceptions and utilisation of maternal, child health and family planning services. The longer duration of marital life may favour higher fertility in the absence of adoption of family planning. However, the couple seems to complete the desired fertility and then adopt family limitation, perhaps with ten years of marital life.

It is presumed that, longer the duration of marriage, the higher will be the fertility. About 15 per cent of respondents had more than 16 years of marital duration. More percentage (38%) of respondents had 6-10 years of marital life. More than one fourth of the sample (26.13%) had 11-15 years of marital duration. One fifth of the sample had below 5 years of marital duration. The data within the districts also presents the similar pattern.

(ii) Fertility Pattern

"To be blessed with children' is the happiest event in women's life". Fertility or child birth of the individuals depends upon the age at marriage, use of contraception and the number of conceptions. Higher number of conceptions reflects the non-use of spacing methods and the inclination for larger family size. The increase in number of conceptions is a detrimental factor on mother's health and exerts great pressure on maternal, child health and family planning services.

This sub-section describes the distribution of variables such as number of conceptions, living children, foetal wastage (still births, abortions) and family size in the study districts as shown in Table—4.5.

(a) Number of Conceptions

The data in the Table—4.5 reveals that more than half (58%) of the respondents had three conceptions and 42 per cent had more than three conceptions. However 12 per cent of women had higher number of conceptions (*i.e.*, six and above). Thus it clearly reflects the non-adoption of family planning methods. The respondents are inclined to have a large family.

The data within the district shows that nearly half of the women in Mahabubnagar district (49%) had more than three conceptions against 36 per cent in Kurnool district. The reasons for higher conceptions in Mahabubnagar district are backwardness, negligence towards their health, ignorance about the problems of large family size, poverty, cultural practices and pressure from their spouse and elders in the families. However the inaccessibility of health providers to educate them in time holds the key.

Table—4.5
The percentage distribution of respondents according to their fertility pattern

Fertility behaviour	*Kurnool District*	*Mahabubnagar District*	*Total*
1	**2**	**3**	**4**
(a) Number of conceptions			
1	14.50 (58)	12.50 (50)	13.50 (108)
2	24.25 (97)	17.25 (69)	20.75 (166)
3	25.50 (102)	21.25 (85)	23.38 (187)
4	14.50 (58)	19.75 (79)	17.13 (137)
5	11.25 (45)	14.50 (58)	12.88 (103)
6 +	10.00 (40)	14.75 (59)	12.39 (99)
(b) Number of living children			
1	24.25 (97)	23.25 (93)	23.75 (190)
2	31.00 (124)	26.25 (105)	28.63 (229)
3	24.00 (96)	21.00 (84)	22.50 (180)
4 +	20.75 (83)	29.50 (118)	25.14 (201)
Mean	2.5475	2.77	2.65875

(Contd . . .)

1	2	3	4
(c) Number of abortions			
Nil	76.25 (305)	75.25 (301)	75.75 (606)
One	15.25 (61)	14.75 (59)	15.00 (120)
Two +	8.50 (34)	10.00 (40)	9.25 (74)
Mean	0.345	0.38	0.3625
(d) Number of still births			
Nil (0)	84.75 (339)	76.25 (305)	80.50 (644)
One	11.00 (44)	18.00 (72)	14.50 (116)
Two +	4.25 (17)	5.75 (23)	5.00 (40)
Mean	0.2075	0.31	0.25875
(e) Family size			
3	15.50 (62)	17.00 (68)	16.26 (130)
4	26.00 (104)	17.00 (68)	21.50 (172)
5	24.75 (99)	20.50 (82)	22.63 (181)
6	14.50 (58)	22.00 (88)	18.25 (146)
7	11.25 (45)	12.00 (48)	11.63 (93)
8	4.50 (18)	7.75 (31)	6.13 (49)
9	2.00 (8)	3.00 (12)	2.50 (20)
10	1.50 (6)	0.75 (3)	1.13 (9)
Total	**100.00 (400)**	**100.00 (400)**	**100.00 (800)**
Mean =	5.08	5.3325	5.20625

(b) Number of Living Children

Nearly half (48%) of the respondents have three or more living children denoting the desire of women for a large family. The remaining 52 per cent of women had two living children.

In Mahabubnagar district, more number of women (118) had more than four children than in Kurnool district (83). It shows that in Mahabubnagar district women are not practising small family norm. More than half of the respondents (52%) had 2 living children. The mean number of living children is 2.55 and 2.77 for Kurnool and Mahabubnagar districts respectively.

(c) Number of Abortions

Abortions and still births indicate the foetal wastage during pregnancy. Nearly one fourth of women (24%) had abortions during their reproductive period indicating bad obstetrical history and poor health status of women. 9 per cent of women had two or more abortions and remaining 15 per cent had one abortion. The percentage of abortions are almost similar (Kurnool—24%; Mahabubnagar—25%) in the districts. The higher percentage of abortions is focusing the need of utilising antenatal services by the women.

(d) The Number of Still Births

Still births denote poor outcome of pregnancy. One fifth of the respondents (20%) had still births in their reproductive life span. The percentage of still births were higher in their Mahabubnagar district (24%) than in Kurnool district (15%) it may be due to malnutrition, early marriages, early child bearing period and poor utilisation of antenatal services.

(e) Family Size

The family size considered here is the total number of persons living in the houses (Couple with their living children). Nearly 40 per cent of respondents had family size of 6 and above. This means the expected goal of 'Health for all by the year 2000 A.D.' (attainment of family size of 2.3) is overstepped by the respondents.

The districts present some wnat different trend. The higher percentage of couples in Mahabubnagar district had larger family size then in Kurnool district. Two thirds of women in Mahabubnagar district (66%) had attained the family size of 5 and above. The mean family size in total is 5.2. It is 5.08 and 5.33 in Kurnool and Mahabubnagar respectively.

The size of the family has relevance for the utilisation of maternal, child health and family planning services. The awareness about small family norm and adoption devices have not caught up with the couples in both districts, since large number of them had beyond 2 children.

Infrastructural Facilities

The utilisation of health services depends on the availability, accessibility, acceptability, suitability and awareness of the community on one hand and the effectiveness of the health care delivery system to reach these beneficiaries on the other. Policies of the government in designing the infrastructure, services, allocation of resources show a direction to health care services. The support of the intersectoral agencies facilitates such planning of health care services.

The objective of reaching the goals of "Health for all by 2000 A.D." particularly maternal child health goals, depends on the level and extent of utilisation of services planned, since provision of services ensure the utilisation. Thus the present study mainly focuses on the utilisation of maternal and child health services to the vulnerable sections of the population, in the study area.

This subsection describes the infrastructural variables, such as awareness of respondents about availability of health agency, adoption of various systems of medicine and accessibility of health services etc which is depicted in Table—4.6.

(i) Awareness about Health Agencies

An attempt was made to find out the awareness of the respondents about the availability, accessibility and adaptability of health services. About 51 per cent of respondents were aware of the agencies providing health services. Among them 40 per cent mentioned the services provided by government agencies in the village. Just 2 per cent of respondents mentioned private agencies. The remaining 8 per cent were aware of both government and private health care agencies which provide health services.

Table—4.6

The percentage distribution of respondents by awareness about health agencies

Awareness about health agencies	*Kurnool District*	*Mahabubnagar District*	*Total*
1	**2**	**3**	**4**
Specification of available health care agency in the study areas			
No health services available within the village	48.75 (195)	49.50 (198)	49.13 (393)
Government agency alone	35.75 (143)	44.25 177)	40.00 (320)
Private agency alone	2.75 (11)	1.50 (6)	2.13 (17)
Both government and private agencies	12.75 (51)	4.75 (19)	8.75 (70)
The distance between the village and the service agency			
< 10 km	56.00 (252)	44.00 (198)	56.25 (450)
> 10 km	42.29 (148)	57.71 (202)	43.75 (350)
Transportation facilities			
Available twice in a day	40.83 (69)	59.17 (100)	21.13 (169)
Once in a day	42.86 (69)	57.14 (92)	20.13 (161)
Not available	65.50 (262)	52.00 (208)	58.75 470)

(Contd . . .)

1	2	3	4
System of medicine approaching, when people are sick			
Allopathy	55.25 (242)	44.75 (196)	54.75 (438)
Homoeopathy	1.75 (7)	2.00 (8)	1.88 (15)
Ayurvedic	3.75 (15)	8.25 (33)	6.00 (48)
Naturopathy	45.48 (136)	54.52 (163)	37.38 (299)
Total	**100.00 (400)**	**100.00 (400)**	**100.00 (800)**

Sub-center and other health facilities were available within the villages and within a distance of 10 km. 56 per cent of respondents were utilising these facilities, Other 44 per cent of respondents have to travel more than 10 km to seek health care services. 41 per cent of respondents told that they had transportation facilities. Out of them 51 per cent had transport facility twice a day, by means of buses. In any case 59 per cent of the respondents has to walk to the service centre since no transportation facilities are available from their villages.

It is interesting to note that the respondents were seeking medical assistance from various systems of medicine like Allopathy, Homoeopathy, Ayurvedic and Naruropathy. Some of them were availing combination of systems also. A contribution of allopathy was observed more in the study area as more than half of the respondents (55%) were utilising allopathy medicines followed by naturopathy treatment (37%) and ayurvedic treatment (6%). It is interesting to note that, less percentage of (1.88%) respondents is using homoeopathy system.

(ii) Information Regarding Health Care Providers and Utilisation of Health Services

The data regarding the delivery of health care services depicted in Table—4.7 shows that in all the selected villages, the health assistant (female) is rendering health services to a large extent whereas other health care providers do not seem to provide major services. Very negligible percentage of sample (4%) received health care services from both health assistants (Male and Female).

Table—4.7
The percentage distribution of respondents by the information about health care providers and utilisation of health services

Health care delivery system and utilisation	*Kumool District*	*Mahabubnagar District*	*Total*
1	**2**	**3**	**4**
(a) The personnel providing the health services			
Health Assistant (Famale)	88.25 (353)	95.00 380)	91.63 (733)
Health Assistant Male and Female	6.25 (25)	2.00 (8)	4.13 (33)
Health Supervisor (Female)	1.50 (6)	0.25 (1)	0.88 (7)
Multipurpose health extension officer	2.25 (9)	2.00 (8)	2.13 (17)
Medical officer	1.75 (7)	0.75 (3)	1.25 (10)
(b) Frequency of visits by health personnel			
Rare	13.25 (53)	19.75 (79)	16.50 (132)
Fortnightly	55.00 (220)	63.75 (255)	59.38 (475)
Monthly	31.75 (127)	16.50 (66)	24.13 (193)
(c) Time of domicillary visits by health personnel)			
Morning	95.00 (380)	95.50 (382)	95.25 (762)
Afternoon/Evening	5.00 (20)	4.50 (18)	4.75 (38)

(Contd . . .)

1	2	3	4
(d) Type of service provided by health personnel			
Preventive services alone	44.50 (178)	58.75 (235)	51.63 (413)
All services	55.50 (222)	41.25 (165)	48.38 (387)
Total	**100.00 (400)**	**100.00 (400)**	**100.00 (800)**

The female health assistants are expected to visit the households once in a month, but in the study area, it is noted that more than half (59%) of them visited the villages fortnightly once. It is a good sign observed. Nearly one fourth (24%) of respondents mentioned that health care providers were visiting their villages monthly once. It is sickening to note that nearly 17 per cent of respondents stated that, the health personnel were visiting their villages very rarely. It is quiet natural that lesser the contacts, lesser will be the utilisation of services. This indicates the gap in the availability of health care providers to the community. Further many visits of health personnel were during morning hours only (95%) which were considered convenient for beneficiaries also.

Health services provided by the health personnel were categorized into three types viz, preventive, promotive and curative. In the study area, the respondents received higher percentage of preventive services (52%) against the promotive and curative services (48%) due to lack of drug supply, transportation facilities and beneficiaries at home.

Among the districts, in Mahabubnagar, health assistant (female) seems to be the only major source (95%) of health services against Kurnool district (88%) Whereas other health care providers do not seem to provide any service. Similarly in both the districts, the fornightly visits seems to be more (55%—Kurnool; 64%—Mahabubnagar), majority of them were (95%) providing the health services during mornings. In Mahabubnagar district the respondents availed more preventive services (59%) than curative services (41%) whereas in Kurnool district the respondents received curative services more (56%) than preventive services (44%).

SECTION—II

II. (A) Utilisation of Antenatal Services and Differentials in Utilisation

Antenatal care is the pivot in which safe motherhood and child survival revolve. It is a vital event in women's reproductive life. Antenatal period begins with conception and continues throughout the pregnancy. Good antenatal care forms the foundation for safe delivery. A healthy mother and a healthy child, depend upon the utilisation of antenatal services. Antenatal care also aims at reducing the morbidity and mortality during pregnancy.

To ensure total health of the mother during antenatal period and a healthy baby, the health personnel have to make early registration of antenatal mothers, conduct regular antenatal checkups which include periodic physical examination, lab investigations, immunization and iron and folic supplementation. Further, organising individual or group health education sessions with regard to nutrition and to improve the health condition of antenatal mother and the foetus. The antenatal care also helps to detect early complications and refer these high risk cases. According to the present study to assess antenatal care the above variables were considered. If any one of those specified services are utilised by the respondents, they are considered as 'utilised category' and if none of the services are utilised, they are labelled as 'non-utilised ' category.

Apart from the service utilisation, certain other information regarding the awareness of respondents, practices that are performed by the respondents during antenatal period (like dietary, cultural, sexual and activities related) and the reasons for non utilisation of antenatal services are also considered in the analysis.

The data related to the utilisation of antenatal services in the study is depicted in the Table—4.8. Inspite of intensive efforts made by the government through education and communication activities and allocation of resources to the outreach villages of the country, it is distressing to note, in the study area that only 54.5 per cent of the respondents have utilised the antenatal services. This is lesser than the findings of National Family Health Survey in India (62.3%) and in Andhra Pradesh State (86.3%). Signifying the efforts to intensify the need of strict supervision and guidance for the implementation of activities and for effective utilisation of health interventions by the beneficiaries in the rural areas.

In the study districts, higher percentage of utilisation (60%) was observed in Kurnool district against 49 per cent in Mahabubnagar district. This is mainly due to inaccessibility of health facilities, non-availability of health personnel, lack of awareness about health services and negligence of respondents about their own health.

(a) Utilisation of Antenatal Services

The antenatal services include antenatal checkups, physical examination, lab investigations, immunisation, provision of iron and folic acid tablets and health education regarding the care of the women during pregnancy, preparation for child birth and contraception etc. It is clear from the Table—4.8 that 46 per cent of respondents did not utilised antenatal services whereas 29 per cent have received antenatal services for first pregnancy. One fourth of respondents have received antenatal services for all pregnancies.

Interestingly among those who received antenatal services, one fourth of the respondents (26%) utilised government services and the remaining 29 per cent received the services from private agencies. The low credibility, accessibility of government services might have affected for low utilisation.

Among the women, who obtained antenatal services, about 42 per cent of the women have undergone fundal height, blood pressure and weight check up. Interestingly 41 per cent of the respondents have gone for lab investigations such as Urine for albumin and sugar, blood for haemoglobin and a few percentage of respondents (14%) have gone for only Urine examination.

These investigations are essential to identify pre-eclamptic toxoemia and anaemia among the pregnant women.

Table—4.8
The percentage distribution of respondents by antenatal service utilisation

Antenatal service utilisation	*Kurnool District*	*Mahabubnagar District*	*Total*
1	2	3	4
Non-utilised	40.25 (161)	50.75 (203)	45.50 (364)
Utilised	59.75 (239)	49.25 (197)	54.50 (436)
Antenatal services received			
Not received	40.25 (161)	50.75 (203)	45.50 (364)
For first pregnancy only	31.25 (125)	27.25 (109)	29.25 (234)
For all pregnancies	28.50 (114)	22.00 (88)	25.25 (202)
(a) Place of services received			
Not received	40.25 (161)	50.75 (203)	45.50 (364)
Government services (Home, S.C., P.H.C.)	35.00 (140)	16.50 (66)	25.75 (206)
Private clinic	24.75 (99)	32.75 (131)	28.75 (230)
(b) Type of services received			
Note received	40.25 (161)	50.75 (203)	45.50 (364)
Fundus examination alone	13.00 (52)	11.25 (45)	12.13 (97)
Fundus+Weight+Blood pressure	46.75 (187)	38.00 (152)	42.38 (339)

(Contd . . .)

1	2	3	4
(c) Lab investigations			
No investigations	40.25 (161)	50.75 (203)	45.50 (364)
Urine test alone	13.75 (55)	14.25 (57)	14.00 (112)
Urine test + Haemoglobin	46.00 (184)	35.00 (140)	40.50 (324)
(d) (T.T.) immunization			
Not applicable	40.25 (161)	50.75 (203)	45.50 (364)
Not obtained	3.25 (13)	1.25 (5)	2.25 (18)
Taken	56.50 (226)	48.00 (192)	52.25 (418)
(e) Health education			
Not applicable	40.25 (161)	50.75 (203)	45.50 (364)
Not obtained	40.50 (162)	38.00 (152)	39.25 (314)
Received	19.25 (77)	11.25 (45)	15.25 (122)
(f) Iron and folic acid tablets			
Not applicable	40.25 (161)	50.75 (203)	45.50 (364)
Not consumed	13.75 (55)	14.25 (57)	14.00 (112)
Consumed	46.00 (184)	35.00 (140)	40.50 (324)
Total	**100.00 (400)**	**100.00 (400)**	**100.00 (800)**

The physical examination and lab investigations of an antenatal mother is very helpful to assess the health status of pregnant women and development of foetus and also to identify the risk factors during antenatal period. Two doses of tetanus toxoid immunization should be given for pregnant women to prevent tetanus for the mother during pregnancy and neonatal tetanus for the child. All pregnant women should be protected with tetanus toxoid immunization. Hence a key goal was identified in Health For All by the year 2000 A.D. 48 per cent of respondents did not receive vaccination during antenatal period. In Kurnool district 44 per cent of antenatal mothers did not receive T.T. immunisation against 52 per cent in Mahabubnagar district. The low coverage of mothers for immunisation against tetanus shows the impending dangers of maternal and neonatal deaths due to tetanus.

Health education is a powerful weapon to increase the awareness of mothers about antenatal, natal and postnatal services. Usually health education will be given by the health personnel regarding various topics eg. nutrition, sleep, rest, activities, contraception, preparation for delivery and child birth. Only 15 per cent of mothers have received health education in the antenatal period which indicates the large gap in awareness for service utilisation.

Another intervention planned for antenatal mothers is iron and Folic acid supplementation to combat nutritional anaemia and to meet additional needs of mothers and foetus. It is assumed that 50 to 80 per cent of antenatal mothers in India are anaemic. In this study, it is noted that, during antenatal period, 55 per cent of respondents received iron and folic acid tablets from health personnel. Among them 14 per cent of respondents did not consume the tablets due to fear of side effects of drugs.

(b) Reasons for Not Seeking Antenatal Care Services

Mothers who have not utilised the antenatal services (45.5% of the sample) from health providers were asked about the reasons for not utilising. The details are presented in Table—4.9. *(See the table in page 88)*. The major factor contributing to the non use of antenatal care were that the respondents had no knowledge about antenatal services (22%). They were inaccessible to health services (10%). About 7 per cent of the women felt that it is not important to go for antenatal checkups and not customary in their families. The family members did not allow them to utilise antenatal services. 6 per cent to the respondents did not use the services due to time constraints as they were busily engaged in occupational activities, when health personnel visited their residence. District wise data does not show any significant difference in this aspect. The findings of the present study is on line with the National Family Health Survey in India 92-93. This survey also stated that, the reasons for non-utilisation of antenatal services were: lack of knowledge of antenatal care (13%), financial cost (7%), uncustomery (6%), objection by elders for checkup (5%) etc.

Table—4.9

The percentage distribution of respondents by reasons for non-utilising antenatal services

Reasons for non-utilisation of antenatal services	*Kurnool district*	*Mahabubnagar district*	*Total*
Non applicable	59.75 (239)	49.25 (197)	54.50 (436)
Time constraints	7.50 (30)	3.75 (15)	5.63 (45)
Social and family causes	4.75 (19)	10.00 (40)	7.38 (59)
Lack of knowledge	17.50 (70)	27.00 (108)	22.25 (178)
Inaccessibility of health services	10.50 (42)	10.00 (40)	10.26 (82)
Total	**100.00** (400)	**100.00** (400)	**100.00** (800)

Antenatal Problems

Usually in the rural areas, when women are suffering with major health problems, they will not expose and don't consider their illness as a disease due to their low status in the family, negligence, and ignorance. Normally during pregnancy, certain physiological changes occur in women. Majority of the women feel that these changes are minor health problems. They will try to tolerate it or they will adjust by adopting diverse activities. But when these problems interfere with regular activities, they seek medical advise. Similar phenomenon was noticed in the study area also. Major percentage of respondents (93%) reported that they did not have any health problems during their antenatal period. Very few women (7%) informed that they had minor health problems. The identified problems were: Morning sickness (4%), preeclamptic toxemia (0.8%), constipation (0.6%), heart burn (0.5%), pain abdomen (0.3%) and piles (0.1%) Only negligible percentage (3%) of respondents sought medical assistance. However as per the investigator's observation it has been found that majority of the women were suffering with anaemia and malnourishment.

Among the districts, the respondents belonging to Kurnool district (10%) suffered more with minor health problems than in Mahabubnagar district (4%). More number of respondents reported morning sickness (31). The other health problems were minimal. It is observed that the respondents in Mahabubnagar district are considering pregnancy as a casual means and they give least importance for their health. (Table not given).

Awareness of Respondents About Clinical Manifestations During Pregnancy

Knowledge about conception and pregnancy is vital for a woman to take efficient care during antenatal period. It is surprising to find that, 42 per cent of women are not aware of signs and symptoms during pregnancy. Whereas more than half of the respondents (55%) consider amenorrhoea as the only one clinical manifestation observed during pregnancy. A very negligible percentage of respondents (3%) mentioned morning sickness as a clinical sign during pregnancy as shown in Table—4.10. *(See the table in page 90).* There is a need to educate the women about clinical manifestations of pregnancy so that they can utilise the antenatal services and antenatal care in a better way.

Same trends are noticed in the two study districts without much variation. This points to the imminent need to educate the women about signs and symptoms of pregnancy and the care to be initiated immediately. The ignorance of majority of rural women about pregnancy and child birth will influence the utilisation of maternal health care services. The focus of group education by the health providers can help to overcome this ignorance.

Table—4.10

The percentage distribution of respondents by their awareness about clinical manifestations during pregnancy

Awareness	*Kurmool District*	*Mahabubnagar District*	*Total*
Knowledge about clinical manifestations of pregnancy			
Do not know	40.25 (161)	44.00 (176)	42.13 (337)
Amenorrhoea and morning sickness	0.25 (1)	0.25 (1)	0.25 (2)
Morning sickness	2.75 (11)	3.25 (13)	3.00 (24)
Amenorrhoea	56.75 (227)	52.50 (210)	54.63 (437)
Total	**100.00** **(400)**	**100.00** **(400)**	**100.00** **(800)**

Practices During Antenatal Period

The practices of the couple, during antenatal period depends upon their socio-cultural background (*eg:* customs, traditions, beliefs, superstitions), way of living, male dominance, need in fulfilling the basic drives like sexual urge, ignorance of complications and negative attitude towards healthier life.

In the present study, the practices related to cultural and desire-fulfilment such as sexual urge are enquired and their responses were described in Table—4.11

Table—4.11
The percentage distribution of respondents by practices during antenatal period

Practices	*Kurnool District*	*Mahabubnagar District*	*Total*
1	2	3	4
(i) Cultural practices			
(a) Celebrating Sreemantham and Naming ceremony			
No	47.00 (188)	55.00 (220)	51.00 (408)
Yes	53.00 (212)	45.00 (180)	49.00 (392)
(b) Going to natal home for delivery			
All	2.75 (11)	3.25 (13)	3.00 (24)
First	73.50 (294)	15.75 (63)	44.63 (357)
Second	7.50 (30)	9.50 (38)	8.50 (68)
None	16.25 (65)	71.50 (286)	43.88 (351)
(c) Period of staying in mothers' home			
Not gone	16.25 (65)	71.50 (286)	43.88 (351)
Within a month	53.50 (214)	15.00 (60)	34.25 (274)
Upto 3 months	30.25 (121)	13.50 (54)	21.88 (175)
II. Sexual Practice			
(a) Period of indulging in sexual intercourse			
Early months of pregnancy (<5 months)	19.75 (79)	23.75 (95)	21.75 (174)

(Contd . . .)

1	2	3	4
Later months of pregnancy (upto 8 months)	72.00 (288)	70.00 (280)	71.00 (568)
Till delivery	8.25 (33)	6.25 (25)	7.25 (58)
III. Dietary Practices			
Modified	53.09 (86)	46.91 (76)	20.25 (162)
Not modified	49.22 (314)	50.78 (324)	79.75 (638)
Total	**100.00 (400)**	**100.00 (400)**	**100.00 (800)**

1. Cultural Practices

In Indian culture, when a woman becomes pregnant, on an auspicious day, usually in odd months (5th, 7th, 9th) both natal and 'inlaws' families will celebrate a cultural function called '*Sreemantham*'. On that day they all enjoy together by sharing happiness and experience unity of all the relatives. They feel 'child bearing' is the happiest vital event in reproductive life of a woman. The elders in the family, offer prayers to God for safe delivery and bless the woman. Depending upon their economic background they will purchase either clothes or ornaments etc., After this function, on a good day, woman will go to natal home for delivery either for first pregnancy alone or for all pregnancies based upon their family circumstances. In natal family, woman feel free, comfortable, happy to stay with parents and siblings, will have rest. She mentally prepares herself to cope up with the stress and strain related to delivery.

Younger women are likely to depend upon their natal home at the time of child birth. This is because they feel quality of maternal and child care services are better there. Mother and daughter relationship is biological and often friendly. The natal family is also involved in her fertility decision-making process in the family. Women prefer to utilise natal family services at the time of child birth.

The other cultural practice followed by the Indian families is 'Naming Ceremony' for the newborn, during postnatal period. This function is celebrated by the members of natal family. On that day, both families will meet together again and enjoy the occasion.

Nearly half of the respondents (49%) celebrate "Sreemantham and naming ceremonies" during antenatal and postnatal period. In Kurnool district more percentage of families (53%) celebrate both functions in contrast, lesser percentage of families (45%) celebrate both functions in Mahabubnagar district because of their socio-economic backwardness.

More percentage of respondents in the study area had gone to natal home for first delivery (44.7%) and 9 per cent of women had their second delivery also at natal home and very negligible percentage (3%) of women went to natal home for all deliveries signifying the preference of the women staying in natal family. They also enjoy the celebration of both functions at natal home. This is a usual ritual prevailing in Indian families. A major percentage (44%) of respondents did not go to natal home even for single delivery. The reason quoted by them was economic backwardness. They have to do occupational activities till delivery and immediately after delivery also.

More than one third (34%) of respondents stayed in mothers' house for few days. 22 per cent of women stayed upto 3 months also in natal home.

The district wise data presents, different trend. Major percentage of women (72%) in Mahabubnagar district did not go to natal home for delivery because of low socio-economic status. In contrast, in Kurnool district nearly three quarters (74%) of respondents had gone to natal home for first delivery as a customary practice and they were back to in-laws' house within a month after delivery as they have to fulfil the family responsibilities and economic burdens.

According to the National Family Health Survey conducted during 1992-93 in all the major states of India, about 74 per cent of the total births in the four years preceding the survey, were delivered at natal home.

2. Sexual Practice

The fulfilment of sexual desire is the basic need among the couple. In rural areas, it is the unique enjoyment for the people, as they were ignorant about the consequences related to excessive coitus in early and later months of pregnancy such as abortions, premature rupture of membranes and premature delivery. They will be indulging in sexual activities during antenatal period, even upto the full term. It is observed that an overwhelming percentage of couple (93%) were indulging in coitus till later months of pregnancy, very few percentage of couple (7%) indulged in sexual intercourse upto delivery also. The two districts are also manifesting the similar trends.

3. Dietary Practices

The dietary practices of women depends upon their family background, food habits, cultural practices, affordability, awareness of respondents about nutrients and its needs. These practices in antenatal period has a bearing effect on the health of the mother, foetal development and safe delivery.

During the antenatal period women are supposed to modify their diet. They should take high caloric and high protein diet to meet the nutritional demands of mother and child, and for growth and development of the foetus. However it does not always happen, inspite of nutritional education and motivational efforts given by health functionaries also. It may be due to traditional beliefs, customs, lack of awareness, affordability and fulfilment of additional responsibility in the family etc.

Determinants of Antenatal Services

Antenatal services utilisation (dependent variable) has been correlated with the following independent variables to find out the crucial determinants of antenatal service utilisation and its differentials.

II. (a) Socio-economic variables and utilisation of antenatal services

(i) Respondents' Education and Utilisation of Antenatal Services

Education brings change in womens' health behaviour. As education increases these awareness of respondents about health aspects also increases. It influences the attitudes and practices, thereby it affects the utilisation of health services also. The data in the Table—4.12 manifests the relationship between education and utilisation of antenatal services. It is observed that education has a significant positive relationship with utilisation of antenatal services. Higher utilisation (75%) was observed among the respondents who studied upto primary school level. It is surprising to note that slightly lesser percentage of utilisation (68%) was observed with the respondents, whom studied middle school and above, than the women with primary level. On the other hand among the illiterates, half of them utilised antenatal services. It is obvious that as education of respondents increases, the percentage of utilisation also increases. Thus the hypothesis is found to be true.

Table—4.12

The percentage distribution of respondents by their education and utilisation of antenatal services

Womens' education	*Kurnool District*			*Mahabubnagar District*			*Total*		
	Non-utilised	*Utilised*	*Total*	*Non-utilised*	*Utilised*	*Total*	*Non-utilised*	*Utilised*	*Total*
Illiterate	44.90 (141)	55.10 (173)	100.00 (314)	52.59 (183)	47.41 (165)	100.00 (348)	48.94 (324)	51.06 (338)	100.00 (662)
Primary School (1-5)	18.18 (18)	81.82 (36)	100.00 (44)	39.13 (9)	60.87 (14)	100.00 (23)	25.37 (17)	74.63 (50)	100.00 (67)
Middle school and above	28.57 (12)	71.43 (30)	100.00 (42)	37.93 (11)	62.07 (18)	100.00 (29)	32.39 (23)	67.61 (48)	100.00 (71)
Total	40.25 (161)	59.75 (239)	100.00 (400)	50.75 (203)	49.25 (197)	100.00 (400)	45.50 (364)	54.50 (436)	100.00 (800)

P.Chi.2(6)=22.0323; Pr=0.001 11.7936; Pr=0.067 25.6902; Pr=0.000

The similar trend is observed in Kumool district. Higher percentage of utilisation was observed with the respondents who studied upto primary school education (82%) followed by middle school education and above (71%) and lesser utilisation among illiterates (55%). In Mahabubnagar district, significant variation was not observed with levels of schooling. However much difference in the utilisation pattern was observed between women with education (62%) and illiterates (47%). The difference in the levels of utilisation between illiterates (51%) and literates (75%) is indicative of the influence of literacy on health behaviour and utilisation of antenatal services.

Respondents Occupation and Utilisation of Antenatal Services

Women are engaged in multiple activities at home and outside. They are taking an active part in assisting their spouses to fulfil the economic needs of families, thus they are sharing the additional responsibility, apart from the traditional vocation *i.e.*, home keeping.

Women from the lower socio-economic strata were seen in varied occupations thus the nature of occupation influences their health and utilisation of antenatal services. As expected the housewives utilised antenatal services to a larger extent (67%) followed by cultivators (57%) and coolies (51%). The hindering factors for low utilisation of antenatal services among the coolies and cultivators are: the cultural, traditional practices and low accessibility to health information. On the otherhand, Housewives will have more time, more accessibility to health information and services, cultural practices, elders at home etc., are influential factors for higher utilisation of antenatal services. Kurmool district manifests similar pattern as per the total population. Thus the hypothesis, higher the level of occupation, higher will be the utilisation of antenatal services is confirmed here. Whereas the data in Mahabubnagar district also presents higher percentage of antenatal services utilisation among housewives (64%) followed by coolies (48%) and cultivators (43%). The study population consists of women who are engaged only in lower category of occupation, hence the general trend that occupation helps women to utilise better health services has been nullified here as depicted in Table—4.13.

Table—4.13
The percentage distribution of respondents by their occupation and utilisation of antenatal services

Womens' education	*Kurnool District*			*Mahabubnagar District*			*Total*		
	Non-utili sed	*Utili-sed*	*Total*	*Non-utili-sed*	*Utili-sed*	*Total*	*Non-utili-sed*	*Utili-sed*	*Total*
Housewives	31.58 (24)	68.42 (52)	100.00 (76)	36.36 (16)	63.64 (28)	100.00 (44)	33.33 (40)	66.67 (80)	100.00 (120)
Cultivation	32.47 (25)	67.53 (52)	100.00 (77)	57.38 (35)	42.62 (26)	100.00 (61)	43.48 (60)	56.52 (78)	100.00 (138)
Petty business + cooly	45.34 (112)	54.66 (135)	100.00 (247)	51.53 (152)	48.47 (143)	100.00 (295)	48.71 264	51.29 (278)	100.00 (542)
Total	40.25 (161)	59.75 (239)	100.00 (400)	50.75 (203)	49.25 (197)	100.00 (400)	45.50 (364)	54.50 (436)	100.00 (800)

P.Chi.2((6)=15.0277; Pr=0.020 12.4549; Pr=0.053 15.4277; Pr=0.017

Type of Activities Performed by the Rural Women During Antenatal Period

Since early ages, women in our nation occupies an unparallel and prestigious position in the families. The womans traditional vocation is held to be marriage and motherhood. There is no vocation that demand more of a person both physically, psychologically and emotionally than motherhood. The activities performed by the rural women is dichotomised into household activities and income generating activities. The household activities includes cooking, child rearing, cleaning the house, washing, house keeping, maintaining home budget, assisting husband to do the job and transporting the entire family etc. The women now-a-days are involved in nearly the same quantum of work as men, ranging from arduous manual labour to top most jobs. Their ranks are bound to swell as a consequence of increased prices and the financial stress. The women from lower economic strata in rural areas function shoulder to shoulder with men engaged in income generating activities and are also expected to carry on the household work on returning from their jobs. An Indian rural woman gets hardly 4-5 hours rest. Increased working hours, customs, ignorance and poverty are influential factors in increasing morbidity and mortality pattern among the focal women group. Usually in rural areas, the women will perform both household and income generating activities throughout pregnancy and immediately after child birth also.

The observation of these facts in the study area is presented in the Table—4.14 which shows 80 per cent of women respondents engage in household activities alone during antenatal period and the remaining 20 per cent of women engage in occupation besides home-making. It is quite desirable for a woman to perform some or other household work at home during pregnancy as a single exercise. However in the later weeks of pregnancy they should resist from heavy and strainful work. It is customary that they attend at home but due care has to be taken to ensure safety.

About 48 per cent of woman does heavy activities till later months of pregnancy implies the need for assistance of women in fulfilling the responsibilities of entire family. However 43 per cent of women performed heavy work until delivery indicates the risks which may affect her health. Perhaps the absence of helping hands at home and husband not sharing much of her burden, might be the reason. In Mahabubnagar district, nearly half of the women (49%) does heavy work till delivery as against just 38 per cent in Kurnool district whereas in Kurnool district, more than half of the women (54%) work upto later months of pregnancy as against 42 per cent in Mahabubnagar district. The reasons for doing heavy work till delivery or later months of pregnancy includes the beliefs among women that if they do the work, they will have easy delivery. Compulsion at home or earning for livelihood is necessary for them.

Even though it is not possible to avoid household work, it is possible to avoid heavy work at full term (9th month). Hence it is necessary to educate the women and community with regard to antenatal care and utilisation of health services, seeking health advices during antenatal period to prevent complications during pregnancy and child birth.

Table—4.14
The percentage distribution of respondents by type of work performed in antenatal period

Type of work performed	*Kurnool District*	*Mahabubnagar District*	*Total*
Household work	77.00 (308)	83.25 (333)	80.13 (641)
Household+ occupational work	23.00 (92)	16.75 (67)	19.88 (159)
P. Chi (1) = 4.9059; Pr = 0.027			
Continuity to do hardwork			
Till delivery	37.50 (150)	49.25 (197)	43.38 (347)
Early months (< 5 months)	8.75 (35)	9.00 (36)	8.00 (71)
Later months (> 5 months upto 9th month)	53.75 (215)	41.75 (167)	47.75 (382)
Total	**100.00 (400)**	**100.00 (400)**	**100.00 (800)**

P. Chi 2(4)=14.3916; Pr: 0.006

Type of Work Performed During Antenatal Period and Utilisation of Antenatal Services

Even though motherhood is considered as a boon for women, the women cannot be idle at home, hence they perform either household activities or a combination of both household and other income generating activities in rural areas. But inspite of their work they have to take care of the health of the foetus and the mother's.

The Table—4.15 *(See the table in page 100)* shows better level of antenatal service utilisation was observed by the women who perform household activity alone (67%) than the women who does both household and other income generating activities (51%). It might be due to the fact that the women who do not have a need to earn, usually stay at home. Most of the educated, belonging to higher economic and social status are available during the visit of health personnel and have the benefit of utilising antenatal services better than those who are engaged in other occupations outside home. Thus nearly half of the respondents (49%), who were engaged in both household and other income generating work, did not utilise antenatal services as they were busy outside their home, most of the time.

Table—4.15
The percentage distribution of respondents by type of work performed in antenatal period and utilisation of antenatal services

Womens' education	*Kurnool District*			*Mahabubnagar District*			*Total*		
	Non-utilised	*Utilised*	*Total*	*Non-utilised*	*Utilised*	*Total*	*Non-utilised*	*Utilised*	*Total*
Household work	28.26 (26)	71.74 (66)	100.00 (92)	40.30 (27)	59.70 (40)	100.00 (67)	33.33 (53)	66.67 (106)	100.00 (159)
Household and other income generating work	43.83 (135)	56.17 (173)	100.00 (308)	52.85 (176)	47.15 (157)	100.00 (333)	48.52 (311)	51.48 (330)	100.00 (641)
Total	**40.25 (161)**	**59.75 (239)**	**100.00 (400)**	**50.75 (203)**	**49.25 (197)**	**100.00 (400)**	**45.50 (364)**	**54.50 (436)**	**100.00 (800)**

P. Chi 2(2) = 13.3478; Pr = 0.001 5.1592; Pr = 0.076 12.4148; Pr = 0.002

In the study districts also, the pregnant women in household work showed greater utilisation of antenatal services, with Kurnool district showing higher utilisation (71%) than the Mahabubnagar district (60%) as against the women who are involved in both household and other income generating activities (Kurnool—56%); Mahabubnagar—47%). It is because, the women were mostly engaged in working and thus earn some income for living. Such expectant mothers will loose the wages if they go for antenatal check up and so they neglect to take regular antenatal services. Thus work status of respondents has shown a negative effect on antenatal services. Thus work status of respondents has shown a negative effect on antenatal service utilisation in the study area.

(iii) Annual Family Income and Utilisation of Antenatal Services

Income is a socio-economic variable which influences the utilisation of health services. Higher level of utilisation was observed in higher income groups among the total sample (65%) as well as within the districts (Kurnool = 73%; Mahabubnagar = 56%); followed by low income group in total (55%), Mahabubnagar (59%) and middle income groups total (52%); Mahabubnagar = 44%). Whereas Kurnool district is exhibiting a different trend, there is a positive association was observed *i.e.*, higher the income levels, higher utilisation levels was noticed. Nearly three fourths sample (74%) belonged to high income group utilised antenatal services followed by middle income groups (59%) and low income groups (51%). It is interesting to note that in the study area, even the low income group of respondents also utilised antenatal services more may be due to increased awareness about antenatal care and improved health consciousness as shown in Table—4.16.

Table—4.16

The percentage distribution of respondents by annual family income and utilisation of antenatal services

Womens' education	*Kurnool District*			*Mahabubnagar District*			*Total*		
	Non-Utili-sed	*Utili-sed*	*Total*	*Non-utili sed*	*Utili-sed*	*Total*	*Non-utili-sed*	*Utili-sed*	*Total*
<10,000/-	49.28 (34)	50.72 (35)	100.00 (69)	41.05 (39)	58.95 (56)	100.00 (95)	44.51 (73)	55.49 (91)	100.00 (164)
10,000/- to 18,000/-	41.20 (110)	58.80 (157)	100.00 (267)	56.10 (138)	43.90 (108)	100.00 (246)	48.34 (248)	51.66 (265)	100.00 (513)
18,001/- and above	26.56 (17)	73.44 (47)	100.00 (64)	44.07 (26)	55.93 (33)	100.00 (59)	34.96 (43)	65.04 (80)	100.00 (123)
Total	40.25 (161)	59.75 (239)	100.00 (400)	50.75 (203)	49.25 (197)	100.00 (400)	45.50 (364)	54.50 (436)	100.00 (800)

P. Chi 2(6) = 17.1100; Pr = 0.009 12.3854; Pr = 0.054 20.6370; Pr = 0.008

II. (b) Socio-cultural Variables and Utilisation of Antenatal Services

(i) Caste and Utilisation of Antenatal Services

Caste is a social stratification variable which influences the utilisation of antenatal services. In the present study it has been hypothesised that higher caste people will utilise the antenatal services in a better way than the lower caste people.

The Table—4.17 reveals that in total, the respondents from forward caste have utilised the antenatal services in higher percentage (63%) than the lower castes (backward caste—53% and scheduled caste and scheduled tribes—54%).

Table—4.17

The percentage distribution of respondents by caste and utilisation of antenatal services

Caste	*Kurnool District*			*Mahabubnagar District*			*Total*		
	Non-Utili-sed	*Utili-sed*	*Total*	*Non-utili-sed*	*Utili-sed*	*Total*	*Non-utili-sed*	*Utili-sed*	*Total*
F.C.	30.77 (24)	69.23 (54)	100.00 (78)	46.67 (21)	53.33 (24)	100.00 (45)	36.59 (45)	63.41 (78)	100.00 (123)
B.C.	44.55 (94)	55.45 (117)	100.00 (211)	50.22 (113)	49.78 (112)	100.00 (225)	47.48 (207)	52.52 (229)	100.00 (436)
SC, ST	38.74 (43)	61.26 (68)	100.00 (111)	53.08 (69)	46.92 (61)	100.00 (130)	46.47 (112)	53.53 (129)	100.00 (241)
Total	**40.25 (161)**	**59.75 (239)**	**100.00 (400)**	**50.75 (203)**	**49.25 (197)**	**100.00 (400)**	**45.50 (364)**	**54.50 (436)**	**100.00 (800)**

P. Chi. 2(4) = 6.8378; Pr = 0.145 3.4527; Pr = 0.750 10.2830; Pr = 0.113

More or less, similar trend is observed in the districts also. In Kurnool district, the utilisation of antenatal services was the highest among the forward castes (69%) followed by scheduled caste and scheduled tribes (61%) and backward caste (55%). In Mahabubnagar district, higher utilisation of antenatal services was noticed among forward caste (53%) followed by backward caste (50%) and scheduled caste and scheduled tribes (47%). Hence the hypothesis, that high utilisation of antenatal services among high caste people, is thus confirmed here.

(ii) Family Structure and Utilisation of Antenatal Services

Some of the functions of the family have been transformed. The family has taken up the additional responsibility of health care service utilisation.

The association between family structure and utilisation of antenatal services is presented in the Table—4.18. The utilisation levels are higher (62%) in joint families, when compared to nuclear families (51%). The reason may be due to the advice and experience of the elders within the family about the utilisation of health services, whereas it is lacking in nuclear families. In joint families, one or other member will be going for occupational activities and so there are chances for antenatal mothers to stay within the house and obtain the antenatal services either at home or at clinic.

Table—4.18

The percentage distribution of respondents by family type and utilisation of antenatal services

Family type	*Kurnool District*			*Mahabubnagar District*			*Total*		
	Non-utili-sed	*Utili-utili*	*Total*	*Non-utili-sed*	*Utili-sed*	*Total*	*Non-utili-sed*	*Utili-sed*	*Total*
Joint	29.06 (34)	70.94 (83)	100.00 (117)	46.67 (63)	53.33 (72)	100.00 (135)	38.49 (97)	61.51 (177)	100.00 (252)
Nuclear	44.88 (127)	55.12 (156)	100.00 (283)	52.83 (140)	47.17 (125)	100.00 (265)	48.72 (267)	51.28 (281)	100.00 (548)
Total	**40.25 (161)**	**59.75 (239)**	**100.00 (400)**	**50.75 (203)**	**49.25 (197)**	**100.00 (400)**	**45.50 (364)**	**54.50 (436)**	**100.00 (800)**

P. Chi. 2(2) = 11.1081; Pr = 0.004 1.8062; Pr = 0.405 7.8230; Pr = 0.020

The districts also show the similar pattern. The non-utilisation levels are high in nuclear families when compared to joint families. Even among both joint and nuclear families higher percentage of utilisation was observed in Kurnool district (60%) as against Mahabubnagar district (49%) (53%—joint and 47 per cent nuclear families).

(iii) Consanguinity and Utilisation of Antenatal Services

The marriages between the relatives like maternal uncle and cousin are categorized as "consanguineous marriages". If no relationship exists among the couples before marriage, they are categorized as "non-consanguineous marriages".

It is interesting to observe that in the total sample, higher percentage of utilisation of antenatal services was observed among non-consanguineous couple (57%) than the consanguineous couple (52%). It may be due to, the elders and family members were looking after antenatal mothers within the houses, as their influence will be more on the mothers. It hinders the percentage of utilisation. In Kurnool district also the similar trend is noticed. Higher percentage of utilisation of antenatal services is observed in non-consanguineous marriages (64%) against the consanguineous marriages (56%). However in Mahabubnagar district no significant difference has been observed between consanguineous and non-consanguineous groups as shown in Table—4.19.

Table—4.19

The percentage distribution of respondents by consanguinity and antenatal service utilisation

Relationship of the respondents with husband	*Kurnool District*			*Mahabubnagar District*			*Total*		
	Non-utilised	*Utilised*	*Total*	*Non-utilised*	*Utilised*	*Total*	*Non-utilised*	*Utilised*	*Total*
1	2	3	4	5	6	7	8	9	10
Related	44.16 (87)	55.84 (110)	100.00 (197)	50.68 (111)	49.32 (108)	100.00 (219)	47.60 (198)	52.40 (218)	100.00 (416)

(Contd . . .)

1	2	3	4	5	6	7	8	9	10
Not related	36.45 (74)	63.55 (129)	100.00 (203)	50.83 (92)	49.17 (89)	100.00 (181)	43.23 (166)	56.77 (218)	100.00 (384)
Total	40.25 (161)	59.75 (239)	100.00 (400)	50.75 (203)	49.25 (197)	100.00 (400)	45.50 (364)	54.50 (436)	100.00 (800)

P. Chi. 2(4) = 7.9328; Pr = 0.094 2.0959; Pr = 0.718 6.7019; Pr = 0.153

(iv) Interspouse Communication and Utilisation of Antenatal Services

Interspouse communication favours the couple to decide health related issues, like utilisation of services, modification of life style practices and behaviour. It brings change in the attitudes and practices of couple.

The data presented in the Table—4.20 *(See the table in page 106)* shows the percentage distribution of respondents by interspouse communication and utilisation of antenatal services. Higher percentage of utilisation of antenatal services (65%) was observed among the respondents who were freely discussed the family size and sexual matters as against the couple who are not discussing (52%). Interspouse communication favours and promotes exchange of their ideas, opinions and decision on the family welfare matters. Timely decisions make them utilise the services properly, to adopt small family norm and to plan future life in a systematic way.

An appreciable percentage of respondents in Kurnool district (67%) were discussing with their lifemates about health care matters as against 60 per cent in Mahabubnagar district. This creates increased awareness in health problems and thereby increase in utilisation of health care services apart from promoting the exchange of ideas, opinions and other factors. Thus the intraspousal communication is observed more in Kurnool district than Mahabubnagar district as people are more socialised, forward with exposure to health care information. The persistence of traditional beliefs, taboos, joint family system leading to lack of privacy, illiteracy, ignorance about the importance of free intraspousal communication, unplanned way of life and backwardness, all these factors hinder the exposure to health information and utilisation pattern of antenatal services in Mahabubnagar district.

Table—4.20

The percentage distribution of respondents by interspouse communication and utilisation of antenatal services

Interspouse Communication about sexual matters and family size limitation	*Kurnool District*			*Mahabubnagar District*			*Total*		
	Non-utilised	*Utilised*	*Total*	*Non-utilised*	*Utilised*	*Total*	*Non-utilised*	*Utilised*	*Total*
Not discussing	43.42 (122)	56.58 (159)	100.00 (281)	52.30 (182)	47.70 (166)	100.00 (348)	48.33 (304)	51.67 (325)	100.00 (629)
Discussing	32.77 (39)	67.23 (80)	100.00 (119)	40.38 (21)	59.62 (31)	100.00 (52)	35.09 (60)	64.91 (111)	100.00 (171)
Total	**40.25 (161)**	**59.75 (239)**	**100.00 (400)**	**50.75 (203)**	**49.25 (197)**	**100.00 (400)**	**45.50 (364)**	**54.50 (436)**	**100.00 (800)**

P. Chi. 2(2) = 4.1390; Pr = 0.126 5.9497; Pr = 0.051 11.6009; Pr = 0.003

(v) Sex Preference and Utilisation of Antenatal Services

In the present study, the women who have more sex preference, utilised the antenatal services in effective manner (66%) as against those who do not have sex preference (52%). The respondents who were having sex preference, will be very anxious and utilise the antenatal services in a better way.

Among the districts also, similar trend was noticed. In Kurnool district higher percentage of utilisation was observed (86%) as against the Mahabubnagar district (54%) among the women who had sex preference. Even among the women who did not have sex preference. Kurnool district shows more percentage (56%) of utilisation than the Mahabubnagar district (48%). It signifies the increased health consciousness, improved awareness about health services and accessibility of health facilities to the respondents in Kurnool district compared with Mahabubnagar district as shown in Table—4.21.

Table—4.21
The percentage distribution of respondents by sex preference and utilisation of antenatal services

Sex Preference	*Kurnool District*			*Mahabubnagar District*			*Total*		
	Non-utilised	*Utilised*	*Total*	*Non-utilised*	*Utilised*	*Total*	*Non-utilised*	*Utilised*	*Total*
Having Sex Preference	14.29 (7)	85.71 (42)	100.00 (49)	45.56 (41)	54.44 (49)	100.00 (90)	34.53 (48)	65.47 (91)	100.00 (139)
No Sex Preference	43.87 (154)	56.13 (197)	100.00 (351)	52.26 (162)	47.74 (148)	100.00 (310)	47.81 (316)	52.19 (345)	100.00 (661)
Total	**40.25 (161)**	**59.75 (239)**	**100.00 (400)**	**50.75 (203)**	**49.25 (197)**	**100.00 (400)**	**45.50 (364)**	**54.40 (436)**	**100.00 (800)**

II. (c) Demographic Variables and Utilisation of Antenatal Services

(1) Women's Actual Age and Utilisation of Antenatal Services

The utilisation of antenatal services by current age is presented in the Table—4.22. *(See the table in page 108).* The data manifests higher percentage of utilisation in the younger age groups than in the older age groups.

The highest percentage of utilisation (63%) is observed in the youngest age group *i.e.* <19 years of age group, which has declined to 53.29 per cent in the next age group (20-24 years). The utilisation is very low (48%) in the higher age group of women who fall in the age group of 30 years and above. The data significantly reflects, that the younger women obviously show greater utilisation than the older age group. Because with the recent universal primary health care approach of government and with the activities of non-governmental organisations, people are more conscious and aware of the importance of health service utilisation.

In Kurnool district, the younger age group of women *i.e.,* below 19 years of age show higher utilisation (67%) followed by 58 per cent by 20-24 years of age group. In Mahabubnagar district, the utilisation among the younger age group (< 19 years) is high (61%) followed by 20-24 years (48%) respectively. However in the higher age groups *i.e.,* 25 years and above the utilisation is around 58 per cent in Kurnool district as against 48 per cent in Mahabubnagar district.

Thus the low level of utilisation is evidently seen in higher age groups (25 years and above), which is significantly low in backward Mahabubnagar district.

The women in the higher age groups who were married a decade back or the earlier, has less access to health information than the younger age groups, who have greater avenues of health information.

Table—4.22
The percentage distribution of respondents by womens' actual age and utilisation of antenatal services

Women's actual age (in years	*Kurnool District*			*Mahabubnagar District*			*Total*		
	Non-utili sed	*Utili-sed*	*Total*	*Non-utili-sed*	*Utili-sed*	*Total*	*Non-utili-sed*	*Utili-sed*	*Total*
<19	32.69 (17)	67.31 (35)	100.00 (52)	39.24 (31)	60.76 (48)	100.00 (79)	36.64 (48)	63.36 (83)	100.00 (131)
20-24	41.62 (72)	58.38 (101)	100.00 (173)	52.17 (84)	47.83 (77)	100.00 (161)	46.71 (156)	53.29 (178)	100.00 (334)
25-29	40.16 (49)	59.84 (73)	100.00 (122)	52.21 (59)	47.79 (54)	100.00 (113)	45.96 (108)	54.04 (127)	100.00 (235)
30-44	43.40 (23)	56.60 (30)	100.00 (53)	61.70 (29)	38.30 (18)	100.00 (47)	52.00 (52)	48.00 (48)	100.00 (100)
Total	**40.25 (161)**	**59.75 (239)**	**100.00 (400)**	**50.75 (203)**	**49.25 (197)**	**100.00 (400)**	**45.50 (364)**	**54.50 (436)**	**100.00 (800)**

P. Chi 2(6) = 2.1726; Pr = 0.903 9.2426; Pr = 0.160 6.8648; Pr = 0334

(ii) Age at Marriage of Respondents and Antenatal Service Utilisation

Age at marriage has great influence over the social values, attitudes and practices of individuals. It influences the demand and utilisation of health services also. Thus age at marriage has relevance in terms of early consummation and child birth that inturn affects the health of the mother and the child.

The utilisation of antenatal services by the age at marriage depicted in the Table—42.3 shows significantly higher level of antenatal services utilisation (76%) among the women who were married at higher ages *i.e.,* 18 years and above than the women who were married at younger ages {<11 years} they show a lowest level (49%) of utilisation. Thus it is obvious, that earlier the age at marriage, lesser will be the utilisation of antenatal services.

Table—4.23
The percentage distribution of respondents by age at marriage and utilisation of antenatal services

Age at marriage (years)	*Kurnool District*			*Mahabubnagar District*			*Total*		
	Non-utilised	*Utili-sed*	*Total*	*Non-utili-sed*	*Utili-sed*	*Total*	*Non-utili-sed*	*Utili-sed*	*Total*
<11	22.22 (4)	77.73 (14)	100.00 (18)	58.73 (37)	41.27 (26)	100.00 (63)	50.62 (41)	49.38 (40)	100.00 (81)
12-13	38.61 (39)	61.39 (62)	100.00 (101)	50.26 (98)	49.74 (97)	100.00 (195)	46.28 (137)	53.72 (159)	100.00 (296)
14-15	46.51 (80)	53.49 (92)	100.00 (172)	49.57 (58)	50.43 (59)	100.00 (117)	47.75 (138)	52.25 (151)	100.00 (289)
16-17	40.00 (32)	60.00 (48)	100.00 (80)	43.75 (7)	56.25 (9)	100.00 (16)	40.63 (39)	59.37 (57)	100.00 (96)
18+	20.69 (6)	79.31 (23)	100.00 (29)	33.33 (3)	66.67 (6)	100.00 (9)	23.68 (9)	76.38 (29)	100.00 (38)
Total	**40.25 (161)**	**59.75 (239)**	**100.00 (400)**	**50.75 (203)**	**49.25 (197)**	**100.00 (400)**	**45.50 (364)**	**54.50 (436)**	**100.00 (800)**

P. Chi 2(2) = 13.0376; Pr = 0.222 6.3603; Pr = 0.784 13.0376; Pr = 0.222

Mahabubnagar district also presents a similar trend. The women who were married at ages <11 years showed lower percentage of (41%) than those who were married at higher age at marriage *i.e.*, 18 years and above (67%). Thus the hypothesis *i.e.*, age at marriage will have a positive association with the utilisation of services is found to be true. This may be because of women at younger ages will have lesser exposure to health information and ignorant about the importance of antenatal care. On the other hand, women who were married after 18 years are mature and are subjected to more health information which in turn increase their awareness to seek the antenatal services in a better way.

However, Kurnool district manifests better utilisation of antenatal services (78%) by women at age <11 years also. Interestingly the women marrying at 18 years and above sought higher percentage of utilisation (79%). However at the ages 12 to 17 years the utilisation is low. It is evident from the table, that the respondents in Kurnool district were more health conscious and exposed to health information at all ages than the respondents in Mahabubnagar district.

IV. Infrastructural Facilities and Utilisation of Antenatal Services

(i) Frequency of Visits and Utilisation of Antenatal Services

Health personnel visit the villages to render health care services to the needy population. The accessibility, availability and delivery of qualitative health services by the health personnel may facilitate greater utilisation thus creates credibility.

In the study area, the visits of health personnel are trichomitised into fortnightly, monthly and rare visits. The frequency of visits made by health personnel will have a bearing over the utilisation pattern. It is observed that, higher the frequency of visits, higher the percentage of utilisation. Thus a positive association was found between the frequency of visits and utilisation of antenatal services confirms the already formulated hypothesis.

It is obvious from the table that higher percentage of utilisation of antenatal services was observed with forthnightly visits (68%) followed by monthly visits (51%) and rare visits (47%) by the health providers.

The district wise data in Table—4.24 also presents the similar trend. However higher percentage of utilisation of antenatal services was observed when compared with other stages of maternity cycle irrespective of the frequency of visits made by the health personnel.

Repeated visits, by the health providers, to the clients creates a feeling of concern among them and may motivate them to seek the services. In a way it generates demand for services. Thus the quality of services and greater utilisation depends upon the frequency and regularity of contacts of the health providers. The health administrators' role is crucial to ensure such visits, by the health providers through administrative and supervisory support.

Table—4.24

The percentage distribution of respondents by visits of health personnel and utilisation of antenatal services

Time of visiting the village by health personnel	*Kurnool District*			*Mahabubnagar District*			*Total*		
	Non-utilised	*Utilised*	*Total*	*Non-utilised*	*Utilised*	*Total*	*Non-utilised*	*Utilised*	*Total*
Rare	52.83 (28)	47.17 (25)	100.00 (53)	53.16 (42)	46.84 (37)	100.00 (79)	53.03 (70)	46.97 (62)	100.00 (132)
Monthly	47.73 (105)	52.27 (115)	100.00 (220)	50.20 (128)	49.80 (127)	100.00 (255)	49.05 (233)	50.95 (242)	100.00 (475)
Fortnightly	22.05 (28)	77.95 (99)	100.00 (127)	50.00 (33)	50.00 (33)	100.00 (66)	31.61 (61)	68.39 (132)	100.00 (193)
Total	**40.25 (161)**	**59.75 (239)**	**100.00 (400)**	**50.75 (203)**	**49.25 (197)**	**100.00 (400)**	**45.50 (364)**	**54.50 (436)**	**100.00 (800)**

P. Chi 2(4) = 30.4720; Pr= 0.000 6.1589; Pr = 0.188 23.2733; Pr = 0.000

II. *(ii) Type of Services Provided by the Health Personnel and Utilisation of Antenatal Services*

The health services provided by the health personnel in the community were trichotomised into preventive, promotive and curative services. Preventive services are aimed at preventing the occurrence of specific diseases. To maintain and improve the beneficiaries health promotive services are provided. The antenatal mothers expect immediate relief for any ailment hence the curative services and the related interventions are accepted and utilised to a larger extent than the promotive services. Under maternal health care, one of the main activities carried out by the female health assistant is, providing antenatal services to the women during antenatal period. The awareness about the need of Tetanus toxoid immunisation to prevent Tetanus disease for mothers and neonatal tetanus for new born and iron and folic acid tablets to prevent nutritional anaemia have motivated the antenatal mothers to accept these preventive services. But the other preventive and promotive services like personal hygiene, diet, regular check ups, mother craft classes etc., are not accepted to the same level. Thus it is true that a combination of preventive, promotive and curative services show a greater utilisation (64%) as against only 46 per cent of preventive services. The districts wise data also exhibit the similar trends with better levels of utilisation in Kurnool district (68.72%) than in Mahabubnagar district (58.18%) when all types of services provided to the beneficiaries as shown in Table—4.25.

Health care providers who shoulder the greater responsibility to bring effective change in the knowledge, attitude and practices among the members of the community and thereby motivate them for utilising the existing services effectively at various levels. Health education can break down the barriers of ignorance, prejudice, fears, phobias and misconceptions regarding various activities carried out by health personnel.

Table—4.25
The percentage distribution of type of services provided by health personnel and utilisation of antenatal services

Type of Services provided by health personnel in A.N. period	Kurnool District			Mahabubnagar District			Total		
	Non-utilised	Utilised	Total	Non-utilised	Utilised	Total	Non-utilised	Utilised	Total
Preventive services alone	47.51 (105)	52.49 (116)	100.00 (221)	57.02 (134)	42.98 (101)	100.00 (235)	54.24 (224)	45.76 (189)	100.00 (413)
Preventive/ Promotive/ Curative services	31.28 (56)	68.72 (123)	100.00 (179)	41.82 (69)	58.18 (96)	100.00 (165)	36.18 (140)	63.82 (247)	100.00 (387)
Total	40.25 (161)	59.75 (239)	100.00 (400)	50.75 (203)	49.25 (197)	100.00 (400)	45.50 (364)	54.50 (436)	100.00 (800)

P. Chi 2(2) = 11.5475; Pr = 0.003 9.1298; Pr = 0.010 28.7264; Pr = 0.000

(iii) Health Education Activities Carried Out by Health Personnel and Utilisation of Antenatal Services

The data in the Table—4.26 *(See the table in page 114)* manifests the percentage distribution of respondents by health education activities conducted by the health personnel and antenatal services utilisation. The overall percentage of utilisation was high (61%) among the respondents who were exposed to health education activities than the women who were not exposed to health education (49%), magnifying the impact of health education over the attitudes and practices of individuals.

The similar trend was seen among the districts also, however Kurnool district shows higher percentage of utilisation than Mahabubnagar district, it is due to non-availability and inaccessibility of health services. Higher percentage of utilisation was observed when the women are exposed to health education activities in both the districts Kurnool—(69%) and Mahabubnagar (54%) as against with the women who are not exposed to health education activities (Kurnool—53%); Mahabubnagar—45%).

Table—4.26
The percentage distribution of respondents by antenatal services utilisation and health education activities carried out by health personnel

Exposure to health education activities	*Kurnool District*			*Mahabubnagar District*			*Total*		
	Non-utilised	*Utilised*	*Total*	*Non-utilised*	*Utilised*	*Total*	*Non-utilised*	*Utilised*	*Total*
Not Exposed to health education activities	47.51 (105)	52.49 (116)	100.00 (221)	55.00 (110)	45.00 (90)	100.00 (200)	51.07 (215)	48.93 (206)	100.00 (421)
Exposed to health education activities	31.28 (56)	68.72 (123)	100.00 (179)	46.50 (93)	53.50 (107)	100.00 (200)	39.31 (149)	60.69 (230)	100.00 (379)
Total	40.25 (161)	59.75 (239)	100.00 (400)	50.75 (203)	49.25 (197)	100.00 (400)	45.50 (364)	54.50 (436)	100.00 (800)

P. Chi. 2(2) = 11.5475; Pr = 0.003 3.5116; Pr = 0.173 11.1485; Pr = 0.004

(iv) Source of Information About Maternal Health Services and Utilisation of Antenatal Services

The community will obtain the health information through various communication channels like health personnel, neighbours, elders in the family, satisfied utilisers and mass media.

The health personnel plays a crucial role in providing the knowledge to the community by organising information, education and communication activities through utilising mass-media.

The data related to antenatal service utilisation and sources of information is presented in the Table—4.27. The women in the rural community will be motivated by different means in utilising the health services. When all the sources are providing information, higher percentage of utilisation of antenatal services will be observed. The same phenomena was noticed in the study area also.

Table—4.27

The percentage distribution of respondents by source of information about maternal health services and utilisation of antenatal services

Source of information	*Kurnool District*			*Mahabubnagar District*			*Total*		
	Non-utili sed	*Utili-sed*	*Total*	*Non-utili-sed*	*Utili-sed*	*Total*	*Non-utili-sed*	*Utili-sed*	*Total*
Neighbours relatives.	58.42 (59)	41.58 (42)	100.00 (101)	61.54 (48)	38.46 (30)	100.00 (78)	59.78 (107)	40.22 (72)	100.00 (179)
Mass-media	44.44 (12)	55.56 (15)	100.00 (27)	69.23 (9)	30.77 (4)	100.00 (13)	52.50 (21)	47.50 (19)	100.00 (40)
Health personnel	34.62 (54)	65.38 (102)	100.00 (156)	48.89 (88)	51.11 (92)	100.00 (180)	42.26 (142)	57.74 (194)	100.00 (336)
All sources	31.03 (36)	68.97 (80)	100.00 (116)	44.96 (58)	55.04 (71)	100.00 (129)	38.37 (94)	61.13 (151)	100.00 (245)
Total	40.25 (161)	59.75 (239)	100.00 (400)	50.75 (203)	49.25 (197)	100.00 (400)	45.50 (364)	54.50 (436)	100.00 (800)

P. Chi 2(6) = 24.3162; Pr = 0.000 8.2070; Pr = 0.0223 24.9027; Pr = 0.000

Higher percentage of utilisation of antenatal services was observed (61%) when all the sources are used as a source of information. The next major effective source of information was health personnel. They will act as powerful weapons to motivate the people, when resulted the higher utilisation of antenatal services (58%). The mass media (48%) and satisfied utilisers (40%) are the other sources of information in utilising antenatal services.

The district wise data also shows the similar trends. The sources of information in relation to antenatal service utilisation in order of priority were: all resources (Kurnool—69%; Mahabubnagar—55%), followed by health personnel (Kurnool—65%, Mahabubnagar—51%), mass media (Kurnool—56%;

Mahabubnagar—31%) and satisfied utilisers (Kurnool—42%, Mahabubnagar—38%) respectively.

(b) Utilization of Natal Services and Differentials in Utilisation

Child birth is a normal physiological process and an occasion of joy in any women's reproductive life, but complications may arise from unskilled and septic manipulations. The need for effective natal care is therefore indispensable, even if the delivery is a normal one. The natal services are concerned with the care of the women and the new born, during and immediately after delivery.

The utilisation of natal services facilitate the safe delivery and a healthy baby. The women in the study area show very low utilisation of natal services. Depending upon the person conducting the delivery, place of delivery and practices during delivery, the utilisation of natal services are categorised as 'utilised' and 'non-utilised'.

In the study area, low percentage of (35%) utilisation of natal services was observed as compared to antenatal service utilisation (54.50%) as shown in Table—4.28. With the districts concerned, in Kurnool district more percentage of respondents have utilised natal services (38%) against their counterparts in the Mahabubnagar district (32%).

The natal services was low in the study area as compared to antenatal services, because in rural areas majority of the community was still practising traditional, cultural practices such as conducting deliveries by untrained personnel/self and other unsafe methods. These are all due to inaccessibility of health facilities and non-availability of health personnel. Another reason observed in the study area was, during antenatal period the health personnel, visits the mother either at clinic or at home which facilitated higher utilisation levels during antenatal period than the natal services.

Apart from the utilisation of natal services, the other information regarding natal care like cultural practices, hygienic care, new born care practices, feeding practices etc. are also gathered.

Tale—4.28
The percentage distribution of respondents by utilisation of natal services

Utilization of Natal services	*Kurnool District*	*Mahabubnagar District*	*Total*
Non-utilised	62.00 (248)	67.75 (271)	64.88 (519)
Utilised	38.00 (152)	32.25 (129)	35.12 (281)
(i) Personnel conducted delivery			
Trained persons	75.00 (300)	25.00 (100)	50.00 (400)
Untrained persons	25.00 (100)	75.00 (300)	50.00 (400)
(ii) Place of delivery			
Home	83.50 (334)	80.75 (323)	82.13 (657)
Institution	16.50 (66)	19.25 (77)	17.88 (143)
Total	100.00 (400)	100.00 (400)	100.00 (400)

Place and Person Conducted Delivery

In Indian setting conduction of delivery is based upon economic background of families, social factors like influence of elders in the families and satisfied utilisers within the community, cultural pattern, traditions followed by the family, availability of health personnel, accessibility and affordability of health services. In rural areas, majority of deliveries will be conducted at home and they will use the services from the personnel whoever will be readily available at that time.

The data related to place and person conducted delivery in the study areas presented in the Table—4.28. As expected, major percentage of deliveries (82%) occurred at home. Nearly one fifth of the respondents utilised institutional services during labour either at primary health centres, government hospitals or private agencies. The data within the districts is manifesting more or less the similar trend.

With regards to persons, conducting the delivery, in the total sample, half of the deliveries (50%) were conducted by trained persons and the remaining half by untrained persons *i.e.*, local dais and elders in the community. The district wise data presents a different trend. In Kurnool district three fourths of deliveries (75%) were conducted by trained persons. Among these, only 17 per cent of respondents utilised institutional services and the remaining 58 per cent of deliveries were conducted by trained birth attendants. Whereas in Mahabubnagar district, major percentage (75%) of deliveries are conducted by traditional birth attendants and only one fourth of respondents (25%) utilised services from trained personnel. Among them 19 per cent utilised institutional deliveries and the remaining six per cent of deliveries were conducted by trained dais at home. The reasons attributed for this are: non-availability of trained personnel, economic backwardness, pressure from elders in the families and socio-cultural pattern. It is shockening to find that in a case, a respondent in Mahabubnagar district had delivery without the assistance of others and gave baby bath immediately after delivery, as no one was around to care for her, because she stay in an interior village and belonged to nuclear family.

Cultural Practices Followed by the Women During Natal Period in the Study Area

Going to natal home for delivery is a common cultural practice observed in Indian society. Depending upon their socio-cultural, economic background they will go to natal home either for first delivery or for all deliveries. Generally the women will go to natal home during the last trimester of pregnancy and they will stay in the natal home upto 1 or 2 months after the delivery according to their convenience, economic status, and responsibilities of women within the family and number of deliveries. In the sample population also similar trend was observed. 30 per cent of women went to natal home for first delivery only, the other 45 per cent of respondents went for all deliveries. Few percentage of respondents (12%) did not go to natal home. The reasons quoted by them were that their parents were no more; they were staying very far from native place and that they quarrelled with natal family members.

More than half of the respondents (59%) stayed for 1-3 months. 19 per cent of women left the natal home within a month. Ten per cent of women stayed upto five months. The district wise data in Table—4.29 also showed more or less the similar trend.

Table—4.29
The percentage distribution of respondents by cultural practices followed during natal period

Cultural practices followed during natal period	*Kurnool District*	*Mahabubnagar District*	*Total*
(a) Going for natal home for deliveries			
All	44.25 (177)	46.50 (186)	45.38 (363)
Few	16.00 (64)	9.50 (38)	12.75 (102)
First delivery alone	32.50 (130)	28.25 (113)	30.38 (243)
None	7.25 (29)	15.75 (63)	11.50 (92)
(b) Period of staying at mother's house			
Not gone	7.25 (29)	15.75 (63)	11.50 (92)
More than 5 months	1.00 (4)	0.25 (1)	0.63 (5)
3-5 months	12.00 (48)	7.75 (31)	9.88 (79)
1-3 months	65.25 (261)	53.50 (214)	59.38 (475)
Within a month	14.50 (58)	22.75 (91)	18.63 (149)
Total	100.00 (400)	100.00 (400)	100.00 (800)

Newborn Practices

From birth to seven days, the child is known as 'Newborn'. During this period, the basic needs *viz.*, feeding, bath, cord care, warmth, protection and rooming in have to be fulfilled.

Common entry of micro organisms in the newborn is through the umbilical cord. It is the direct entry of microbes into the blood stream, so the cord should be kept clean and dry until it falls off. If the cord is left exposed to the air, without any application of dusting powder, it dries up and falls of much earlier. However, some applications to the umbilical stump is generally noticed. More percentage of respondents (63%) were in the practice of applying turmeric powder, as they felt that it keeps clean stump because of antiseptic nature. Few percentage of women (8%) applied oil to the umbillical cord as it keeps dry. It is surprising to notice the prevalence of hazardous practice in the study area *i.e.*, applying cow dung (8%) over the umbilical stump which leads to chances of getting Tetanus infection as shown in Table—4.30.

Table—4.30
The percentage distribution of respondents by newborn care practices

Newborn care practices	*Kurnool District*	*Mahabubnagar District*	*Total*
1	**2**	**3**	**4**
Cord Care			
Nothing	20.00 (80)	12.50 (50)	16.25 (130)
Turmeric Powder	60.50 (242)	66.25 (265)	63.38 (507)
Caster Oil	8.25 (33)	4.25 (17)	6.25 (50)
Coconut oil	1.25 (5)	1.25 (5)	1.25 (10)
Talcum powder	4.50 (18)	0.50 (2)	2.50 (20)

(Contd . . .)

1	2	3	4
Ointment	4.50 (18)	0.00 (0)	2.25 (18)
Cow dung	1.00 (4)	15.25 (61)	8.13 (65)
Bath			
Once daily	45.00 (180)	28.75 (115)	36.88 (295)
Twice daily	50.75 (203)	69.25 (277)	60.00 (480)
Alternative days once	2.50 (10)	2.00 (8)	2.25 (18)
Weekly twice	1.75 (7)	0.00 (0)	0.88 (7)
Feeding			
Demand	96.25 (385)	99.00 (396)	97.63 (781)
Scheduled	3.75 (15)	1.00 (4)	2.38 (19)
Rooming in			
Yes	99.00 (396)	98.75 (395)	98.88 (791)
No	1.00 (4)	1.25 (5)	1.13 (9)
Warmth			
Yes	99.00 (396)	98.75 (395)	98.88 (791)
No	1.00 (4)	1.25 (5)	1.13 (9)
(i) Breast feeding practices			
(a) Knowledge of Colostrum			
Not known	76.00 (304)	78.50 (314)	77.25 (618)
Known	24.00 (96)	21.50 (86)	22.75 (182)

(Contd . . .)

1	2	3	4
(b) Initiation of breast feeing			
After 24 hours	82.50 (330)	92.50 (370)	87.50 (700)
Within 3 hours	6.25 (25)	2.50 (10)	4.38 (35)
Within half an hour	11.25 (45)	5.00 (20)	8.13 (65)
(c) Substitution of foods other than breast feeding for first 3 days			
Not given	12.75 (51)	15.75 (63)	14.25 (114)
Sugar Water	2.25 (9)	2.75 (11)	2.50 (20)
Honey	0.75 (3)	1.25 (5)	1.00 (8)
Glucose water	11.25 (45)	7.25 (29)	9.25 (74)
Cow milk	7.50 (30)	5.25 (21)	6.38 (51)
Goat milk	10.50 (42)	13.25 (53)	11.88 (95)
Buffalow milk	2.25 (9)	1.25 (5)	1.75 (14)
Nursing mother's milk	48.00 (192)	52.25 (209)	50.13 (401)
Caster oil	4.75 (19)	1.00 (4)	2.88 (23)
Total	**100.00** **(400)**	**100.00** **(400)**	**100.00** **(800)**

More than half of the respondents (60%) were giving bath to their babies twice a day, a good practice, which was noticed. They mentioned that bath keeps the baby fresh, removes dirt, provides cleanliness and promotes rest and sleep.

Feeding of newborn is also very much needed, in order to meet the nutrition needs of the child. An overwhelming percentage of respondents (98%) breast fed their babies on demand basis.

Maintenance of newborn body temperature is to be maintained by keeping the baby warm through achieving a balance between heat production and heat loss. Rooming in (latching in) is placing the baby by the side of mother as it establishes the mother-child close relationship and bondage but the mother is conversant with the art of baby care so that she can assume full care of the baby when at home. It as an expression of love, provides emotional security for the child, beneficial effect on the temperament of the child and expression of maternal instincts. Cuddling of the baby, warmth and rooming in etc., practices were universally followed by the postnatal mothers in the study area (99%). The district wise data also showed similar trend.

(i) Breast Feeding Practices

Breast feeding practices of the mothers influence the growth and development of the child. It is one of the best means of protecting the life of the babies in early infancy and childhood. Faulty breast feeding practices may lead to early childhood morbidity and mortality. This again interacts with fertility behaviour of the couple. The early initiation of breast feeding and continuation for a period beyond six months within proper weaning intervention protects the health of the child and enhances survival of the child. Duration of breast feeding depends upon the weaning and other cultural practices. It has great influence on prevention of infection, provides nutrients and antibodies to enhance the child survival and decreases child morbidity and mortality. Breast feeding practice is almost universally observed in the study area. From sixteenth week of pregnancy, the colostrum is produced. It contains immunoglobulins which protects the child from infections and also gives nourishment to the newborn.

Even though 77 per cent of women were aware about the importance of colostrum, a major percentage (88%) of women initiated breast feeding after 24 hours only. Thereby they avoided to give colostrum for their babies. The common practice noticed in the rural areas was that, for the first three days after the child birth they will not give breast feeding for their babies but other nursing mother's milk will be given as a major substitute for feeding, in majority of cases. In the study area also, half of the sample were having the same practice. 14 per cent of the women did not give any feed for new born as they believe that whatever swallowed by the foetus in the mother's womb, that will come out for first 3 days. The other common substitutes given were: sugar water, honey, cow's milk, goat and buffalo's milk. A few percentage of women (8%) have initiated breast feeding within half an hour which is a good sign noticed in the study sample.

Determinants of Utilization of Natal Services

I. *Socio-economic Variables and Utilisation of Natal Services*

The socio-economic variables such as education, family income, occupation in relation to utilisation of natal services were discussed.

(i) Respondent's Education and Utilisation of Natal Services

Education increases the health consciousness and modifies the behaviour of the individuals. Thereby it influences indirectly the utilisation of natal services, irrespective of level of schooling.

The distribution of respondents by education and utilisation of natal services is presented in the Table—4.31. It shows a positive association between education and utilisation of natal services. In the present study education shows a drastic effect over the utilisation of natal services.

The respondents with certain level of schooling (either primary or middle school and above) exhibit higher percentage of utilisation (54%) over the illiterates (31%).

In Kurnool district, the data manifested similar trend *i.e.,* higher percentage of utilisation was observed among the respondents who had middle school education (62%) followed by primary school education (52%) and illiterates (33%). Whereas the Mahabubnagar district shows a different trend. The level of education did not show any impact over the utilisation pattern. More than half of the respondents (57%) who had primary school education utilised natal services. The percentage of utilisation was less among the women with middle school and above (41%) followed by illiterates (30%) but better with the respondents who had primary school education. (56.25%). The identified reasons for this type of behaviour are that women with primary school education are very conscious, anxious about their health pattern and child birth for minor problems also they cannot manage and taken assistance from health resources. These made them for higher utilisation of natal services, to whereas the mothers with middle school and above were able to manage themselves, it may been the cause for low utilisation when compared to woman with primary school education.

Table—4.31

The percentage distribution of respondents' by education and utilisation on natal services

Respondents' Education	*Kurnool District*			*Mahabubnagar District*			*Total*		
	Non-utilised	*Utilised*	*Total*	*Non-utilised*	*Utilised*	*Total*	*Non-utilised*	*Utilised*	*Total*
Illiterate	67.20 (211)	32.80 (103)	100.00 (314)	70.11 (244)	29.89 (104)	100.00 (348)	68.73 (455)	31.27 (207)	100.00 (662)
Primary School	47.73 (21)	52.27 (23)	100.00 (44)	43.48 (10)	56.52 (13)	100.00 (23)	46.27 (31)	53.73 (36)	100.00 (67)
Middle school and above	38.10 (16)	61.90 (26)	100.00 (42)	58.62 (17)	41.38 (12)	100.00 (29)	46.68 (33)	53.52 (38)	100.00 (71)
Total	62.00 (248)	38.00 (152)	100.00 (400)	67.75 (271)	32.25 (129)	100.00 (400)	64.88 (519)	35.12 (281)	100.00 (800)

P. Chi. 2(6) = 43.3660; Pr = 0.000 22.6804; Pr = 0.001 65.6950; Pr = 0.000

(ii) Occupation and Utilisation of Natal Services

Occupation is a socio-economic variable and developmental indicator of the nation. The data in the Table—4.32 manifests the trends in utilisation of natal services by the occupation of women.

The percentage of utilisation was high among housewives (50%) followed by cultivators (40%) and coolies (31%). The district wise data also manifest the same trend. Kurnool district exhibits higher percentage of utilisation than Mahabubnagar district. In both the districts coolies and cultivators show almost similar percentage of utilisation of natal services.

Housewives will have more chances for health information, more awareness about health agencies and higher chances of interaction with health personnel etc. On the other hand lower utilisation was noticed among coolies and cultivators due to inaccessibility of health services, negligence and lack of time for the respondents to approach the health agencies.

Table—4.32

The percentage distribution of respondents by occupation and utilisation of natal services

Respondents' occupation	*Kurnool District*			*Mahabubnagar District*			*Total*		
	Non-utilised	*Utilised*	*Total*	*Non-utilised*	*Utilised*	*Total*	*Non-utilised*	*Utilised*	*Total*
Housewives	47.37 (36)	52.63 (40)	100.00 (76)	54.55 (24)	45.45 (20)	100.00 (44)	50.00 (60)	50.00 (60)	100.00 (120)
Cultivation	54.55 (42)	45.45 (35)	100.00 (77)	67.21 (41)	32.79 (20)	100.00 (61)	60.14 (83)	39.86 (55)	100.00 (138)
Cooly+ petty business	68.83 (170)	31.17 (77)	100.00 (247)	69.83 (206)	30.17 (89)	100.00 (295)	69.37 (376)	30.63 (166)	100.00 (542)
Total	**62.00 (248)**	**38.00 (152)**	**100.00 (400)**	**67.75 (271)**	**32.25 (129)**	**100.00 (400)**	**64.88 (519)**	**35.12 (281)**	**100.00 (800)**

P. Chi. 2(6) = 26.1363; Pr = 0.000 7.2725; Pr = 0.296 26.1212; Pr = 0.000

(iii) Annual Family Income and Utilisation of Natal Services

Income is an indicator of economic development which influences the utilisation of services directly. The economic backwardness may deter the women from utilisation of natal services to some extent.

The higher percentage of utilisation was observed in higher income groups (44%) followed by middle income group (34%) and low income group (33%) as depicted in Table—4.33. Thus a positive association was observed between income and utilisation of services. The reasons observed were: affordability. and accessibility of health services.

Table—4.33
The percentage distribution of respondents by annual family income and utilisation of natal services

Annual family income (Rs.)	*Kurnool District*			*Mahabubnagar District*			*Total*		
	Non-utili sed	*Utili-sed*	*Total*	*Non-utili-sed*	*Utili-sed*	*Total*	*Non-utili-sed*	*Utili-sed*	*Total*
<10,000/-	69.57 (48)	30.43 (21)	100.00 (69)	65.26 (62)	34.25 (33)	100.00 (95)	67.07 (110)	32.93 (54)	100.00 (164)
10,001/- 14,000/-	67.09 (106)	32.91 (52)	100.00 (158)	70.87 (90)	29.13 (37)	100.00 (127)	68.77 (196)	31.23 (89)	100.00 (285)
14,001/- 18,000/-	55.05 (60)	44.95 (49)	100.00 (109)	70.59 (84)	29.41 (35)	100.00 (119)	63.16 (144)	36.84 (84)	100.00 (228)
18,001/-+	53.13 (34)	46.87 (30)	100.00 (64)	59.32 (35)	40.68 (24)	100.00 (59)	56.10 (69)	43.90 (54)	100.00 (123)
Total	**62.00 (248)**	**38.00 (152)**	**100.00 (400)**	**67.75 (271)**	**32.25 (129)**	**100.00 (400)**	**64.88 (519)**	**35.12 (281)**	**100.00 (800)**

P. Chi. 2(6) = 15.7386; Pr = 0.0015 7.8625; Pr = 0.248 17.4165; Pr = 0.026

The district wise data manifests different pattern in the utilisation of natal services based on income. Kurnool district exhibits positive association *i.e.,* higher percentage of utilisation was noticed in higher income groups (47%) followed by middle income group (38%) and low income group of respondents

(30%). On the other hand Mahabubnagar district exhibits a different trend. However better utilisation was noticed in high income groups (41%) followed by low income groups (34%) and middle income group (29%).

II. Socio-cultural Variables and Utilisation and Natal Services

(i) Caste and Utilisation of Natal Services

Caste is a social variable, which influences the cultural and traditional practices and the utilisation of natal services. The respondents who belong to forward community, have utilised the natal services in a better way (47%) than the respondents of backward communities (B.C.—35%; SC/ST—29%). The districts wise data in Table—4.34 also showed similar trend. The forward communities have utilised natal services (47%) more than the lower community (B.C.—36% Kurnool, Mahabubnagar—35%); S.C. and S.T.—Kurnool 35%; Mahabubnagar—23%). The hypothesis, higher the caste, higher will be the utilisation of natal services is thus confirmed here.

Table—4.34

The percentage distribution of respondents by caste and utilisation of natal services

Caste	*Kurnool District*			*Mahabubnagar District*			*Total*		
	Non-utilised	*Utilised*	*Total*	*Non-utilised*	*Utilised*	*Total*	*Non-utilised*	*Utilised*	*Total*
Forward caste	52.56 (41)	47.44 (37)	100.00 (78)	53.33 (24)	46.67 (21)	100.00 (45)	52.85 (65)	47.15 (58)	100.00 (123)
Backward caste	63.98 (135)	36.02 (76)	100.00 (211)	65.33 (147)	34.67 (78)	100.00 (225)	64.68 (282)	35.32 (154)	100.00 (436)
Scheduled caste and scheduled tribe	64.86 (72)	35.14 (39)	100.00 (111)	76.92 (100)	23.08 (30)	100.00 (130)	71.37 (172)	28.63 (69)	100.00 (241)
Total	**62.00 (248)**	**38.00 (152)**	**100.00 (400)**	**67.75 (271)**	**32.25 (129)**	**100.00 (400)**	**64.88 (519)**	**35.12 (281)**	**100.00 (800)**

P. Chi 2(4) = 12.6613; Pr = 0.013 15.4671; Pr = 0.017 16.9379; Pr = 0.010

The forward communities are socio-economically advanced, hence they are more health conscious and spare their time to seek the health services, whereas the hindering factors for low utilisation of natal services among the women in lower community are: sharing additional responsibilities such as assisting their spouse in economic activities, neglecting their health and ignorance of health factors and considering all life events in a casual way etc.

(ii) Type of Family and Utilisation and Natal Services

Family will have a definite role in the utilisation of natal services. Family members are the final decision-makers to decide the place and person conducting the delivery. Family structure and exposure to health information have a definite influence on utilisation of natal services.

Interestingly, slightly better utilisation was observed in joint families (38%) than the nuclear families (34%). It is because of the pressure of the elders, their previous experience, sharing of responsibilities in the family and motivation by health personnel during natal period.

A similar trend is observed even at the district level also presented in Table—4.35 (*See the table in page 130*). Joint families were showing more percentage of utilisation (Kurnool—39%); Mahabubnagar—38%) than in the nuclear families. However the nuclear families in Mahabubnagar show a low utilisation (30%) than in Kurnool district (38%) which can be attributed to backwardness.

Eventhough it is expected that nuclear families are more prone to greater utilisation, the rural background, poverty and lack of exposure to health information might have affected utilisation of natal services. The joint family system with its traditions and customs is set for a change. Hence better utilisation is desired. The social change taking place in the society should percolate into rural families. The joint family is on the decline, hence the nuclear families should bestow greater care and attention for its members. Greater thrust should be given by the health care providers about the need and utilization of natal services.

Table—4.35
The percentage distribution of respondents by the type of family and utilisation of natal services

Womens' education	*Kurnool District*			*Mahabubnagar District*			*Total*		
	Non-utili-sed	*Utili-sed*	*Total*	*Non-utili-sed*	*Utili-sed*	*Total*	*Non-utili-sed*	*Utili-sed*	*Total*
Joint	60.54 (72)	39.46 (45)	100.00 (117)	62.96 (85)	37.04 (50)	100.00 (135)	62.30 (157)	37.70 (95)	100.00 (252)
Nuclear	62.19 (176)	37.81 (107)	100.00 (283)	70.19 (186)	29.81 (79)	100.00 (265)	66.06 (362)	33.94 (186)	100.00 (548)
Total	**62.00 (248)**	**38.00 (152)**	**100.00 (400)**	**67.75 (271)**	**32.25 (129)**	**100.00 (400)**	**64.88 (519)**	**35.12 (281)**	**100.00 (800)**

(iii) Interspouse Communication and Utilisation of Natal Services

The communication between the couple is a positive motivational and influential factor in the decision-making process relating to health care and effective utilisation of natal services.

The utilisation of natal services is observed to be high (47%) among the couples who had interaction and free discussion, than the couple who were not discussing (32%). It is evident that, the interspouse communication promotes positive attitude and enhances greater utilisation of natal services. The districts also exhibit the same trend. However greater utilisation of natal services is observed in Kurnool district with couple interact (50%). But it is less in Mahabubnagar district (42%), (Table—4.36)

The inhibitions with the couple for discussion on health related issues, lack of awareness about the need and availability of services coupled with customs and traditional practices, might have prevented interaction between the couple. Thus it is obvious that the efforts are to be focused on equipping the couple with adequate health information and promote interaction between the couple. Involvement of satisfied utilisers, local dais, health personnel to promote interspouse communication are the needs of the day, because they enhance wider utilisation of natal services.

Table—4.36

The percentage distribution of respondents by interspouse communication and utilisation of natal services

Internal spousal communication	*Kurnool District*			*Mahabubnagar District*			*Total*		
	Non-utilised	*Utilised*	*Total*	*Non-utilised*	*Utilised*	*Total*	*Non-utilised*	*Utilised*	*Total*
Not discussing	66.90 (188)	33.10 (93)	100.00 (281)	69.25 (241)	30.75 (107)	100.00 (348)	68.20 (429)	31.80 (200)	100.00 (629)
Discussing	0.42 (60)	49.58 (59)	100.00 (119)	57.69 (30)	42.31 (22)	100.00 (52)	52.63 (90)	47.37 (81)	100.00 (171)
Total	**62.00 (248)**	**38.00 (152)**	**100.00 (400)**	**67.75 (271)**	**32.25 (129)**	**100.00 (400)**	**64.88 (519)**	**35.12 (281)**	**100.00 (800)**

P. Chi 2(2) = 9.9512; Pr = 0.007 3.6703; Pr = 0.160 14.9615; Pr = 0.001

(iv) Sex Preference and Utilisation of Natal Services

The data related to the association between sex preference and utilisation of natal services, is depicted in the Table 4.37 (*See the table in page 132)*. It was observed that there is no variation on the utilisation of natal services in the total sample based on sex preference. However the districts present a slight difference in the utilisation of natal services.

In Mahabubnagar district, a higher level of utilisation was noticed among the respondents with sex preference (36%) than the couple who do not have any sex preference (31%). Perhaps the women in this district, because of sex preference, might have given weightage for the service utilisation in the hope of having a preferred child. It is interesting to note that in Kurnool district, a reverse trend is observed *i.e.* higher percentage of utilisation of natal services is observed among the couple who were not having sex preference (38%) against the couple who were having sex preference (35%).

The desire to have a child of their preferred sex may motivate the women for greater utilisation of natal services. Their hope to have a child of their choice related to sex, stimulates them to have a healthy baby. However this is not a dominating factor, since the sex of the child is not predetermined besides the women who are modernized and educated may not prefer sex. At the same time, they may utilise the services in a better way. Hence the service utilisation is not greatly affected due to sex preference in the study area.

Table—4.37

The percentage distribution of respondents by sex preference and utilisation of natal services

Sex preference	*Kurnool District*			*Mahabubnagar District*			*Total*		
	Non-utilised	*Utilised*	*Total*	*Non-utilised*	*Utilised*	*Total*	*Non-utilised*	*Utilised*	*Total*
Having sex Preference	65.31 (32)	34.69 (17)	100.00 (49)	64.44 (58)	35.56 (32)	100.00 (90)	64.75 (90)	35.25 (49)	100.00 (139)
Not having sex preference	61.54 (216)	38.46 (135)	100.00 (351)	68.71 (213)	31.29 (97)	100.00 (310)	64.90 (429)	35.10 (232)	100.00 (661)
Total	**62.00 (248)**	**38.00 (152)**	**100.00 (400)**	**67.75 (271)**	**32.25 (129)**	**100.00 (400)**	**64.88 (519)**	**35.12 (281)**	**100.00 (800)**

P. Chi 2(2) = 0.2596; Pr = 0.878 0.9364; Pr = 0.626 0.8562; Pr = 0.652

IV. Infrastructual Facilities and Utilisation of Natal Services

(i) Visits of the Health Personnel and Utilisation of Natal Services

Health personnel visit the villages to render health care services to the needy population within the community. If the health personnel are accessible, available and acceptable to the community and provide quality health care services, their credibility will be high with the community. Thus the beneficiaries have a good rapport with the health care providers, because the beneficiaries are more interested to utilise the services to a large extent.

The visits made by the health personnel were trichotomised into weekly/fortnight visits, monthly visits and rare visits. A significant positive association is found between the frequency of visits made by the health personnel and utilisation of natal service is noticed in Table—4.38.

Table—4.38

The percentage distribution of respondents by the visits of health personnel and utilisation of natal services

Visits by health personnel	*Kurnool District*			*Mahabubnagar District*			*Total*		
	Non-utili sed	*Utili-sed*	*Total*	*Non-utili-sed*	*Utili-sed*	*Total*	*Non-utili-sed*	*Utili-sed*	*Total*
Rare	75.47 (40)	24.53 (13)	100.00 (53)	70.89 (56)	29.11 (23)	100.00 (79)	72.73 (96)	27.27 (36)	100.00 (132)
Monthly	70.00 (154)	30.00 (66)	100.00 (220)	68.24 (173)	31.76 (82)	100.00 (255)	69.05 ((327)	31.15 (148)	100.00 (475)
Weekly/ Fortnightly	42.52 (54)	57.48 (73)	100.00 (127)	62.12 (42)	37.88 (24)	100.00 (66)	49.22 (96)	50.78 (97)	100.00 (193)
Total	**62.00 (248)**	**38.00 (152)**	**100.00 (400)**	**67.75 (271)**	**32.25 (129)**	**100.00 (400)**	**64.88 (519)**	**35.12 (281)**	**100.00 (800)**

P. Chi 2(4) = 31. 1749; Pr = 0.000 30.490; Pr = 0.550 29.3048; Pr = 0.000

As per the visits of health personnel to the villages concerned, more than half of the respondents (59%) informed that health care providers are visiting the villages monthly once followed by weekly visits. The remaining 17 per cent of respondents told that, the health personnel are rarely visiting the villages. It is quite natural that lesser the contacts, lesser will be the utilisation of services. This indicates the gap in the availability of health care providers to the community. The female health assistant, who is responsible to provide natal services to the community is supposed to visit every antenatal woman, atleast once in a month. However it seems to be different in the present study because of which the utilisation of natal service is also less. However the levels of utilisation show an upward trend from rare to monthly and fortnightly visits by the health providers.

It is evident from the data that higher percentage of utilisation of natal services is observed, when the health personnel visited them fortnightly (51%), followed by monthly visits (31%) and rare visits (27%). However much variation is not observed in utilisation pattern when the health personnel visited them either monthly once or rare, but a significant improvement in the utilisation pattern observed when they were visited by health personnel regularly. Thus the hypothesis higher the number of visits, higher will be the level of utilisation of natal services is found to be true.

The district wise data also observed a similar picture. However the respondents in Kurnool district show better utilisation than in Mahabubnagar district, when the health personnel visited them regularly *i.e.,* fortnightly once (Kurnool 57%; Mahabubnagar 38%), whereas a reverse trend in utilisation pattern was noticed during rare and monthly visits *i.e.,* Mahabubnagar district shows a better level of utilisation during rare visits (29%) and monthly visits (32%) than Kurnool district (25%—rare; 30%—monthly).

(ii) Type of Health Services Provided by Health Personnel and Utilisation of Services

In the rural community, the health personnel provide preventive, promotive and curative health services. Generally if the health personnel provide all types of health services, the utilisation of natal services will be better.

Higher level of utilisation was observed (42%) when all types of services are provided by the health personnel, but less utilisation was observed if they provide preventive services alone (29%). Significant association was found between the types of services provided by the health personnel and utilisation of health services. The district wise data in the Table—4.39 also presents a similar picture.

In Kurnool district higher percentage of utilisation was observed (48%) when all types of health services are provided but not so much in Mahabubnagar district (33%). But in Mahabubnagar district better percentage of utilisation was observed when preventive services alone provided (32%) than in Kurnool district (26%). It is observed that in Mahabubnagar district, majority of women were receiving preventive services only by the health personnel.

Table—4.39

The percentage distribution of respondents by type of health services provided by health personnel and utilisation of natal services

Type of services provided by health personnel	*Kurnool District*			*Mahabubnagar District*			*Total*		
	Non-utili sed	*Utili-sed*	*Total*	*Non-utili-sed*	*Utili-sed*	*Total*	*Non-utili-sed*	*Utili-sed*	*Total*
Preventive services alone	74.16 (132)	25.84 (46)	100.00 (178)	68.51 (161)	31.49 (74)	100.00 (235)	70.94 (293)	29.06 (120)	100.00 (143)
Preventive, promotive and curtative services	52.25 (116)	47.75 (106)	100.00 (222)	66.67 (110)	33.33 (55)	100.00 (165)	58.40 (226)	41.60 (161)	100.00 (387)
Total	62.00 (248)	38.00 (152)	100.00 (400)	67.75 (271)	32.25 (129)	100.00 (400)	64.88 (519)	35.12 (281)	100.00 (800)

P. Chi 2(2) = 21.1516; Pr = 0.000 0.1509 Pr = 0.927 29.3048; Pr = 0.000

(iii) Health Education Activities Carriedout by the Health Personnel and Utilisation of Natal Services

The health information will be disseminated to the community by the health personnel by conducting health educational activities. The beneficiaries in turn procure adequate knowledge and motivated themselves to utilise the health services effectively.

When the women are exposed to health educational activities, naturally they will utilise the services in a better way

(38%) than the women who are not exposed to health educational activities (33%). The district wise data presented in Table—4.40 also presents the similar pattern. Higher level of utilisation of natal services was observed when the women are exposed to health education activities (Kurnool = 40%); Mahabubnagar = 36%} than their counterparts (Kurnool = 36%, Mahabubnagar = 29%). It is interesting to note that the women who are not exposed to health educational activities also utilised the services (Kurnool = 36%, Mahabubnagar = 29%) due to self motivation and health consciousness.

Table—4.40

The percentage distribution of respondents by health education activities carried out by health personnel and utilisation of natal services

Health education activities carried out	*Kurnool District*			*Mahabubnagar District*			*Total*		
	Non-utili sed	*Utili-sed*	*Total*	*Non-utili-sed*	*Utili-sed*	*Total*	*Non-utili-sed*	*Utili-sed*	*Total*
Not Carried out	63.80 (141)	36.20 (80)	100.00 (221)	71.50 (143)	28.50 (57)	100.00 (200)	67.46 (284)	32.54 (137)	100.00 (421)
Carried out	59.78 (107)	40.22 (72)	100.00 (179)	64.00 (128)	36.00 (72)	100.00 (200)	62.01 (235)	37.99 (144)	100.00 (379)
Total	**62.00 (248)**	**38.00 (152)**	**100.00 (400)**	**67.75 (271)**	**32.25 (129)**	**100.00 (400)**	**64.88 (519)**	**35.12 (281)**	**100.00 (800)**

P. Chi 2(2) = 1.1904; Pr = 0.551 4.4732 Pr = 0.107 2.6323; Pr= 0.268

(iv) The Source of Health Information and Utilisation of Natal Services

The community will acquire the health information by different sources like neighbours, relatives, mass-media activities and health personnel. They will be acting as channels of health information. Neighbours and relatives act as primary source of health information with regard to natal service utilisation (50%) followed by health personnel (39%), combination of all sources (36%) and mass-media activities (24%).

The community which includes family members, neighbours and relatives *i.e.*, satisfied utilisers, will act as powerful vehicles or channels of communication by transferring the information. They are the best influencing agencies for effective utilisation of health services. Hence now a days, in the implementation of national health programmes, community participation, community mobilisation and their involvement are taken up. The health personnel will be disseminating the health information to the community with the help of mass-media activities. They act as second major source of information in the study area.

The district wise data in Table—4.41 presents a different trend *i.e.*, in both the districts mass-media activities act as primary source (Kurnool—52%, Mahabubnagar—46%) followed by health personnel (Kurnool—43%), Mahabubnagar—36%) and neighbours and relatives (Kurnool—21%, Mahabubnagar—29%).

Table—4.41

The percentage distribution of respondents by source of information about maternal and child health services and utilisation of natal services

Source of information	*Kurnool District*			*Mahabubnagar District*			*Total*		
	Non-utilised	*Utilised*	*Total*	*Non-utilised*	*Utilised*	*Total*	*Non-utilised*	*Utilised*	*Total*
Neighbours, relatives	79.21 (80)	20.79 (21)	100.00 (101)	71.79 (56)	28.21 (22)	100.00 (78)	50.00 (20)	50.00 (20)	100.00 (40)
Mass-media alone	48.15 (13)	51.85 (14)	100.00 (27)	53.85 (7)	46.15 (6)	100.00 (13)	75.98 (136)	24.02 (43)	100.00 (179)
Health personnel	57.05 (89)	42.95 (67)	100.00 (156)	64.44 (116)	35.56 (64)	100.00 (180)	61.01 (205)	38.99 (131)	100.00 (336)
Combination of all sources	56.90 (66)	43.10 (50)	100.00 (116)	73.32 (92)	26.68 (37)	100.00 (129)	64.49 (158)	35.51 (87)	100.00 (245)
Total	**62.00 (248)**	**38.00 (152)**	**100.00 (400)**	**67.75 (271)**	**32.25 (129)**	**100.00 (400)**	**64.88 (519)**	**35.12 (281)**	**100.00 (800)**

P. Chi 2(6) = 19.8478; Pr = 0.003 14.8703 Pr = 0.021 21.7710; Pr = 0.001

C. Utilisation of Postnatal Services and Differentials in Utilisation

The period from immediately after delivery to six weeks, is known as "Puerperal period" or "Postnatal period". It includes the care of the mother and the newborn. Postnatal care ensures sound maternal health and child survival. Thus the availability and utilisation of postnatal services become a key factor in reducing maternal and infant morbidity and mortality.

During postnatal period the female health assistant has to visit the postnatal mother twice a day, during first three days of delivery and daily once upto 7 days, (till the umbilical cord drops off). During her visits she checks fundal height and vital signs observes lochia, checks vital signs and educates the mother about, child rearing, feeding and dietary practices, breast and perrineal hygience, postnatal exercises and the need of contraception. If postnatal mother suffers with minor illness, she will render curative services. If need arises, they will refer the case of referral institutions. In the present study, if the mother receives either one or other service the mother is categorised as 'utilised category' and if none of the services is availed the mother is categorised as 'non-utilised category'.

Apart from the utilisation of postnatal services, the other relevant information pertaining to postnatal period like the practices such as cultural, hygienic, dietary (breast feeding, weaning practices) and, the type of activities performed during postnatal period etc. is gathered.

The percentage of services utilisation in the present study, significantly decreased from antental period (54.5%) followed by natal period (35%) and postnatal period (30%). The identified reasons for this pattern are: ignorance, less exposure to the health information, inaccessibility and non-availability of health functionaries and low economic status of the respondents. During antenatal period, the health worker visits the mother atleast once. But they may not take proper care in natal and postnatal period, which results in the low utilisation of the services (Table—4.42).

In total, more than one fourth of the respondents (30%) have utilised postnatal services. The districts show just a marginal variation in the utilisation in this aspect. In Kurnool district, better percentage of utilisation (32%) was noticed against Mahabubnagar district (28%) due to accessibility of health services, availability of health personnel and higher exposure to mass-media activities.

Table—4.42
The percentage distribution of respondents according to postnatal service utilisation

Postnatal service utilisation	*Kurnool District*	*Mahabubnagar Distrct*	*Total*
1	**2**	**3**	**4**
Non-utilised	68.00 (272)	72.00 (288)	70.00 (560)
Utilised	32.00 (128)	28.00 (112)	30.00 (240)
(i) Postnatal visits by health personnel			
Dire	32.00 (128)	28.00 (112)	30.00 (240)
Not done	68.00 (272)	72.00 (288)	70.00 (560)
(ii) Postnatal services received			
Not applicable	68.00 (272)	72.00 (288)	70.00 (560)
Received	11.25 (45)	7.25 (29)	9.25 (74)
Not received	20.75 (83)	20.75 (83)	20.75 (166)
(iii) Health education activities carried out by health personnel during postnatal period			
Not applicable	68.00 (272)	72.00 (288)	70.00 (560)
Carried out	3.00 (12)	2.00 (8)	2.50 (20)
Not carried out	29.00 (116)	26.00 (104)	27.00 (220)

(Contd . . .)

1	2	3	4
(iv) Identified health problems during potnatal period			
No problems	84.75 (339)	81.75 (327)	83.25 (666)
Medical problems	9.25 (37)	8.00 (32)	8.63 (69)
Exclusively reproductive problems	6.00 (24)	10.25 (41)	8.13 (65)
(v) Remedy for postnatal problems			
Not applicable	84.75 (339)	81.75 (327)	83.25 (666)
Remedy not taken	0.75 (3)	5.00 (20)	2.88 (23)
Remedy taken	14.50 (58)	13.25 (53)	13.88 (111)
Total	**100.00** **(400)**	**100.00** **(400)**	**100.00** **(800)**

Utilisation of Postnatal Services

The female health assistant plays an eminent role in educating and guiding the women to protect their health during postnatal period. In the present study the respondents were asked whether they received these services during postnatal period or not.

In the present analysis, only 30 per cent of respondents were visited by health professionals during their postnatal period. A slight variation in utilisation pattern was observed between the study districts (Kurnool—32%, Mahabubnagar—28%), eventhough 30 per cent of mothers are visited by health personnel. It is surprising to find that only 9 per cent of women received services by them, the remaining 21 per cent of respondents were visited by female health assistant only to register the birth of child. No other service was provided by her. In Kurnool district, 11 per cent of mothers received postnatal services out of 32 per cent of women who were visited by health personnel, whereas in Mahabubnagar district only 7 per cent of women received postnatal services out of 28 per cent of women by health personnel during postnatal period. Only a little percentage of women (3%) received health information during postnatal period regarding perennial care and breast hygiene. It clearly points out a big gap between expected services from health personnel and the percentage of service delivered by them.

Only 17 per cent of women had problems during postnatal period, among them, half of the women suffered from medical problems (9%) whereas other half suffered exclusively from reproductive problems (8%). Only 14 per cent of women sought medical treatment.

These facts throw light on the state of health services and the usefulness of the health personnel. There is little scope to enhance the credibility of the health care providers in such situations. This is contrary to the wide publicity given by government about the maternal and child health care and its concern for the health of mother and child. There is no second opinion about the inaccessibility and poor quality of services. These facts point to the bad state of provision of maternal and child health services in the study area which needs immediate attention to streamline the system for qualitative maternal and child health care.

PRACTICES OF WOMEN DURING POSTNATAL PERIOD

I. Hygienic Practices

During postnatal period, hygienic care is very essential to prevent sepsis and other complications. Information on three items namely bath, perennial and breast care were gathered. The bath will be given immediately after delivery. The family will celebrate "Purudu" function when the mother is given a bath during postnatal period either on 3rd day, 5th day, 7th day and 9th day. After this day the mother attends to regular activities. Nearly one fourth of total sample took bath immediately after delivery (24%) or on the first day of delivery (28%), which is a good practice. More than one third (32%) of mothers took bath on the third day also, remaining women were in the practice of taking bath after third day only. An overwhelming percentage of mothers (94%) in Mahabubnagar district took bath after four days as against the mothers in Kurnool district (74%).

Breast and perinneal hygiene are essential to prevent infections. Half of the women took perinneal care once daily. A good practice was also observed by the women in the study area *i.e.* 18 per cent of women were taking perinneal care, including care about wet pads. Breast hygiene was also practised whenever they gave feed to the child.

18 per cent of mothers did not understand about hygienic practices, even after probing. They did not also give any response for the study.

II. Activities Carriedout by Women During Postnatal Period

In Indian culture, during postnatal period, women will carry out the regular as well as occupational activities after celebrating 'purudu'. More than one fourth of women (29%) resumed to normal household work after 10 days, 35 per cent of women resumed to household activities between 10-15 days, the remaining 36 per cent of women informed the household activities after 16 days. In nuclear families the mother attends to the household work quite early. The districts wise data presented in Table—4.43 also represents more or less the similar trend. This finding emphasises the need of assistance to mothers in the families.

With regards to resumption of work outside the house, more than one third of the sample (32%) does outside work within a month and majority of the women performed the outside activities within 3 months (83%). Almost all the respondents resumed the outside work within five months. It clearly emphasises the need of assistance in the families which are economically backward. The data within the districts presents a different trend. In Mahabubnagar district, major percentage of women (89%) resumed outside work within three months as against the women in Kurnool district (77%). It clearly denotes in both the districts that the rural women have to perform outside work even within the puerperal period also. The reasons quoted by them were: supplementing the economy and shouldering the burden of the family as well as sharing the duties of the spouse.

Table—4.43
The percentage distribution of respondents by postnatal practices

Practices of women during postnatal period	*Kurnool District*	*Mahabubnagar District*	*Total*
1	2	3	4
I. Hygienic Practices			
(a) Bath			
On the day of delivery	4.75 (59)	33.25 (133)	24.00 (192)
Next day	29.00 (116)	27.25 (109)	28.13 (225)
3rd day	30.00 (120)	33.00 (132)	31.50 (252)
5th day	17.00 (68)	3.75 (15)	10.38 (83)
7th day	6.50 (26)	1.75 (7)	4.13 (33)
>9th day	2.75 (11)	1.00 (4)	1.88 (15)
(b) Perinneal and breast care			
Not taken	4.50 (18)	3.50 (14)	4.00 (32)
Twice a day	13.00 (52)	7.75 (31)	10.38 (83)
Once daily	53.25 (213)	47.00 (188)	50.13 (401)
Whenever wets	18.75 (75)	16.25 (65)	17.50 (140)
Do not know	10.50 (42)	25.50 (102)	18.00 (144)

(Contd . . .)

1	2	3	4
II. Activities Carriedout by Women During Postnatal Period			
(a) Resuming normal work in postnatal period			
Before 10 days	33.10	26.25	28.63
	(124)	(105)	(229)
10-15 days	33.50	36.00	34.75
	(134)	(144)	(278)
> 16 days	35.50	37.75	36.63
	(142)	(151)	(293)
(b) Resuming outside work			
Within a month	34.50	28.75	31.63
	(138)	(115)	(253)
1-3 months	42.00	60.50	51.25
	(168)	(242)	(410)
> 4 months	23.50	10.75	17.13
	(94)	(43)	(137)
III. Dietary Practices			
(i) Modified	41.00	29.00	35.00
	(164)	(116)	(280)
Not modified	59.00	71.00	65.00
	(236)	(284)	(520)
(a) Reasons for modification			
For healthy mother and healthy baby	53.78 (64)	46.22 (55)	42.50 (119)
For breast milk production	62.11 (100)	37.89 (61)	57.50 (161)
(b) Additional foods consumed			
Not applicable	59.00 (236)	71.00 (284)	65.00 (520)
Garlic	31.25 (125)	13.50 (54)	22.38 (179)

(Contd . . .)

1	2	3	4
Mutton	5.25 (21)	7.50 (30)	6.38 (51)
Fruits	1.00 (4)	2.25 (9)	1.63 (13)
Bitter gourd	2.25 (9)	3.25 (13)	2.75 (22)
Milk	1.25 (5)	2.50 (10)	1.88 (15)
(c) Foods avoided			
Not applicable	59.25 (237)	76.50 (306)	67.88 (543)
Butter milk	25.25 (101)	7.50 (30)	16.38 (131)
Brinzol	12.00 (48)	7.00 (28)	9.50 (76)
Gongura	2.50 (10)	7.00 (28)	4.75 (38)
Chillies	1.00 (4)	2.00 (8)	1.50 (12)

III. Dietary Practices

During postnatal period, the women generally require high caloric and high protein diet to meet the nutritional needs of the child, to regain mothers' health and to increase the production of the breast milk.

In the present study, more than one third of the sample modified their diet in postnatal period (35%), for breast milk production (58%) and for the health of mother and child (42%), on the other hand nearly two thirds of sample (65%) did not modify their diet in postnatal period because of cultural taboos, beliefs, ignorance and poverty. In Kurnool district more percentage of women (41%) modified their diet in postnatal period against their counterparts in Mahabubnagar district (29%). The change in the dietary pattern usually depends upon the availability of food, economic condition, influence of elders within the family and other cultural practices of the families.

35 per cent of respondents consumed additional foods during postnatal period, they are: garlic (22%), mutton (6%), fruits (2%), bittergourd (3%) and milk (2%). They felt that these food items are essential for mothers' and childs' health. 32 per cent of respondents avoided certain cold and hot foods during postnatal period. They believe that cold foods cause allergy and other infections *eg:* buttermilk (16%), brinjal (10%), hot foods such as chillies (2%) and "Gongura" (5%). These are avoided as they cause diarrhoea in child and allergy for mothers and children.

DETERMINANTS OF POSTNATAL SERVICES

I. Socio-economic Variables and Utilisation of Postnatal Services

(i) The Respondents' Education and Utilisation of Postnatal Services

The education upto five years of schooling may or may not have significant impact over the attitude of the couple but higher education will have definite influence over the health consciousness of women.

The data in the Table—4.44 depicts the association between the education and utilisation of postnatal service. It is clearly evident from the data that the women with the education upto middle school and above, utilised the postnatal services in a better way (46%) than the other two groups (28%). No difference in the utilisation pattern was noticed among the illiterates and the women with primary level of education. From the district wise data it is observed that in Kurnool district, as the education shoots up, the percentage of utilisation also increased, thus manifesting positive association between education and utilisation of postnatal services and was significant at 0.001 level, whereas in Mahabubnagar district, it is observed that the percentage of utilisation was high among illiterates (28%) than the mothers with primary level of education (17%), but a sharp increase in utilisation of postnatal services was noticed among the women, who are educated upto middle school and above (35%). It denotes that in the backward community, to bring modification of behaviour, more years of schooling is essential.

Table—4.44
The percentage distribution of respondents by their education and utilisation of postnatal services

Womens' Education	*Kurnool District*			*Mahabubnagar District*			*Total*		
	Non-utilised	*Utilised*	*Total*	*Non-utilised*	*Utilised*	*Total*	*Non-utilised*	*Utilised*	*Total*
Illiterate	71.34 (224)	28.66 (90)	100.00 (314)	71.84 (250)	28.16 (98)	100.00 (348)	71.60 (474)	28.40 (188)	100.00 (662)
Primary school	65.91 (29)	34.09 (15)	100.00 (44)	82.61 (19)	17.39 (4)	100.00 (23)	71.64 (48)	28.36 (19)	100.00 (67)
Middle school and above	45.24 (19)	54.76 (23)	100.00 (42)	65.52 (19)	34.48 (10)	100.00 (13)	53.52 (38)	46.48 (33)	100.00 (33)
Total	68.00 (272)	32.00 (128)	100.00 (400)	72.00 (288)	28.00 (112)	100.00 (400)	70.00 (560)	30.00 (240)	100.00 (800)

P. Chi. 2(6) = 37.7912; Pr = 0.000 13.9289; Pr = 0.030 43.4867; Pr = 0.000

(ii) Occupation and Utilisation of Postnatal Services

Occupation is a socio-economic variable which affects the health behaviour of the couple. Eventhough government is assisting the low socio-economic women during antenatal and postnatal period by giving maternity benefit funds, to meet the additional nutritional demands of mother and child, still major percentage of rural women were going for risky labour work during the puerperal period itself to meet the economic needs of the entire family. Depending upon the occupational activities, the women will spare their time and put efforts to seek the health care services during postnatal period. When they go for field work they will neglect their own health and child's health also. All these factors may contribute for low utilisation of postnatal services among coolies and cultivators.

Table—4.45 presents postnatal services utilization based on occupational categories, higher percentage of utilisation was observed among housewives (42%) followed by cultivators (33%) and coolies (27%). Housewives will have more accessibility to the health agencies. Because they will be available at home when health personnel visits them. They also go to the health agencies and avail the health services. With regard to the cultivators because of their sound economic position they can stay at home upto the puerperal period and avail postnatal services to some extent. The identified cause for low utilisation among coolies is to fulfill the economic necessity by going for occupational activities immediately after delivery.

Table—4.45
The percentage distribution of respondents by occupation and utilisation of postnatal services

Respondents' occupation	*Kurnool District*			*Mahabubnagar District*			*Total*		
	Non-utilised	*Utilised*	*Total*	*Non-utilised*	*Utilised*	*Total*	*Non-utilised*	*Utilised*	*Total*
Housewives	56.58 (43)	43.42 (33)	100.00 (76)	61.36 (27)	38.64 (17)	100.00 (44)	58.33 (70)	41.67 (50)	10.00 (120)
Coolies	74.09 (183)	25.91 (64)	100.00 (247)	72.88 (215)	27.12 (80)	100.00 (295)	73.43 (398)	26.57 (144)	100.00 (542)
Cultivators	59.74 (46)	40.26 (31)	100.00 (77)	75.41 (46)	24.59 (15)	100.00 (61)	66.67 (92)	33.33 (46)	100.00 (138)
Total	**68.00 (272)**	**32.00 (128)**	**100.00 (400)**	**72.00 (288)**	**28.00 (112)**	**100.00 (400)**	**70.00 (560)**	**30.00 (240)**	**100.00 (800)**

P. Chi. 2(6) = 14.5312; Pr = 0.024 6.0873; Pr = 0.413 15.3877; Pr = 0.017

With the district differences considered, Kurnool district exhibits the similar pattern as with the total sample. Higher percentage of utilisation was observed among housewives (43%) followed by cultivators (40%) and coolies (26%). Mahabubnagar district shows different trends. Higher percentage of utilisation was observed among housewives (39%) followed by coolies (27%) and cultivators (25%).

Socio-cultural Variables and Utilisation of Postnatal Services

(i) Caste and Utilisation of Postnatal Services

The utilisation of postnatal services by respondents' caste is presented in the Table—4.46. It clearly manifests a higher percentage of utilisation by higher caste *i.e.*, forward caste (37%) followed by backward caste (31%) and schedule caste and scheduled tribes (26%). This clearly shows a positive relationship between caste and postnatal service utilisation.

Table—4.46

The percentage distribution of respondents by caste and postnatal services utilisation

Caste	*Kurnool District*			*Mahabubnagar District*			*Total*		
	Non-utili sed	*Utili-sed*	*Total*	*Non-utili-sed*	*Utili-sed*	*Total*	*Non-utili-sed*	*Utili-sed*	*Total*
Forward Caste	64.10 (50)	35.90 (28)	100.00 (78)	62.22 (28)	37.78 (17)	100.00 (45)	63.41 (78)	36.59 (45)	100.00 (123)
Backward Caste	67.77 (143)	32.23 (68)	100.00 (211)	71.11 (160)	28.44 (65)	100.00 (225)	69.50 (303)	30.50 (133)	100.00 (436)
Scheduled Caste and scheduled Tribes	71.17 (79)	28.83 (32)	100.00 (111)	76.92 (100)	23.08 (30)	100.00 (130)	74.27 (179)	25.73 (62)	100.00 (241)
Total	68.00 (272)	32.00 (128)	100.00 (400)	72.00 (288)	28.00 (112)	100.00 (400)	70.00 (560)	30.00 (240)	100.00 (800)

P. Chi 2(4) = 1.6046; Pr = 0.808 12.5870; Pr = 0.050 11.8094; Pr = 0.066

The district wise data also shows a similar trend. The forward caste exhibits higher percentage of postnatal service utilisation (Mahabubnagar—38%; Kurnool—36%) followed by backward castes (Kurnool—32%; Mahabubnagar—28%) and scheduled castes and scheduled tribe (Kurnool—29%; Mahabubnagar—23%).

The low socio-economic status compel the low caste women to engage in income generating activities outside the home, thus making them non-available when health providers visit their homes. The inaccessibility of health facilities and non-availability of health personnel which are the weakest link in primary health care facilitated for low utilisation. Further the traditional practices and apathy also come in the way of utilisation of postnatal services.

(ii) Type of Family and Utilisation of Postnatal Services

The data related to family type and utilisation of postnatal services is presented in the Table—4.47. Joint families show better level of postnatal service utilisation (35%) against the nuclear families (28%). The data in Kurnool district also is depicting the similar trend. Joint families exhibit more percentage of utilisation (41%) than nuclear families (28%) whereas, Mahabubnagar district shows marginal difference in the utilisation pattern based on family type *i.e.,* 29 per cent of respondents belonging to joint families utilised postnatal services against 28 per cent of women in nuclear families. Low percentage of utilisation was observed in Mahabubnagar district. The cultural taboos, beliefs and the feeling of good health resulted in not seeking health advice etc.

In nuclear families, specially in lower income groups, majority of women go for work till delivery and immediately after delivery also. The hindering factors for low utilisation of postnatal services are: non-availability of health personnel, ignorance about health, economic necessity, negligence and absence of persons to look after, to guide and to support them. At the same time they will not feel it as a need to utilize the health services etc. The joint family no doubt, seems to be more secure for its members. The favourable factors for better utilisation in these families are: guidance and motivation from elders to seek health care services and acceptance of traditional practices for postnatal care.

The communication between the spouses and with other couples facilitates the diffusion of information, discussion related to utilisation of services and other issues of postnatal care. Thus greater interspouse communication favours higher utilisation of services.

Table—4.47
The percentage distribution of respondents by type of family and utilisation of postnatal services

Type of family	*Kurnool District*			*Mahabubnagar District*			*Total*		
	Non-utili sed	*Utili-sed*	*Total*	*Non-utili-sed*	*Utili-sed*	*Total*	*Non-utili-sed*	*Utili-sed*	*Total*
Joint family	58.97 (69)	41.03 (48)	100.00 (117)	71.11 (96)	28.89 (39)	100.00 (135)	65.48 (165)	34.52 (87)	100.00 (252)
Nuclear family	71.73 (203)	28.27 (80)	100.00 (283)	72.45 (192)	27.55 (73)	100.00 (265)	72.08 (395)	27.98 (153)	100.00 (548)
Total	**68.00 (272)**	**32.00 (128)**	**100.00 (400)**	**72.00 (288)**	**28.00 (112)**	**100.00 (400)**	**70.00 (560)**	**30.00 (240)**	**100.00 (800)**

P. Chi 2(2) = 6.2511; Pr = 0.044 0.1262; Pr = 0.939 3.6524; Pr = 0.161

(iii) Interspouse Communication and Utilisation of Postnatal Services

The relationship between interspouse communication and utilisation of postnatal services are depicted in the Table—4.48. *(See the table in page 152)*. The couple who were discussing openly and frankly about the health care matters will have an open environment to exchange their ideas and modify their bevhaviour. This favours for higher utilisation of postnatal services (33%) as noticed in the total sample, against the couple, who does not have any intercepts communication (29%). In Kurnool district, data reveals similar pattern. Significant difference was noticed with districts data *i.e.,* 37 per cent of respondents utilised postnatal services after discussion against those who did not interact (30%). Whereas in Mahabubnagar district, reverse trend was noticed. More percentage of respondents (29%) utilised potnatal services after discussion against those who did not interact (23%).

The social environment, exposure to information through mass media, visits of health personnel and utilising the services facilitate intraspouse communication. Intensive efforts have to be emphasised by the health personnel to facilitate intraspouse communication and diffusion of health ideas among the couples.

Table—4.48

The percentage distribution of respondents by interspouse communication and the utilisation of postnatal services

Inter spousal commu- nication	*Kurnool District*			*Mahabubnagar District*			*Total*		
	Non- utili sed	*Utili- sed*	*Total*	*Non- utili- sed*	*Utili- sed*	*Total*	*Non- utili- sed*	*Utili- sed*	*Total*
Not dis- cussing	70.11 (197)	29.89 (84)	100.00 (281)	71.26 (248)	28.74 (100)	100.00 (348)	70.75 (445)	29.25 (184)	100.00 (629)
Discu- ssing	63.03 (75)	36.97 (44)	100.00 (119)	76.92 (40)	23.08 (12)	100.00 (52)	67.25 (115)	32.75 (56)	100.00 (171)
Total	68.00 (272)	32.00 (128)	100.00 (400)	72.00 (288)	28.00 (112)	100.00 (400)	70.00 (560)	30.00 (240)	100.00 (800)

P. Chi 2(2) = 5.7282; Pr = 0.057 0.6315; Pr = 0.729 6.5087; Pr = 0.039

Infrastructural Facilities and Utilisation of Postnatal Services

(i) The Visits of the Health Personnel and Utilisation of Postnatal Services

The female health assistant visits the villages to render the health care services according to the time schedule, approved plan of work, need of the community and the convenience of the assistant. She is mainly responsible to deliver maternal and child health services in her jurisdiction. The regularity of visits of health personnel to the households, has a bearing effect over the utilisation of services by the community.

If the health personnel are visiting the villages regularly, they win the confidence of the community where they serve, in reciprocal manner the community also comes forward to utilise the services rendered by health personnel. Based on the availability of health personnel, the beneficiaries feel accessible and approach them to obtain their services and seek advises from them, whenever the need arises. The similar pattern was noticed in the data presented in the Table—4.51, which represents the association between the visits of health personnel and utilisation of postnatal services. In the total sample, higher percentage of postnatal services utilisation was observed when the health personnel visit them fortnightly (38%), followed by rare visits (30%) and monthly visits (27%).

The district wise data presented in Table—4.49 shows different trend. In Kurnool district, positive association was noticed between the frequency of visits and utilisation of postnatal services *i.e.*, higher the number of visits, higher the percentage of utilisation. Hence higher percentage of utilisation was seen during fortnight visits (43%) followed by monthly (27%) and rare visits (26%). Thus a marginal variation was noticed in the utilisation pattern during monthly and rare visits.

Table—4.49

The percentage distribution of respondents by frequency of visits of health personnel and utilisation of postnatal services

Visits of health personnel	*Kurnool District*			*Mahabubnagar District*			*Total*		
	Non-utilised	*Utilised*	*Total*	*Non-utilised*	*Utilised*	*Total*	*Non-utilised*	*Utilised*	*Total*
Rare	73.58 (39)	26.42 (14)	100.00 (53)	67.09 (53)	32.91 (26)	100.00 (79)	69.70 (92)	30.30 (40)	100.00 (132)
Monthly	72.73 (160)	27.27 (60)	100.00 (220)	74.12 (189)	25.88 (66)	100.00 (255)	73.47 (349)	26.53 (126)	100.00 (475)
Fortnightly	57.48 (73)	42.52 (54)	100.00 (127)	69.70 (46)	30.30 (20)	100.00 (66)	61.66 (119)	38.34 (74)	100.00 (193)
Total	**68.00 (272)**	**32.00 (128)**	**100.00 (400)**	**72.00 (288)**	**28.00 (112)**	**100.00 (400)**	**70.00 (560)**	**30.00 (240)**	**100.00 (800)**

P. Chi 2(4) = 13.1134; Pr = 0.011 4.3295; Pr = 0.363 10.6003; Pr = 0.031

Mahabubnagar district presents a different pattern, higher percentage of postnatal service utilisation was noticed during rare visits of health personnel (33%) followed by fortnightly visits (30%) and monthly visits (26%). The respondents in Mahabubnagar district informed that the health personnel visits them rarely, to render the postnatal services. So the women are admitted in institutions and obtain the postnatal services.

The data in the districts as well as in the total sample emphasises the need of regular visits by the health personnel to the beneficiaries to provide necessary services and advice to the needy population at community level. Then the people in the community also should think that their own health is their prime responsibility and so should cooperate with health personnel in seeking services.

(ii) Type of Services Provided by Health Personnel and Postnatal Service Utilisation

The health personnel are expected to deliver preventive, promotive and curative services to the community. If they provide all these services, the community also utilise them to a large extent. The utilisation of postnatal services is higher (36%) when the health personnel provide all services, than the preventive services (25%) as depicted in Table—4.50.

The utilisation of postnatal services increase, when comprehensive (Preventive, Promotive and Curative) services were provided rather than preventive services. The need based services are always desirable and acceptable to the clients. These trends are obviously seen among the districts of the study. In Kurnool district, a higher percentage of utilisation was observed when all types of services provided (40%) as against in Mahabubnagar district (30%). Mahabubnagar district shows better level of postnatal service utilisation, when the health personnel are providing preventive services alone (27%) contrary to Kurnool district (22%)

During maternal, child health clinics and home visits, the health personnel educate the public, especially the women, regarding care during antenatal, natal, postnatal period and child care, for effective utilisation of health services by the community.

Table—4.50

The percentage distribution of respondents by type of services provided by health personnel and utilisation of postnatal services

Type of services provided by the health personnel	*Kurnool District*			*Mahabubnagar District*			*Total*		
	Non-utili sed	*Utili-sed*	*Total*	*Non-utili-sed*	*Utili-sed*	*Total*	*Non-utili-sed*	*Utili-sed*	*Total*
Preventive services alone	78.09 (139)	21.91 (39)	100.00 (178)	73.19 (172)	26.81 (63)	100.00 (235)	75.30 (311)	24.70 (102)	100.00 (413)
All types of services	59.91 (133)	40.09 (89)	100.00 (222)	70.30 (116)	29.70 (49)	100.00 (165)	64.34 (249)	35.66 (138)	100.00 (387)
Total	**68.00 (272)**	**32.00 (128)**	**100.00 (400)**	**72.00 (288)**	**28.00 (112)**	**100.00 (400)**	**70.00 (560)**	**30.00 (240)**	**100.00 (800)**

(iii) Health Education Activities Carried Out by Health Personnel and Utilisation of Postnatal Services

Naturally a better level of utilisation is observed among the women, who are exposed to health education activities (34%) than the women who are not exposed to health information (26%). The data within the districts also shows the similar pattern. More percentage of women utilised postnatal services, when they are exposed to health education activities (Kurnool—36%; Mahabubnagar—33%) than the mothers who are not exposed to health information (Kurnool—29%; Mahabubnagar—24%). The non-utilisation is found to be higher (66%) even among the respondents who are exposed to health education activities. It may be due to non-availability of health personnel and inaccessibility of health facilities.

It is evident from the data in Table—4.51 *(See table on page 156)* that health education has influenced the utilisation of postnatal services. However, even without health education more than one fourth of respondents utilised the services. This is mainly due to the information gained through neighbours, friends and others.

Table—4.51
The percentage distribution of respondents by health education activities carried out by the health personnel and utilisation of postnatal services

Health Education activities	*Kurnool District*			*Mahabubnagar District*			*Total*		
	Non-utilised	*Utilised*	*Total*	*Non-utilised*	*Utilised*	*Total*	*Non-utilised*	*Utilised*	*Total*
Not carried out	71.44 (158)	28.56 (63)	100.00 (221)	76.50 (153)	23.50 (47)	100.00 (200)	73.87 (311)	26.13 (110)	100.00 (421)
Carried out	63.69 (114)	36.31 (65)	100.00 (179)	67.50 (135)	32.50 (65)	100.00 (200)	65.70 (249)	34.30 (130)	100.00 (379)
Total	68.00 (272)	32.00 (128)	100.00 (400)	72.00 (288)	28.00 (112)	100.00 (400)	70.00 (560)	30.00 (240)	100.00 (800)

P. Chi 2(2) = 3.9850; Pr = 0.136 5.4119; Pr = 0.067 8.3905; Pr = 0.015

(iv) Source of Information and Utilisation of Postnatal Services

The information on health, as to be disseminated to bring a desirable change in the health behaviour of the community. Health facilities are obtained from the various resources for the dissemination of health information. Health personnel will organise several health education programmes through Information, Education, Communication activities with the help of mass-media. Neighbours, as utilisers will also act as motivators. Sometime one or more resources as a combination will act as powerful resource for effective utilisation of health care services.

In postnatal service utilisation, the major source of health information is found to be combination of all resources (37%) followed by mass-media (30%), health personnel (28%) and satisfied utilisers (25%).

The district wise data in Table—4.52 showed a different pattern. In Mahabubnagar district, satisfied utilisers in the community are found to be the major source of health information (32%) followed by the remaining resources *viz.*, health personnel and mass-media activities (23%). Whereas in Kurnool district, the resources for health information in order of priority are, combination of resources (41%), health personnel, mass-media (33%) and satisfied utilisers in the community (18%). So the data in both districts emphasize the need of health education programmes to create the awareness within the community, especially the target group with regard to postnatal services.

Table—4.52

The percentage distribution of respondents by source of information about maternal, child health services and utilisation of postnatal services

Health Education activities	*Kurnool District*			*Mahabubnagar District*			*Total*		
	Non-utilised	*Utilised*	*Total*	*Non-utilised*	*Utilised*	*Total*	*Non-utilised*	*Utilised*	*Total*
Mass media alone	66.67 (18)	33.33 (9)	100.00 (27)	76.92 (10)	23.08 (3)	100.00 (13)	70.00 (28)	30.00 (12)	100.00 (40)
Neighbours and others	81.91 (82)	18.09 (19)	100.00 (101)	67.95 (53)	32.05 (25)	100.00 (78)	75.42 (135)	24.58 (44)	100.00 (179)
Health personnel	66.67 (104)	33.33 (5)	100.00 (156)	76.67 (138)	23.33 (42)	100.00 (180)	72.02 (242)	27.98 (94)	100.00 (336)
Combination	58.62 (68)	41.38 (48)	100.00 (116)	76.67 (87)	23.33 (42)	100.00 (129)	63.27 (155)	36.73 (90)	100.00 (245)
Total	**68.00 (272)**	**32.00 (128)**	**100.00 (400)**	**72.00 (288)**	**28.00 (112)**	**100.00 (400)**	**70.00 (560)**	**30.00 (240)**	**100.00 (800)**

P. Chi. 2(6) = 16.2470: Pr = 0.12 5.5926: Pr = 0.470 11.2842: Pr = 0.080

D. Utilisation of Child Health Services and Differentials in Utilisation

Children are future citizens of the country. The foundations for the personality of citizen are laid in the formative years of life. We must ensure a healthy start for each of them. The involvement in child health is a direct entry point to improve socio-economic development, cultural background and above all the quality of life of the nation.

Care for the child starts even before conception, through postponement of first pregnancy until the mother herself has reached full physical maturity. Through spacing of birth, child care continues from conception through suitable care during pregnancy, child birth and childhood. Therefore, an investment in child development is an investment in the future of action.

Early childhood is a period of rapid growth and development which largely depends on the interaction of heredity and environmental factors. Any deficiency during this period may cause irreparable damage to the future development of the child. Specially in developing countries, the child must be protected by the required interventions particularly from the childhood (fatal) diseases.

Generally in the Indian families, much importance is given for child and his welfare. People will think child as an asset to the family. The primary caretakers in the families are, usually the mothers. They neglect their health also, for the care of children. The entire family will pay much attention and concern for their children. The similar pattern was observed in the study area also, as shown in Table—4.53. Higher percentage of utilisation of child health services was observed (64%) in contrast to maternal health services *i.e.*, antenatal (55%), natal (35%) and postnatal services (30%). The district wise data also presents similar trend which is the utilisation of better child health services (Kurnool—68%; Mahabubnagar—61%) compared to the utilisation of maternal services *i.e.*, antenatal (Kurnool—60%, Mahabubnagar—49%), natal (Kurnool—38%, Mahabubnagar—32%), and postnatal services (Kurnool—32%, Mahabubnagar—28%).

Apart from the utilisation of child health services the other factors related to the care of the child such as feeding practices (breast feeding, weaning) were studied.

Table—4.53

The percentage distribution of respondents by utilisation of child health services

Districts	*Levels of utilisation*		*Total*
	Utilised	*Non-utilised*	
Kurnool	67.50 (270)	32.50 (130)	64.37 (515)
Mahabubnagar	61.25 (245)	38.75 (155)	35.63 (285)
Total	**100.00** **(400)**	**100.00** **(400)**	**100.00** **(800)**

Utilisation of Immunization Services

Under five children constitute about 14 per cent of total population in our country. They are highly prone for morbidity and mortality (33.4%). The national health programmes like Expanded Programme of Immunization (1978) and Universal Immunization Programme (1985) were launched to protect the children against vaccine preventable diseases. Vast campaigns are conducted and the health information was disseminated throughout the country through intensive information, education and communication activities to increase the awareness and utilise the immunization services by the beneficiaries in the community.

The information regarding the awareness of respondents about vaccine preventable diseases, vaccines, utilisation of immunisation services, immunization status of children. Identified problems after immunization, follow-up services by the health personnel etc are gathered and presented in the Table—4.54. *(See the table in page 161).*

When the investigator inquired with the respondents, about the vaccine preventable diseases, more than half of the mothers (57%) are aware of Polio and Tetanus. Very negligible percentage of respondents are aware of Tuberculosis and Measles. Only 4 per cent of respondents are able to list all (six) killer diseases. Again only 3 per cent of respondents are able to name the Pertusis disease. Much differentials were not observed in the data pertaining to the study districts. The low awareness has a bearing effect over the utilisation of immunization services.

More than half of the respondents (57%) are aware of Polio and D.P.T vaccines. One tenth of the mothers (10%) are also mentioned BCG vaccine against Tuberculosis and very few percentage (5%) are mentioning Measles vaccine for measles. Negligible percentage of mothers (3%) are able to list all vaccines.

Health personnel (64%), family members (14%) and neighbours (10%) were the major source of information to motivate the people to utilize the services. Mass-media (0.7%) is quoted as the poorest source of motivation in the study area. Hence information, education and communication activities by the health care providers have to be intensified.

It is interesting to note that in the study area, among the total sample, more than three fourths of women (77%) immunised their children either fully (32%) or partially (45%). Nearly one fourth of the women respondents (23%) did not immunise their children. The district wise data presents more or less the similar trend. In Kurnool district more percentage of women had fully immunised children (46%) compared to the women in Mahabubnagar district (35%). Nearly 45% percentage of women had partially immunised children in both the districts. More than one fourth of the sample (26%) in Kurnool district and one fifth of the respondents (20%) in Mahabubnagar district did not immunise their children. The reasons quoted by them were that their children are healthy (10%) that they are busy in occupational activities (8%), and that they don't have time to take their children to the health centre (5%).

Generally the child won't suffer from any problem after immunization. Sometimes certain problems were observed after it. 65 per cent of respondents' children did not have any problem after immunization. Nearly one fifth of the respondents' children (22%) suffered from fever. This is a normal response due to antigen and antibody reaction. 2 per cent of children had abscess formation after DPS immunisation and negligible percentage (1%) of respondents' children suffered with pain at the site of injection. It is observed that, half of the respondents' children (52%) were visited by the health personnel after immunisation.

Table—4.54
The percentage distribution of respondents' by utilisation of immunization services

Utilisation of immunisation services	*Kurnool District*	*Mahabubnagar District*	*Total*
1	**2**	**3**	**4**
(i) Knowledge of vaccine preventable diseases			
Polio	21.50 (86)	21.00 (84)	21.25 (170)
Tuberculosis	1.00 (4)	1.75 (7)	1.38 (11)
Measles	0.50 (2)	0.00 (0)	0.25 (2)
Pertusis	3.75 (15)	2.75 (11)	3.25 (26)
Tetanus	0.50 (2)	1.00 (4)	0.75 (6)
Polio and Tetanus	52.25 (209)	62.00 (248)	57.13 (457)
Polio, Tuberculosis, Measles, Tetanus	14.25 (57)	10.00 (40)	12.13 (97)
All	6.25 (25)	1.50 (6)	3.88 (31)

(Contd . . .)

1	2	3	4
(ii) Knowledge of vaccines			
Oral Polio	25.00 (100)	21.25 (85)	23.13 (185)
Measles	0.75 (3)	0.25 (1)	0.50 (6)
B.C.G.	1.25 (5)	0.25 (1)	0.75 (6)
D.P.T.	0.75 (3)	0.25 (1)	0.50 (4)
Polio and DPT	52.75 (211)	61.75 (247)	57.25 (458)
Polio, BCG, DPT	9.25 (37)	11.25 (45)	10.25 (82)
Polio, Measels, DPT	4.75 (19)	4.25 (17)	4.50 (36)
All	4.50 (18)	0.75 (3)	2.63 (21)
None	1.00 (4)	0.00 (0)	0.50 (4)
(iii) Immunisation status			
Fully Immunized	46.12 (119)	34.75 (139)	32.25 (258)
Partially immunized	44.25 (177)	45.00 (180)	44.63 (357)
Not immunized	26.00 (104)	20.25 (81)	23.13 (185)
(iv) Motivation for utilisation of immunization services			
Not applicable	0.25 (1)	4.00 (16)	2.13 (17)
Health personnel	69.50 (278)	59.75 (239)	63.88 (511)
Previous experience	1.25 (5)	0.50 (2)	0.88 (7)

(Contd . . .)

1	2	3	4
Family members	14.25 (57)	14.25 (57)	14.25 (114)
Neighbours	5.75 (23)	14.25 (57)	10.00 (80)
Self	2.00 (8)	1.00 (4)	1.50 (12)
Mass media	1.25 (5)	0.00 (0)	0.63 (5)
Others	0.25 (1)	0.00 (0)	0.13 (1)
Not motivated	5.50 (22)	6.25 (25)	5.88 (47)
(v) Identified problems after immunization			
Not applicable	9.00 (36)	10.50 (42)	9.75 (78)
No problems	60.25 (241)	70.25 (282)	65.38 (523)
Fever	27.50 (110)	15.75 (63)	21.63 (173)
Pain at site	0.75 (3)	1.25 (5)	1.00 (8)
Abscess	2.50 (10)	2.00 (8)	2.25 (18)
(vi) The time of follow-up visit after immunization			
Non follow-up visit	42.50 (170)	42.75 (171)	42.63 (341)
After one month	47.25 (189)	56.25 (225)	51.75 (414)
Within a week	10.25 (41)	1.00 (4)	5.63 (45)
Total	**100.00 (400)**	**100.00 (400)**	**100.00 (800)**

P. Chi. 2(2) = 33.5556; Pr = 0.000

Child Morbidity

Children below five years are at greater risk than any other in population. Factors like low immunity, physiological immaturity etc., will lead to childhood problems. The under-five children usually face certain problems *viz.*, acute respiratory infection, Diarrhoeal diseases, malnutrition and the six killer diseases. The data related to child morbidity in the study area is depicted in the Table—4.55. The morbidity pattern among children are divided into child with no problems, child with one problem and child with multiple problems. The morbidity pattern among under-five children in the study area were collected from the past preceding five years.

Major percentage of children (71%) in the study area suffered from diarrhoea and small percentage of children (8%) suffered from multiple problems. Among them 3 per cent of children suffered from few attacks of acute respiratory tract infections, measles (3%) and polio (2%). The district wise data presents more or less the similar trend.

Even though major percentage of children (79%) had health problems, only 48 per cent of them sought medical treatment. More respondents in Kurnool district (45%) obtained medical treatment than in Mahabubnagar district (36%). The reasons might be economic constraints, ignorance, negligence, belief in fatalism and non-availability of health facilities in the study area.

Table—4.55
The percentage distribution of respondents by child morbidity

Child morbidity	*Kurnool District*	*Mahabubnagar District*	*Total*
1	**2**	**3**	**4**
No problem	16.25 (65)	26.50 (106)	21.38 (171)
One problem	74.00 (296)	67.00 (268)	70.50 (564)
Multiple problems	9.75 (39)	6.50 (26)	8.12 (65)

(Contd . . .)

1	2	3	4
Acute respiratory tract infections	2.50 (10)	3.75 (15)	3.00 (25)
Measles	2.50 (10)	3.75 (15)	3.00 (25)
Polio	2.00 (8)	1.75 (7)	2.00 (15)
Total	**100.00 (400)**	**100.00 (400)**	**100.00 (800)**
(i) Remedy for childhood problems			
No problem	16.25 (65)	26.50 (106)	21.38 (171)
Treatment not obtained	38.75 (155)	37.50 (150)	38.13 (305)
Treatment obtained	45.00 (180)	36.00 (144)	40.50 (324)
Total	**100.00 (400)**	**100.00 (400)**	**100.00 (400)**

Knowledge and Practices of Women in Treating Diarrhoeal Diseases

Dehydration caused by frequent passage of loose watery stools is the most common cause of deaths among under-five children. Every year, the child will have atleast 3 or 4 attacks of diarrhoea. Faulty feeding techniques, poor personal hygiene, unhygienic practices, malnutrition and neglected child rearing practices are the pre-disposing causes for diarrhoea. Every year 10 lakh deaths are resulting with diarrhoeal diseases. The child should be rehydrated depending upon the degree of dehydration. A wide coverage of campaigns with intensive information, education and communication activities are conducted to improve the awareness of community throughout the country.

During mild diarrhoea, the child will be supplemented with oral rehydration solution and other home made liquids. It is very surprising to note that, in the study area more than half (53%)

of the respondents do not know how to treat the children with oral rehydration solution when they suffered from diarrhoeal diseases. Only 41 per cent of respondents replaced the fluids, 59 per cent of mothers did not gave any liquids.

Major percentage of children (79%) were not referred to hospitals for their sickness. Hence there is a need to conduct the health education sessions by the health personnel in the study area to increase the awareness of mothers with regard to prevention and treatment of diarrhoeal diseases (Table—4.56).

Table—4.56

The percentage distribution of respondents by knowledge and treatment of diarrhoeal diseases

Knowledge and practices in treating diarrhoeal diseases	*Kurnool District*	*Mahabubnagar District*	*Total*
Awareness about ORS			
Not known	50.50 (202)	55.50 (222)	53.00 (424)
Known	49.50 (198)	44.50 (178)	47.00 (376)
During dehydration knowledge of fluid replacement			
Do not know	18.25 (73)	29.25 (117)	23.75 (190)
Not given	34.50 (138)	35.75 (143)	35.13 (281)
Given	47.25 (189)	35.00 (140)	41.13 (329)
Referral Yes	3.75 (15)	3.25 (13)	3.50 (28)
No	96.25 (385)	96.75 (387)	96.50 (772)
Total	**100.00 (400)**	**100.00 (400)**	**100.00 (800)**

Child Mortality

Infant and childhood mortality are comparatively very high in developing countries. In India, the child mortality which was 33.40 per cent in 1991 has declined to 10 per cent in 1995, due to the introduction of Child Survival and Safe Motherhood Programme. Even now it has a major impact on determining the acceptance of small family norm, as successful reproduction requires high fertility to offset the high mortality. The child mortality constitute an important dimension of population growth and fertility behaviour.

The percentage distribution of respondents according to the number of child deaths in the study area are presented in the Table—4.57. The data is shown in three categories *i.e.*, one child death, death of two children in a single family and more child deaths. Major percentage of families did not experience any child deaths (90%) and only 10 per cent of women experience child deaths.

Table—4.57
The percentage distribution of respondents by child mortality

Child mortality	*Kurnool District*	*Mahabubnagar District*	*Total*
1	**2**	**3**	**4**
(a) No. of children died			
0	91.75 (367)	89.00 (356)	90.38 (723)
1	6.25 (25)	9.50 (38)	7.88 (63)
2	1.50 (6)	0.75 (3)	1.13 (5)
>3	0.50 (2)	0.75 (3)	0.63 (5)
(b) Causes for death			
Not applicable	91.75 (367)	89.00 (356)	90.38 (723)

(Contd . . .)

1	2	3	4
Accident	0.25 (1)	1.00 (4)	0.63 (5)
Severe malnutrition	0.25 (1)	1.00 (4)	0.63 (5)
Diarrhoea	1.50 (6)	2.00 (8)	1.75 (14)
6 Killer diseases	0.75 (3)	1.00 (4)	0.88 (7)
Prematurity	1.50 (6)	1.25 (5)	1.38 (11)
Jaundice	1.00 (4)	1.50 (6)	1.25 (10)
Prolonged labour	0.25 (1)	0.00 (0)	0.13 (1)
Vomitings	0.25 (1)	0.25 (1)	0.25 (1)
Asphyxia	2.50 (10)	3.00 (12)	2.75 22)
(c) Age of death			
Not applicable	91.75 (367)	89.00 (356)	90.38 (723)
Below 6 months	5.50 (22)	8.00 (32)	6.75 (54)
6-12 months	1.75 (7)	1.50 (6)	1.63 (13)
1-2 years	1.00 (4)	1.25 (5)	1.13 (9)
More than 2 years	0.00 (0)	0.25 (1)	0.13 (1)
Total	**100.00 (400)**	**100.00 (400)**	**100.00 (800)**

Kurnool and Mahabubnagar districts shows marginal variation, which is not significant. In Mahabubnagar district the percentage of one child death (9.5%) is slightly higher than in Kurnool district (6%), whereas 2 or more number of child deaths happened to be observed in Kurnool district (2%) than in Mahabubnagar district (1.5%). Asphyxia, and Diarrhoea appears to be the major causes of deaths occurring in the study area.

Feeding Practices

(i) Breast Feeding Practices

The total duration of breast feeding noticed in the study area was, that nearly 40 per cent of women fed their babies for 18-24 months, 22 per cent of the women fed for 9-12 months of duration and nearly one forth of women fed their babies with breast feeding, for more than 30 months. The district wise data in Table—4.58 also present the similar, Kurnool district shows better feeding practices than Mahabubnagar district.

(ii) Weaning Practices

Supplementary feeding is a gradual process of introducing additional nutrients to the child to meet the demands of growth and development. It should be around the age of 3-4 months. Weaning foods in the form of liquids (eg. animal milk, glucose water, fruit juices, dhal water, vegetable and bone soups etc.) will be given in early weaning period (3-5 months). After that (5th and 8th month), semi-solid diet in the form of soft rice, banana, biscuits in the milk, gruel etc. will be given. From 8th month onwards, solid diet will be supplemented, like half boiled egg, soft boiled cereals, pulses, liver, fish etc. At the age of one year, the child will eat the type of diet as the adults eat. Proper care regarding supplementary foods play a vital role in maintaining child's health. Timely weaning promotes the childs' development pattern, protects against infection and prevents malnutrition. Certain times, early weaning practices without maintaining proper hygienic practices lead to infections. Late weaning practices induces malnutrition and its consequences. Hence it is very crucial to supplement the childs' nutrition in the form of timely weaning practices.

The weaning practices among the respondents presented in the Table—4.58 show that 11 per cent of respondents have started liquids other than breast milk from 3rd month onwards which is a good sign unserved in the study area. Nearly half of the mothers (46%) gave semi-solids to their children from 5th month onwards and one third of the sample (30%) started semi-solids from 7th month onwards.

Table—4.58

The percentage distribution of respondents by child feeding practices

Feeding practices	*Kurnool District*	*Mahabubnagar District*	*Total*
1	**2**	**3**	**4**
Breast Feeding Practices			
(a) Total duration of breast feeding			
Not given	4.00 (16)	2.75 (11)	3.38 (27)
< 5 months	2.00 (8)	1.25 (5)	1.63 (13)
6-8 months	2.25 (9)	3.25 (13)	2.75 (22)
9-12 months	17.50 (70)	26.75 (107)	22.13 (177)
13-18 months	9.25 (37)	10.00 (40)	9.63 (77)
18-24 months	45.25 (181)	29.75 (119)	37.50 (300)
24-30 months	4.00 (16)	3.25 (13)	3.63 (29)
30-36 months	13.00 (52)	18.00 (72)	15.50 (124)
> 36 months	2.75 (11)	5.00 (20)	3.88 (31)

(Contd . . .)

1	2	3	4
(ii) Weaning Practices			
(a) Liquids			
Not applicable	88.50 (354)	89.50 (358)	89.00 (712)
From birth	3.00 (12)	2.25 (9)	2.63 (21)
2nd month onwards	2.75 (11)	3.75 (15)	3.25 (26)
3rd month onwards	5.75 (23)	4.50 (18)	5.13 (41)
(b) Semi-solids			
Not applicable	14.00 (56)	8.00 (32)	11.00 (88)
5th-6th month	46.25 (185)	45.75 (183)	46.00 (368)
7th-8th month	29.50 (118)	30.50 (122)	30.00 (240)
More than 9 months	10.25 (41)	5.75 (63)	13.00 (104)
(c) Solids			
Not applicable	4.00 (16)	1.25 (5)	2.63 (21)
7th month	4.50 (18)	5.50 (22)	5.50 (40)
8th month	15.75 (63)	7.50 (30)	11.63 (93)
9th month	22.75 (91)	12.50 (50)	17.63 (141)
More than 9 months	53.00 (212)	73.25 (293)	63.13 (505)
Total	**100.00 (400)**	**100.00 (400)**	**100.00 (800)**

Around 13 per cent of respondents started weaning diet to their children after completion of 9th month. 63 per cent of mothers gave solid foods after 9th month only, depicting late weaning practices. These respondents felt that breast milk alone is sufficient to meet the needs of the child. 11 per cent of mothers did not supplement any additional food other than breast milk for their children. Hence there is a need on the part of health personnel to conduct health education sessions for mothers, about the importance of weaning and the consequences of late weaning practices.

DETERMINANTS OF CHILD HEALTH SERVICES

(a) Socio-economic Variables and Utilisation of Child Health Services

(i) Respondents' Education and Utilisation of Child Health Services

The relationship between education and utilisation of child health services is shown in the Table—4.59. The data table denotes a positive association between education and utilisation. Thus higher percentage of utilisation (72%) was observed among the respondents who studied middle school and above, followed by the respondents with primary school education (69%) and illiterates (63%). The percentage of non-utilisation was high among illiterates.

Educated women will have more chances of exposure to health information and their awareness will be increased accordingly. They have more curiosity about childs' welfare and utilise the services effectively.

The respondents in Kurnool district manifests higher percentage of utilisation in all education levels than in Mahabubnagar district.

Table—4.59
The percentage distribution of respondents by annual family income and utilisation of child health services

Womens' education	Kurnool District			Mahabubnagar District			Total		
	Non-utilised	Utilised	Total	Non-utilised	Utilised	Total	Non-utilised	Utilised	Total
Illiterate	34.39 (108)	65.61 (206)	100.00 (314)	39.08 (136)	60.92 (212)	100.00 (348)	36.86 (244)	63.14 (418)	100.00 (662)
Primary school	25.00 (11)	75.00 (33)	100.00 (44)	43.48 (10)	56.52 (13)	100.00 (23)	31.34 (21)	68.66 (46)	100.00 (67)
Middle School and above	26.19 (11)	73.81 (31)	100.00 (42)	31.03 (9)	68.97 (20)	100.00 (29)	28.17 (20)	71.83 (51)	100.00 (71)
Total	32.50 (130)	67.50 (270)	100.00 (400)	38.75 (155)	61.25 (245)	100.00 (400)	35.63 (285)	64.37 (515)	100.00 (800)

P. Chi. 2(6) = 5.9848; Pr = 0.425 8.8149; Pr = 0.184 5.2094; Pr = 0.517

(ii) Respondents' Occupation and Utilisation of Child Health Services

The Table—4.60 *(See the table in page 173)* describes the relationship between respondents' occupation and utilisation of child health services.

In toto, mothers who belong to cultivation category of occupation exhibits the highest percentage of utilisation (73%) followed by housewives (69%) and coolies (61%). Housewives and cultivators usually stay long time in the houses comparatively than the coolies. So low utilisation was observed among coolies.

The district wise data shows similar trend of the total sample. Better levels of utilisation was observed in Kurnool district than in Mahabubnagar district in all three categories of occupation. Increase awareness and accessibility of health facilities favour better level of utilisation in Kurnool district.

Table—4.60
The percentage distribution of respondents by their occupation and utilisation of child health services

Respondents occupation	*Kurnool District*			*Mahabubnagar District*			*Total*		
	Non-utilised	*Utilised*	*Total*	*Non-utilised*	*Utilised*	*Total*	*Non-utilised*	*Utilised*	*Total*
Housewives	25.00 (19)	75.00 (57)	100.00 (76)	39.08 (136)	70.92 (212)	100.00 (348)	31.67 (38)	69.33 (82)	100.00 (120)
Cooly	37.65 (93)	62.35 (154)	100.00 (247)	41.67 (15)	58.33 (21)	100.00 (36)	38.75 (210)	61.25 (332)	100.00 (542)
Cultivation	23.38 (18)	76.62 (59)	100.00 (77)	25.00 (4)	75.00 (12)	100.00 (16)	26.81 (37)	73.19 (101)	100.00 (138)
Total	**32.50 (130)**	**67.50 (270)**	**100.00 (400)**	**38.75 (155)**	**61.25 (245)**	**100.00 (400)**	**35.63 (285)**	**64.37 (515)**	**100.00 (800)**

P. Chi. 2(6) = 18.9720; Pr = 0.004 8.8149 Pr = 0.184 5.2094 Pr = 0.517

(iii) Annual Family Income and Utilisation of Child Health Services

It is assumed that the high income groups are associated with better nutritional intake and good medical facilities, which may lead to low morbidity and mortality. Hence, the income of the family has a crucial role in influencing the survival of children.

In the total sample, nearly two thirds of children in all income groups utilised child health services. The district wise data in Table—4.61 presents more or less the same. In Kurnool district a positive association is observed between income and utilisation of child health services *i.e.*, lower utilisation levels are observed in lower income group (58%). It shoots upto major extent of utilisation in higher income group (81%). In Mahabubnagar district higher percentage of utilisation is observed in middle income group (64%) followed by high income group (61%) and low income group (59%).

Table—4.61
The percentage distribution of respondents by annual family income and utilisation of child health services

Annual Family income	Kurnool District			Mahabubnagar District			Total		
	Non-utilised	Utilised	Total	Non-utilised	Utilised	Total	Non-utilised	Utilised	Total
<10,0000/-	42.03 (29)	57.97 (40)	100.00 (69)	41.05 (39)	58.95 (56)	100.00 (95)	35.37 (58)	64.63 (106)	100.00 (164)
10,001/— 14,000/-	43.04 (68)	56.96 (90)	100.00 (158)	36.22 (46)	63.78 (81)	100.00 (127)	35.00 (100)	65.00 (185)	100.00 (285)
>14,001/-	19.08 (33)	80.92 (140)	100.00 (173)	39.33 (70)	60.67 (108)	100.00 (178)	36.18 (127)	63.82 (224)	100.00 (351)
Total	**32.50 (130)**	**67.50 (270)**	**100.00 (400)**	**38.75 (155)**	**61.25 (245)**	**100.00 (400)**	**35.63 (285)**	**64.37 (515)**	**100.00 (800)**

(B) Socio-cultural Variables and Utilisation of Child Health Services

(i) Caste and Utilisation of Child Health Services

As expected, higher caste will be utilising the services in a better way than the lower caste. Higher percentage of utilisation was noticed among the forward caste (73%) followed by lower caste community, but the difference observed here is that, scheduled caste people utilised the services in a better way (65%) than the backward caste (63%). In Kurnool district also similar phenomena was observed, whereas in Mahabubnagar district clear differentiation in utilisation pattern among different caste (*i.e.*, the higher the caste, higher the utilisation) was noticed. Higher percentage of utilisation was observed in forward caste (76%) followed by backward castes (60.5%) and scheduled caste and scheduled tribes (58%). Generally the higher caste people are socio-economically in better condition than the low caste people, hence, it is obvious to confirm the utilisation of services among high caste people is high.

The main evidence noticed in the study sample as shown in Table—4.62 is that, though we are reaching 21st century, still the persistence of traditions, customs, culture and social values are playing a role in utilising the resources and modifying the behaviour of the community. The health educators have to insist the community to practice healthy concepts, whatever the pattern of community it may be.

Table—4.62

The distribution of respondents by Caste and utilisation of child health services

Annual family income	*Kurnool District*			*Mahabubnagar District*			*Total*		
	Non-utilised	*Utilised*	*Total*	*Non-utilised*	*utilised*	*Total*	*Non-utilised*	*Utilised*	*Total*
Forward caste	28.21 (22)	71.79 (56)	100.00 (78)	24.44 (11)	75.56 (34)	100.00 (45)	26.83 (33)	73.17 (90)	100.00 (641)
Backward caste	35.07 (74)	64.93 (137)	100.00 (211)	39.56 (89)	60.44 (136)	100.00 (225)	37.39 (163)	62.61 (273)	100.00 (436)
Scheduled caste and Scheduled tribes	30.63 (34)	69.37 (77)	100.00 (111)	42.31 (55)	57.69 (75)	100.00 (130)	35.27 (85)	64.73 (156	100.00 (241)
Total	37.50 (130)	62.50 (270)	100.00 (400)	38.75 (155)	61.25 (245)	100.00 (400)	35.63 (285)	64.37 (515)	100.00 (800)

P. Chi. 2(4) = 6.2247; Pr = 0.183 7.8386; Pr = 0.183 9.6152; Pr = 0.142

(ii) Family Type and Utilisation of Child Health Services

A marginal variation in utilisation pattern was observed based on family type. Nuclear families show a better percentage of utilisation (65%) against the joint families (63%). Mahabubnagar district also shows similar trend. Nuclear families show better level of utilisation (62%) than joint families (59%).

In Kurnool district similar percentage of utilisation was noticed (68%) in both types of families (Table—4.63).

In Nuclear families, the parents seek health care advice whenever the need arises, and they are very anxiety and feel childs' health is more precious whereas in joint families, the elders within the family will manage and take care. Many times they will opt the traditional methods, leading to lesser utilisation of health services.

Table—4.63

The percentage distribution of respondents by the type of family and utilisation of child health services

Type of Family (years)	Kurnool District			Mahabubnagar District			Total		
	Non-utilised	Utilised	Total	Non-utilised	Utilised	Total	Non-utilised	Utilised	Total
Joint	32.48 (38)	67.52 (79)	100.00 (117)	40.74 (55)	59.26 (80)	100.00 (135)	36.90 (93)	63.10 (159)	100.00 (252)
Nuclear	32.31 (92)	67.69 (191)	100.00 (283)	37.74 (100)	62.26 (165)	100.00 (265)	35.04 (192)	64.96 (356)	100.00 (548)
Total	**32.35 (130)**	**67.65 (270)**	**100.00 (400)**	**38.75 (155)**	**61.25 (245)**	**100.00 (400)**	**35.63 (285)**	**64.37 (515)**	**100.00 (800)**

P. Chi. 2(4) = 0.0351; Pr = 0.983 0.6324; Pr = 0.729 0.2744; Pr = 0.872

(iii) Sex Preference and Utilisation of Child Health Services

The data in the Table—4.64 *(See the table in page 178)* depicts the association between sex preference and child health service utilisation. Higher percentage of utilisation was noticed by the couple who do not have sex preference (66%) against the couple who have sex preference (57%). Similar phenomenon was noticed in the districts of study. Higher percentage of utilisation was noticed in Kurnool district than in Mahabubnagar district.

Table—4.64
The percentage distribution of respondents by sex preference and utilisation of child health services

Sex preference	Kurnool District			Mahabubnagar District			Total		
	Non-utilised	Utilised	Total	Non-utilised	Utilised	Total	Non-utilised	Utilised	Total
Having sex preference	38.78 (19)	61.22 (30)	100.00 (49)	45.56 (41)	54.44 (49)	100.00 (90)	43.17 (60)	56.83 (79)	100.00 (139)
Not having sex preference	31.52 (111)	68.38 (240)	100.00 (351)	36.77 (114)	63.23 (196)	100.00 (310)	34.04 (225)	65.96 (436)	100.00 (661)
Total	**32.50 (130)**	**67.50 (270)**	**100.00 (400)**	**38.75 (155)**	**61.25 (245)**	**100.00 (400)**	**35.63 (285)**	**64.37 (515)**	**100.00 (800)**

P. Chi. 2(2) = 1.8337; Pr = 0.400 4.5644; Pr = 0.102 5.8808; Pr = 0.053

Demographic Variables and Utilisation of Child Health Services

(i) Age at Marriage of Respondents and Utilisation of Child Health Services

The data in Table—4.65 shows the relationship between age at marriage and utilisation of child health services.

It is very clear from the table that the mothers who married at younger ages (below 15 years) have utilised the services at a higher level (64%) because they are inexperienced, very eager and cautious about child care. The percentage of utilisation levels decreased to 58 per cent in the middle group based on age at marriage. It further shoots up to very high in utilisation pattern (79%) among the women who married after 17 years as the women were physically, psychologically mature and exposed to different services of health information.

The district wise data also manifests the similar trend in utilisation of child health services, in relation to respondents' age at marriage.

Table—4.65
The percentage distribution of respondents by age at marriage of respondents and utilisation of child health services

Age at marriage of resp-ondents (in years)	*Kurnool District*			*Mahabubnagar District*			*Total*		
	Non-utilised	*Utilised*	*Total*	*Non-utilised*	*Utilised*	*Total*	*Non-utilised*	*Utilised*	*Total*
Below 13	36.13 (43)	63.87 (76)	100.00 (119)	34.88 (90)	65.12 (168)	100.00 (258)	35.28 (133)	64.72 (244)	100.00 (377)
15	29.65 (51)	70.35 (121)	100.00 (172)	45.30 (53)	54.70 (64)	100.00 (117)	35.99 (104)	64.01 (185)	100.00 (289)
17	38.75 (31)	61.25 (49)	100.00 (80)	56.25 (9)	43.75 (7)	100.00 (16)	41.67 (40)	58.33 (56)	100.00 (96)
20	17.24 (5)	82.76 (24)	100.00 (29)	33.33 (3)	66.67 (6)	100.00 (9)	21.05 (8)	78.95 (30)	100.00 (38)
Total	**32.50 (130)**	**67.50 (270)**	**100.00 (400)**	**38.75 (155)**	**61.25 (245)**	**100.00 (400)**	**35.63 (285)**	**64.37 (515)**	**100.00 (800)**

P. Chi. 2(10) = 8.9491; Pr = 0.537 15.2900; Pr = 0.122 12.8094; Pr = 0.235

(d) Infrastructural Facilities and Utilisation of Child Health Services

(i) Visits of Health Personnel and Utilisation of Child Health Services

Generally the visits made by the health personnel facilitate the beneficiaries to utilise the health services. The Table—4.66 *(See the table in page 180)* presents the association between the visits of the health personnel and utilisation of child health services. Nearly two thirds of respondents utilised child health services in the total sample, irrespective of frequency of visits. It denotes the interests of the parents towards the care of their children.

The district wise data also presents the similar trend. It is interesting to note in Mahabubnagar district that a higher percentage of utilisation (70%) was observed during rare visits of health personnel when compared to regular visits *i.e.,* fortnight and monthly visits (59%). In Kurnool district higher percentage of utilisation of child health services was noticed during monthly visits (71%) against fortnight visits (64%) and rare visits (62%). The data manifests clearly that parents seek health services as and when the need arise irrespective of visits by the health personnel, as the parents are more interested towards their children's health.

Table—4.66

The percentage distribution of respondents by visits of health personnel and utilisation of child health services

Age at marriage of respondents (in years)	*Kurnool District*			*Mahabubnagar District*			*Total*		
	Non-utili sed	*Utili sed*	*Total*	*Non-utili-sed*	*Utili-sed*	*Total*	*Non-utili-sed*	*Utili-sed*	*Total*
Rare	37.74 (20)	62.26 (33)	100.00 (53)	30.38 (24)	69.52 (55)	100.00 (79)	33.33 (41)	66.67 (88)	100.00 (132)
Monthly	29.09 (64)	70.91 (156)	100.00 (220)	40.78 (104)	59.22 (151)	100.00 (255)	35.37 (168)	64.63 (307)	100.00 (475)
Fortnightly	36.22 (46)	63.78 (41)	100.00 (127)	40.91 (27)	59.09 (39)	100.00 (66)	37.82 (73)	62.18 (120)	100.00 (193)
Total	32.50 (130)	67.50 (270)	100.00 (400)	38.75 (155)	61.25 (245)	100.00 (400)	35.63 (285)	64.37 (515)	100.00 (800)

P. Chi. 2(4) = 5.7891; Pr = 0.215 3.4383 Pr = 0.487 4.6522; Pr = 0.325

(ii) The Type of Services Provided by Health Personnel and Utilisation of Child Health Services

The data presented in the Table—4.67 shows the relationship between the type of services provided by the health personnel and utilisation of child health services.

The health personnel will provide preventive services like immunisation, supply of Iron and Folic acid tablets, Vitamin-A and other nutrients to prevent the occurrence of diseases like malnutrition and six killer diseases.

They promote services like nutritional, educational activities etc. They will also provide remedial measures when the child is suffering from various diseases.

If the health personnel are providing all types of services, the women will gain confidence and readily consult the health personnel whenever the need arise. 69% of respondents utilised all types of services from the health functionaries. Nearly two thirds of sample utilised (60%) preventive services alone. The data within the districts also presents the similar trend. When all types of services are provided, higher utilisation was observed in both the districts (Kurnool—71%, Mahabubnagar—67%) against preventive services alone (Kurnool—63%, Mahabubnagar-57%).

Table—4.67

The percentage distribution of respondents by the type of services provided by health personnel and utilisation of child health services

Type of services provided by health personnel	*Kurnool District*			*Mahabubnagar District*			*Total*		
	Non-utili sed	*Utili sed*	*Total*	*Non-utili-sed*	*Utili-sed*	*Total*	*Non-utili-sed*	*Utili-sed*	*Total*
Preventive services alone	37.08 (66)	62.92 (112)	100.00 (178)	42.55 (100)	57.45 (135)	100.00 (235)	40.19 (166)	59.81 (247)	100.00 (413)
Total services (Preventive curative, promotive)	28.83 (64)	71.17 (158)	100.00 (222)	33.33 (55)	66.67 (110)	100.00 (165)	30.75 (119)	69.25 (268)	100.00 (387)
Total	32.50 (130)	67.50 (270)	100.00 (400)	38.75 (155)	61.25 (245)	100.00 (400)	35.63 (285)	64.37 (515)	100.00 (800)

P. Chi. 2(2) = 7.5506; Pr = 0.023 7.7845; Pr = 0.020 18.9245 Pr = 0.000

(iii) Health Education Activities Carried Out by the Health Personnel and Child Health Service Utilisation

Usually the health personnel will conduct the health education sessions for the beneficiaries to improve their awareness and mould their behaviour by changing the attitudes and practices which improve the utilisation of child health services.

In the study area also the same phenomenon is observed. Higher percentage of utilisation (67%) was noticed, among the respondents with health education activities than the respondents who are not exposed to health education activities (62%). Even then a high percentage of utilisation was seen (62%) signifying the parents' interest, eagerness and concern towards their children's safety.

The data within the districts in Table—4.68 also shows the similar trend but higher percentage of utilisation was noticed in Kurnool district than in Mahabubnagar district in both the groups.

Table—4.68

The percentage distribution of respondents by health education activities carried out by the health personnel and utilisation of child health services

Health of education activities carried out by health personnel	*Kurnool District*			*Mahabubnagar District*			*Total*		
	Non-utilised	*Utilised*	*Total*	*Non-utili-sed*	*Utili-sed*	*Total*	*Non-utili-sed*	*Utili-sed*	*Total*
Not carried out	35.29 (78)	64.71 (143)	100.00 (221)	41.50 (83)	58.50 (117)	100.00 (200)	38.24 (161)	61.76 (260)	100.00 (421)
Carried out	29.05 (52)	70.95 (127)	100.00 (179)	36.00 (72)	64.00 (128)	100.00 (200)	32.72 (124)	67.28 (255)	100.00 (379)
Total	**32.50 (130)**	**67.50 (270)**	**100.00 (400)**	**38.75 (155)**	**61.25 (245)**	**100.00 (400)**	**35.63 (285)**	**64.37 (515)**	**100.00 (800)**

P. Chi. 2(2) = 1.91521; Pr = 0.384 1.8564; Pr = 0.395 3.0490; Pr = 0.218

(iv) Source of Information About Maternal and Child Health Services and Utilisation of Child Health Services

Among child health service utilisation, combination of all sources influenced higher percentage of utilisation of services (67%) followed by health personnel (64%), mass-media (63%) and the community (62%).

Table—4.69

The percentage distribution of respondents by source of health information about maternal and child health services and utilisation of child health services

Source of Informa-tion	*Kurnool District*			*Mahabubnagar District*			*Total*		
	Non-utili sed	*Utili sed*	*Total*	*Non-utili-sed*	*Utili-sed*	*Total*	*Non-utili-sed*	*Utili-sed*	*Total*
Mass-media alone	29.63 (8)	70.37 (19)	100.00 (27)	53.85 (7)	46.15 (6)	100.00 (13)	37.50 (15)	62.50 (25)	100.00 (40)
Neighbours	37.62 (38)	62.38 (63)	100.00 (101)	39.74 (31)	60.26 (47)	100.00 (78)	38.55 (69)	61.45 (110)	100.00 (179)
Health Personnel	30.13 (47)	69.87 (109)	100.00 (156)	40.56 (73)	59.44 (107)	100.00 (180)	35.71 (120)	64.29 (216)	100.00 (336)
Combination	31.90 (37)	68.10 (79)	100.00 (116)	34.11 (44)	65.89 (85)	100.00 (129)	33.06 (81)	66.94 (164)	100.00 (245)
Total	32.50 (130)	67.50 (270)	100.00 (400)	38.75 (155)	61.25 (245)	100.00 (400)	35.63 (285)	64.37 (515)	100.00 (800)

P. Chi. 2(6) = 2.4209; Pr = 0.877 10.7268; Pr = 0.097 4.6981; Pr = 0.583

As per the district differentials considered, in Mahabubnagar district mass-media is the poorest source of information (46%) among all other sources. The reasons are: non-availability of health facilities, health personnel and ignorance. Community occupies equal weightage along with health personnel in motivating the people for higher percentage of utilisation (60%).

In Kurnool district higher percentage of the respondents were exposed to mass-media activities (70%). Health personnel also acted as effective motivators (70%) in utilising child health services.

E. Utilisation of Family Planning Services and Differentials in Utilisation

This sub-section begins with an appraisal of women's knowledge of: contraceptive methods, ideal family size, benefits of small family, and decision making. Special attention is focused on adoption status, reasons for utilisation and non-utilisation on family planning services, pattern of adoption and attitude of couple towards exceeding ideal family size. The influence of socio-economic, socio-cultural, demographic and infrastructural variables over the current adoption status of family planning services are also studied.

Awareness of Respondents about Contraceptive Methods

Government of India is utilising all resources to disseminate health information for the needy population by organising the information, education and communication activities to increase their awareness specifically related to contraceptive behaviour through conducting population education programmes.

The investigator made an attempt to assess the awareness of women regarding contraceptive methods. It is clearly evident from the table, that an overwhelming percentage of women (91%) were aware of contraceptive methods, few percentage (9%) of women were reluctant to give response, because of shyness and stigma attached to it.

Table—4.70 shows higher percentage of respondents in Kurnool district (94%) were aware of contraceptive methods, contrary to the respondents of Mahabubnagar district (88%). The knowledge of permanent methods was high, among the respondents belonging to Kurnool district (81%) against Mahabubnagar district (63%).

The National Family Health Survey (1992-93) conducted in states and at national level also manifests the same. Higher percentage of women were aware of permanent methods, as against the spacing methods.

Table—4.70

The percentage distribution of respondents by awareness about contraceptive methods

Awareness	*Kurnool District*	*Mahabubnagar District*	*Total*
(a) Aware	93.75 (375)	87.50 (350)	90.63 (725)
Permanent methods	81.25 (325)	62.50 (250)	71.88 (575)
Temporary methods	6.25 (25)	12.50 (50)	9.38 (75)
Both	6.25 (25)	12.50 (50)	9.38 (75)
(b) No response	6.25 (25)	12.50 (50)	9.38 (75)
Total	**100.00 (400)**	**100.00 (400)**	**100.00 (800)**

Decision-making

The lower social status, inequality of women and male dominance in the society influence the decision-making role of women in the affairs of the family, particularly the family size limitation and family health care matters. The minimal opportunities of income for women and her role as wife, restrict the women's participation in the social development. People who make the decisions at home or in the community are particularly important gate keepers for practising healthy behaviour within the community.

Men make many demands and wives oblige, because of the all encompassing involvement of men in the family and society. Men are able to provide realistic views than women. They can decide fertility related behaviour and family size preferences. Lineage structure tends to keep the spousal link with male dominance in the society. All these factors will influence the decision-making process within the families.

The decision making for the family lamitation and acceptance of family planning methods still wrests with the husband as is seen in Table—4.71. In majority of families, the decisions were taken over by husband alone (77%). In Mahabubnagar district, dominance is greater for men (86%) than in Kurnool district (69%). Elders within the family among the total sample also influence the decision-making process (9.5%). This phenomenon is predominantly seen in joint family system.

Table—4.71

The percentage distribution of respondents by decision maker within the family

Decision maker within the family	*Kurnool District*	*Mahabubnagar District*	*Total*
Husband alone	69.25 (277)	85.50 (342)	77.38 (619)
Elders in the family	9.00 (36)	10.00 (40)	9.50 (76)
Both couple	21.75 (87)	4.50 (18)	13.13 (105)
Total	**100.00 (400)**	**100.00 (400)**	**100.00 (800)**

The status of women depends upon education, employment, age at marriage, their participation in affairs of the family and decision-making are added dimensions. The autonomy a woman enjoys, facilitates her participation in decision-making process. Woman has the key role in home-making process, bearing and rearing of children. Her decision to regulate and limit fertility is more desirable and well appreciated. However the interaction of the couple in the decision-making process to limit the family size is very much desirable. It is appreciable, if couple are taking active part in the decision-making process. About 13 per cent of the couple in the study area were found to be discussing and deciding their family size matter, specially accepting contraceptive to limit their families. In Kurnool district 22 per cent of respondents are involved in such discussions. Lack of interaction between the spouses affect the health status and family planning adoption leading to large families and poverty. The apathy of the males and tradition interfere with such interaction.

The Respondents Opinion about the Number of Children in an Ideal Family Based on Sex Preference

Acceptance of small family with two children is a precondition to lead a healthy family life and for the bright future of their children.

The idea of two child family is catching up slowly with younger couples. However the sex preference demotivates them particularly to son preference.

The Government of India and state governments are keeping intensive efforts to increase the awareness of community, about welfare concept, by conducting health campaigns through information, education and communication activities, even to the remote corners of the country. Hence to find out the opinion of respondents regarding preference of children in an ideal family, an attempt was made and the data was depicted in the Table—4.72. *(See the table in page 188)* Majority of the women (73%) preferred only two children. Out of them, 37 per cent desire to have one male and one female child within the ideal families, so that they can complete all types of cultural tasks and economic fulfilments in life. However 36 per cent did not have any sex preference. Significantly 27 per cent of respondents preferred, male children alone.

Inspite of the desire, the couples have exceeded their number because of unwillingness of husbands, pressure of the elders, inaccessibility to reach health facilities, non-availability of health services, insurance effect, fear of death of children, economic advantage, desire for male child and conservatism.

Table—4.72
The percentage distribution of respondents by sex preference of children in an ideal family

Preference of children	*Kurnool District*	*Mahabubnagar District*	*Total*
Both sons	22.75 (91)	30.50 (122)	26.63 (213)
1 Male + 1 female child	39.50 (158)	35.00 (140)	37.25 (298)
2 Children without any sex preference	37.75 (151)	34.50 (138)	36.13 (289)
Total	**100.00** **(400)**	**100.00** **(400)**	**100.00** **(800)**

Opinion of Couples about Small Family Norm

The idea of small family norm (two child) is disseminated through multi-media, to change the attitude and practices of couples, to raise the standards of living.

The data related to the opinion of respondents about small family norm is depicted in the Table—4.73. The various reasons quoted by the respondents for the small family norm reflect their perception, which includes; 48 per cent for effective child rearing followed by the total family welfare (30%) and for limiting the family size (13%). Of course 9 per cent of the respondents did not hear about a small family norm at all. The districts data also manifests that 13 per cent of respondents in Mahabubnagar district were unaware of small family norm against 6 per cent in Kurnool district. Rest of the respondents have quoted the similar reasons as seen in the total sample.

Table—4.73

The percentage distribution of respondents by their opinion about small family norms

Opinion about small family norm	*Kurnool District*	*Mahabubnagar District*	*Total*
For effective child rearing	47.50 (190)	48.25 (193)	47.88 (383)
To limit family size	10.25 (41)	16.00 (64)	13.13 (105)
For welfare of total family	36.00 (144)	23.25 (93)	29.63 (237)
No response	6.25 (25)	12.50 (50)	9.38 (75)
Total	**100.00 (400)**	**100.00 (400)**	**100.00 (800)**

Status of Respondents by Contraceptive Adoption

The national goal of attaining a couple protection rate of sixty per cent by 2000 A.D., prompts the acceptance of two child norm by the couples. Unless, the survival of all the children is ensured, the family planning acceptance will not increase, for which the utilisation of maternal and child health services are crucial.

The Table—4.74 *(See the table in page 190)* presents the adoption status of respondents. The total adoption of family planning seems to be very low (29%) in the present sample, when compared to the couple protection rate of 46.5 per cent at the state level average.

In consonance of the level of development, the districts also differ in the acceptance of family planning. Kurnool district manifests 38 per cent of family planning adoption against 20 per cent in Mahabubnagar district. However, the data compiled in 1991 shows a couple protection rate of 30.6 per cent and 39.6 per cent in Mahabubnagar and Kurnool districts respectively.

Table—4.74
The percentage distribution of respondents by contraceptive adoption

Adoption Status	*Kurnool District*	*Mahabubnagar District*	*Total*
1	**2**	**3**	**4**
Non-adopted	62.00 (248)	80.00 (320)	71.00 (568)
Adopted	38.00 (152)	20.00 (80)	29.00 (232)
(a) Method on adoption Temporary methods			
Oral Pills	0.25 (1)	0.50 (2)	0.38 (3)
I.U.C.D.	3.25 (13)	1.25 (5)	2.25 (18)
Nirodh/Condom	Nil	Nil	Nil
Permanent methods			
Tubectomy	34.50 (138)	18.25 (73)	26.38 (211)
Vasectomy	Nil	Nil	Nil
(b) Advising family planning methods to others			
No	44.25 (177)	18.75 (75)	31.50 (252)
Yes	55.75 (223)	81.25 (325)	68.50 (548)
(c) Pattern of utilisation of family planning services			
(i) Reasons for contraceptive adoption			
Not applicable	62.00 (248)	80.00 (320)	71.00 (568)
Appricable	32.00 (152)	20.00 (80)	29.00 (232)

(Contd . . .)

1	2	3	4
To limit the family size	55.26 (84)	68.75 (55)	58.16 (139)
For effective child rearing	22.37 (34)	12.50 (10)	18.97 (44)
For the health of mother	10.53 (16)	11.25 (9)	10.78 (25)
For the welfare of the family	3.29 (5)	0.00 (0)	2.16 (5)
For spacing	8.55 (13)	7.50 (6)	8.19 (19)
(ii) Preacceptance education			
Given by health personnel	78.95 (120)	65.00 (52)	74.14 (172)
Motivated by satisfied adopters and community	13.26 (20)	25.00 (20)	17.20 (40)
Self	7.89 (12)	10.00 (8)	8.62 (20)
(iii) Place of family planning services obtained			
At home	0.66 (1)	2.50 (2)	1.29 (3)
Sub-centre	1.97 (3)	3.75 (3)	2.59 (6)
Private sector	3.95 (6)	7.50 (6)	5.17 (12)
Primary health centre	32.89 (50)	31.25 (25)	32.33 (75)
Mandal hospital	60.53 (92)	55.00 (44)	58.62 (136)
(iv) Satisfaction in utilisation of family planning method			
Satisfied	90.13 (137)	87.50 (70)	89.22 (207)
Dissatisfied	9.87 (15)	12.50 (10)	10.78 (25)

(*Contd . . .*)

1	2	3	4
(v) Follow-up services after family planning adoption			
Received	90.13 (137)	87.50 (70)	89.22 (207)
Not received	9.87 (15	12.50 (10)	10.78 (25)
(vi) Identified problems after contraceptive adoption			
No Problems	82.24 (125)	82.50 (66)	82.33 (191)
Intermittent bleeding	1.32 (2)	3.75 (3)	2.16 (5)
Backache	5.26 (8)	7.50 (6)	6.03 (14)
White discharge	0.66 (1)	1.25 (1)	0.86 (2)
Body pains	4.61 (7)	0.00 (0)	08.75 (7)
Infection	0.66 (1)	0.00 (0)	0.43 (1)
Pain abdomen	5.26 (8)	5.00 (4)	5.17 (12)
Total	**100.00 (152)**	**100.00 (80)**	**100.00 (232)**

In India, the promotion and acceptance of contraception, right from the beginning was on permanent methods to a large extent. The acceptance of spacing methods like oral pills, intrauterine contraceptive device and condom are not encouraging, particularly in the rural areas. This has resulted in the acceptance of permanent methods of family planning by couples, after two or more children. After the set back received during emergency in 1976, the vasectomies have almost become negligible. The bias related to vasectomy resulted in higher percentage adoption of female sterilisation, which is clearly manifested in the study area also. 29 per cent of the couple adopted contraceptive methods, among which, 26 per cent adopted female sterilisation, the remaining three per cent of couple adopted temporary methods *viz.*, oral pills (0.38%) and IUCD (2.25%). Surprisingly no male member adopted any contraceptive method either condom of vasectomy. The continuation of spacing methods is also doubtful. The motivation by the health personnel with emphasis on tubectomy and apprehension of these respondents have resulted in the present situation. The health personnel have to intensify the health education programmes and organise health education activities in the community, to motivate the target group of couple to adopt contraceptive methods, specially by male.

The data within the districts reveals, better adoption status among the respondents of Kurnool district (38%) against 20 per cent in Mahabubnagar district. Higher percentage of couple adopted permanent methods in Kurnool district (35%) against to Mahabubnagar district (18%). Very negligible percentage of couples in both the districts (Kurnool—4%; Mahabubnagar—2%) adopted temporary methods. The identified factors for low family planning adoption in Mahabubnagar were: inaccessibility of health services, non-availability of health functionaries, the persisted beliefs, taboos, cultural practices, child value dimensions, poverty, low literacy and low standards of living etc. Whereas in Kurnool district, the status of women and standards of living are comparatively high as more avenues for health information etc., facilitate the better level of contraceptive adoption status.

More than two thirds of the mothers (69%) were interested to motivate the target eligible couple to adopt family planning, whereas one third of the sample (31%) was not interested, as they think that couples can take decisions on their own.

Pattern of Contraceptive Adoption in the Study Area

About 29 per cent of respondents have utilised contraception among the total sample.

The reasons for utilisation of family planning services among the adopters were, to limit the family size (58%), for effective child rearing (19%); for the health of the mother (11%) and for spacing (8%).

The major source of pre-acceptance education was by the health personnel (74.14%). They motivate the eligible couple to adopt contraception depending upon, their family background and social structure. The satisfied adopters and the community also play a vital role in influencing the eligible couple to utilise the family planning services (17.24%). However 8.62 per cent of the respondents were self-motivated to utilise the services because of their education and exposure to health information.

Oral pill users received the pills from health personnel during their home visits (1.29%). The Health Assistant (F) inserted IUCD to the respondents either at sub-centre or at P.H.C. only. A small percentage of respondents (5.17%) have gone to private agency for IUCD insertion. About 26 per cent of respondents underwent tubectomy either at primary health centre or at mandal hospital.

Follow-up of adopters, is usually done by the health personnel, to monitor the health of the mother, to reassure the women about the method and to clarify the doubts. About 89 per cent of the adopters have received follow-up services through health personnel and are satisfied with these services, whereas 11 per cent of the respondents were not satisfied with the follow-up services as no health personnel visited them and no advice was given after adoption.

Majority of the respondents (82%) did not have any problem after contraceptive adoption, except backache (6%) and intermittent bleeding (2%) immediately after IUD insertion, these subsided in course of time.

After tubectomy operation, about 5 per cent of women experienced pain in the abdomen, white discharge (0.86%) and body pains (9%). These are not directly related to tubectomy.

Reasons for Non-adoption of Contraceptive Devices

Information on reasons for non-adoption of contraceptive methods is crucial for designing appropriate strategies for motivation of eligible couple. The information was gathered among the women who are not using any contraceptive method in the study area and are presented in Table—4.75. The reported reasons are fear of side effects (23%), need of more children (20%) and unwillingness of husbands (20%).

Table—4.75

The percentage distribution of respondents by the reasons for non-adoption of contraceptive methods

Reasons for non-adoption of contraceptive methods	*Kurnool District*	*Mahabubnagar District*	*Total*
Fear of side effects after adopting contraceptive devices	28.63 (71)	18.13 (58)	22.71 (129)
Lack of awareness	0.40 (1)	0.00 (0)	0.18 (1)
Waiting for male child	2.82 (7)	25.63 (82)	15.67 (89)
Elders are not willing	4.84 (12)	6.25 (20)	5.63 (32)
Waiting for female child	6.05 (15)	16.56 (53)	11.97 (68)
Need of more children	27.02 (67)	14.38 (46)	19.89 (113)
Husband is not willing	24.60 (61)	16.25 (52)	19.89 (113)
Lack of faith in contraceptives	5.65 (14)	2.81 (9)	4.05 (23)
Total	**100.00 (248)**	**100.00 (320)**	**100.00 (568)**

District wise data reported slightly different reasons. In Mahabubnagar district, where 26 per cent of respondents quoted that they are waiting for male child, 18 per cent expressed fear of side effects and husband's unwillingness (16%). Whereas in Kurnool district the respondents expressed fear of side effects as the first reason (29%) followed by 27 per cent desiring more children and husband's unwillingness (25%).

The data points to the stigma attached with family planning adoption. These were related to fear and apprehension about contraception and sterilisation, male dominance in deciding family size, the fear of child deaths, fatalism etc. All these reasons promote for larger families.

The National Family Health Survey conducted in India (1992-93) quoted the reasons for non-adoption of contraceptive methods. They are: 52 per cent of respondents felt the need of more children, specifically the need for a male child, religious apprehensions (8%), husband's unwillingness (10%) impotency after use of sterilisation or spacing methods (26%) and lack of knowledge (4%). The National Family Health Survey in Andhra Pradesh showed the reasons for non-adoption of contraceptive methods in order of priority are: the need of more children (59%) either in general or because for want of a child of a particular sex, lack of knowledge (33%); health not permitting for use of family planning methods (7%).

DETERMINANTS OF UTILISATION OF FAMILY PLANNING SERVICES

I. Socio-economic Variables and Family Planning Adoption

(i) Education and Family Planning Adoption

The data in the Table—4.76 depicts the relationship between education of respondents by family planning adoption. A positive association was observed in the total sample. As education increases, the percentage of adoption also increases, but the increase was not significant. Only a slight increase in percentage of family planning adoption was observed among the illiterates over literates, The differentials in adoption are not conspicuous perhaps due to highest percentage of illiterates among the sample population.

Only one per cent difference was observed among the illiterates and respondents with primary school education and a marginal 12.3 per cent of increase was observed between the illiterates and higher levels of schooling.

The difference in the districts observed is that in Kurnool district, a positive association was noticed as better levels of family planning adoption (43%) among the respondents, who completed middle school and above than the illiterates (38%) implying the need to promote higher literacy among women population.

Table—4.76

The percentage distribution of respondents by education and family planning adoption

Respondents education	*Kurnool District*			*Mahabubnagar District*			*Total*		
	Non-Adopted	*Adopted*	*Total*	*Non-Adopted*	*Adopted*	*Total*	*Non-Adopted*	*Adopted*	*Total*
Illiterate	62.42 (196)	37.58 (118)	100.00 (314)	79.60 (277)	20.40 (71)	100.00 (348)	71.45 (473)	28.55 (189)	100.00 (662)
Primary School	63.64 (28)	36.36 (16)	100.00 (44)	82.61 (19)	17.39 (4)	100.00 (23)	70.15 (47)	29.85 (20)	100.00 (67)
Middle School and above	57.14 (24)	42.86 (18)	100.00 (42)	82.76 (24)	17.24 (5)	100.00 (29)	59.15 (42)	40.85 (29)	100.00 (71)
Total	**62.00 (248)**	**38.00 (152)**	**100.00 (400)**	**80.00 (320)**	**20.00 (80)**	**100.00 (400)**	**71.00 (562)**	**29.00 (238)**	**100.00 (800)**

P. Chi. 2(3) 0.5284 Pr = 0.913; 0.7725; Pr = 0.856; 1.9008; Pr = 0.593

But in Mahabubnagar district, the reverse trend was noticed. Education does not show any improvement over family planning adoption, as illiterates were adopting higher percentage (20%) than the literates (17%). The trend in Mahabubnagar district denotes the influence of tradition, culture, illiteracy and strong desire for large families. It signifies the need to organise health education programmes in the study area. The health functionaries have to keep intensive efforts and organise the IEC activities in order to bring behavioural modifications by raising the intellectual knowledge and cultivating of healthy practices among the couple.

The National Family Health Survey (1992-93) in India showed positive relationship between education and current use of family planning methods. 33 per cent of illiterate women were currently using family planning methods, compared to 51-55 in literate women. Female sterilisation is also lower among illiterate women than among women who had education lesser than high school level.

The National Family Health Survey (1992-93) in Andhra Pradesh also showed positive association between education and family planning adoption. 20 per cent of illiterates adopted family planning methods whereas the higher percentage of adoption was observed among the literates (56%). Illiterate women adopted only female sterilisation whereas a small with higher levels of education used the temporary contraceptive device like IUD, oral pill and condom.

(ii) Respondents' Occupation and Family Planning Adoption

The occupation of wife tends to influence the adoption of family planning. Among the total adopters, housewives show higher acceptance (37%), followed by coolies (28%) and cultivators (25%). Housewives with higher social status, literacy, income, standard of living have more chances for higher exposure to the health information leading to high family planning adoption. Coolies have broader chances of exposing to mass-media activities for adopting contraception. The phenomenon of more children contribute for more hands to fulfill the future family inspirations, social inhibitions, traditions, lack of time to reach the health services, holding responsibilities in the home as well as in the field, fear of side-effects of operations, influence for low adoption among coolies and cultivators. The districts in the study area also manifesting the similar phenomenon (Table—4.77).

Table—4.77
The percentage distribution of respondents by their occupation and family planning adoption

Respondents education	*Kurnool District*			*Mahabubnagar District*			*Total*		
	Non-Adopted	*Adopted*	*Total*	*Non-Adopted*	*Adopted*	*Total*	*Non-Adopted*	*Adopted*	*Total*
Housewives	55.26 (42)	44.74 (34)	100.00 (76)	77.27 (34)	22.73 (10)	100.00 (44)	63.33 (76)	36.67 (44)	100.00 (120)
Cooly	62.35 (154)	37.65 (93)	100.00 (247)	79.32 (234)	20.68 (61)	100.00 (295)	71.59 (388)	28.41 (154)	100.00 (542)
Cultivation	67.53 (52)	32.47 (25)	100.00 (77)	85.25 (52)	14.75 (9)	100.00 (61)	75.36 (104)	24.64 (34)	100.00 (138)
Total	62.00 (248)	38.00 (152)	100.00 (400)	80.00 (320)	20.00 (80)	100.00 (400)	71.00 (568)	29.00 (232)	100.00 (800)

P. Chi. 2(3) 2.5510; Pr = 0.466 1.8766; Pr = 0.598 2.2803; Pr = 0.516

(iii) Annual Family Income and Family Planning Adoption

The Table—4.78 *(See the table in page 200)* presents the relationship between income and family planning adoption. The income influences the individual's behaviour, raising the standards of living. But reverse trend was observed in the study area. More percentage of adoption (33%) was observed among the respondents with low income group than the higher income groups (Middle income group—29%; high income group—27%). Thus it is evident from the table, a negative association was noticed with income and family planning adoption among total sample. The districts are manifests similar trend as higher income groups show low family planning adoption against higher income groups. Thus it contradicts with already formulated hypothesis *i.e.*, increase in the level of annual income of the family would increase the family planning adoption. It is very much appreciable in the study area that the dissemination of family planning information was high among in the low income group also.

Table—4.78
The percentage distribution of respondents by annual family income and family planning adoption

Annual Family Income (Rs.)	*Kurnool District*			*Mahabubnagar District*			*Total*		
	Non-Adopted	*Adopted*	*Total*	*Non-Adopted*	*Adopted*	*Total*	*Non-Adopted*	*Adopted*	*Total*
<10,000/-	55.07 (38)	44.93 (31)	100.00 (69)	75.79 (72)	24.21 (23)	100.00 (95)	67.07 (110)	32.93 (54)	100.00 (164)
10,000/- 14,000/-	62.66 (99)	37.34 (59)	100.00 (158)	81.10 (103)	18.90 (24)	100.00 (127)	70.88 (202)	29.12 (83)	100.00 (285)
>14,001/-	64.16 (111)	35.84 (62)	100.00 (173)	81.46 (145)	18.54 (33)	100.00 (178)	72.93 (256)	27.07 (95)	100.00 (351)
Total	**62.00 (248)**	**38.00 (152)**	**100.00 (400)**	**80.00 (320)**	**20.00 (80)**	**100.00 (400)**	**71.00 (568)**	**29.00 (232)**	**100.00 (800)**

P. Chi 2(3) 2.2260, Pr = 0.527 1.9817, Pr = 0.576 28.3290, Pr = 0.000

II. Socio-cultural Variables and Family Planning Adoption

(i) Religion and Family Planning Adoption

The religion-wise adoption of family planning is depicted in the Table—4.79. In the total sample, the prevalent rate of adoption is high among the Hindus (29%), followed by the Christians (24%) and the Muslims (22%). As expected, Muslims show lowest acceptance due to religious influence and low literacy levels. However the sample is inadequate to draw generalisations. The data within the districts depicts the similar pattern. Higher percentage of adoption was observed in Hindus (Kurnool—39%); Mahabubnagar—21%) followed by Muslims (Kurnool—33%; Mahabubnagar—14%). Very few percentage of Christians were found in the study area. The data emphasises the need to plan health education activities by the health personnel to remove religious apprehensions and to cultivate healthy practices.

The National Family Health Survey in India (1992-93) shows, highest adoption of family planning among Jains (63%) followed by Christians (48%), Hindus (42%) and Muslims (28%).

The National Family Health Survey in Andhra Pradesh also manifests the highest prevalence rate of adoption among Christians (52%), followed by Hindus (47%) ad Muslims (45%).

Table—4.79

The percentage distribution of respondents by religion and family planning adoption

Religion	*Kurnool District*			*Mahabubnagar District*			*Total*		
	Non-Adop-ted	*Adop ted*	*Total*	*Non-Adop-ted*	*Adop-ted*	*Total*	*Non-Adop-ted*	*Adop-ted*	*Total*
Hindus	**61.46 (228)**	**38.54 (143)**	**100.00 (371)**	**79.47 (298)**	**20.53 (77)**	**100.00 (375)**	**70.51 (526)**	**29.49 (220)**	**100.00 (746)**
Muslim	**66.67 (10)**	**33.33 (5)**	**100.00 (15)**	**86.36 (19)**	**13.64 (3)**	**100.00 (22)**	**78.38 (29)**	**21.62 (8)**	**100.00 (37)**
Christian	**74.43 (10)**	**28.57 (4)**	**100.00 (14)**	**100.00 (3)**	**0.00 (0)**	**100.00 (400)**	**76.47 (13)**	**23.53 (4)**	**100.00 (17)**
Total	**62.00 (248)**	**38.00 (152)**	**100.00 (400)**	**80.00 (320)**	**20.00 (80)**	**100.00 (400)**	**71.00 (568)**	**29.00 (232)**	**100.00 (800)**

P. Chi (2) 0.7136, Pr = 0.700 1.3735, Pr = 0.503 2.7628, Pr = 2.251

(ii) Caste and Family Planning Adoption

Caste will have influence over the attitudes, practices and healthy behaviour of the couple. The data related to Caste and family planning adoption is depicted in the Table—4.80. *(See the table in page 202)*. A higher percentage of adoption was noticed among forward caste (37%) followed by backward caste (29%) and scheduled caste and scheduled tribes (25%) clearly confirming the hypothesis of higher the caste, higher will be the family planning adoption.

Table—4.80
The percentage distribution of respondents by caste and family planning adoption

Caste	*Kurnool District*			*Mahabubnagar District*			*Total*		
	Non-Adopted	*Adopted*	*Total*	*Non-Adopted*	*Adopted*	*Total*	*Non-Adopted*	*Adopted*	*Total*
Forward Caste	53.85 (42)	46.15 (36)	100.00 (78)	77.78 (35)	22.22 (10)	100.00 (45)	62.60 (77)	37.40 (46)	100.00 (123)
Backward Caste	63.98 (135)	36.02 (76)	100.00 (211)	77.78 (175)	22.22 (50)	100.00 (225)	71.10 (310)	28.90 (126)	100.00 (436)
S.C. and S.T.	63.96 (71)	36.04 (40)	100.00 (111)	84.62 (110)	15.38 (20)	100.00 (130)	75.10 (181)	24.90 (60)	100.00 (241)
Total	**62.00 (248)**	**38.00 (152)**	**100.00 (400)**	**80.00 (320)**	**20.00 (80)**	**100.00 (400)**	**71.00 (568)**	**29.00 (232)**	**100.00 (800)**

P. Chi. 2(2) 2.7343, Pr = 0.255 2.7733, Pr = 0.428 6.518, Pr = 0.104

The district show differences in the level of family planning adoption. In Kurnool district, the forward caste is showing higher percentage of adoption (46%). The lower percentage of adoption (36%) was observed in the lower caste communities. Whereas in Mahabubnagar district, no difference in the family planning adoption was observed between forward and backward castes (22%) and low percentage of adoption (15%) was observed among scheduled caste and scheduled tribes because of illiteracy, ignorance and low standards of living.

National Family Health Survey in India and Andhra Pradesh (1992-93) also observed lower percentage of adoption among the low caste communities. In India, the practice of family planning is lower in scheduled caste and scheduled tribe population (33-35%) than non scheduled caste and scheduled tribe women (42%).

The survey conducted by NFHS in Andhra Pradesh, also depicts the same, *i.e.*, the practice of family planning is much higher among non-scheduled caste/scheduled tribe women (50%), than among those from scheduled castes (36%) and scheduled tribe (37%).

(iii) Type of Family and Family Planning Adoption

Type of family is a socio-cultural variable, which affects the values, decisions and the system of entire family. The analysis of family planning adoption by the type of family is depicted in the Table—4.81 which shows that the couples from nuclear families manifest a higher percentage of family planning adoption (31%) than joint families (24%). The district wise data also exhibits a similar trend. The percentage of family planning adoption was high in nuclear families (Kurnool—41%; Mahabubnagar—21%) than in joint families (Kurnool—31%); Mahabubnagar—18%). The reasons for higher adoption in nuclear families were: quick decision making by the couple within limited time, people's views about quality of children and standard of living. The data clearly depicts the impact of social change and modernisation by the couples even in the rural areas. Whereas in joint families, the factors like conservatism, traditions, cultural barriers, influence of elders within the families etc. contribute for low family planning adoption.

Table—4.81
The percentage distribution of respondents by family type and family planning adoption

Caste	*Kurnool District*			*Mahabubnagar District*			*Total*		
	Non-Adop-ted	*Adop ted*	*Total*	*Non-Adop-ted*	*Adop-ted*	*Total*	*Non-Adop-ted*	*Adop-ted*	*Total*
Joint	69.23 (81)	30.77 (36)	100.00 (117)	82.22 (111)	17.78 (24)	100.00 (135)	76.19 (192)	23.81 (60)	100.00 (252)
Nuclear	59.01 (167)	40.99 (116)	100.00 (283)	78.87 (209)	21.13 (56)	100.00 (265)	68.61 (376)	31.39 (172)	100.00 (548)
Total	**62.00 (248)**	**38.00 (152)**	**100.00 (400)**	**80.00 (320)**	**20.00 (80)**	**100.00 (400)**	**71.00 (568)**	**29.00 (232)**	**100.00 (800)**
P. Chi 2(1) 3, 6699,		**Pr = 0.055**		**0.6289, 0.428**			**0.0676, 0.795**		

(iv) Interspouse Communication about Family Size Limitation and Family Planning Adoption

Interspouse communication is a predictor of closeness of conjugal relationship and plays a vital role in decision making process, especially related to family size limitation and adoption of small family norm. Greater interspouse communication facilitates better understanding, wider perception and timely adoption of family planning methods and small family norm. Interspouse communication also facilitates the change in their attitudes and practices.

Women will have certain ideas, opinions, interest about their own family. If they have freedom to express their views, with their spouse, they plan their future and reach the desired goals in life. Male dominance pushes the women to an insignificant position. The interspouse communication paves the way for dissemination of information about healthy family life, standard of living and small family norm.

The adoption of family planning is higher (33%) when the couple interact with each other against 28 per cent of couples going for family planning without any interaction (Table—4.82).

The interspouse communication seems to have a marginal effect on adoption of family planning in Kurnool district and almost insignificant influence in Mahabubnagar district. Still men hold the key for decision on family size limitation in the communities. This shows the secondary role of women in decision-making on family size.

The communication between couples can be improved by enhancing the status of women, particularly by improving their level of education. This would not only expose women to new knowledge about child bearing and rearing but also improve interspouse communication on various issues including family planning, thereby paving the way to contraceptive acceptance. Health personnel have to encourage the couple for greater interaction and provide them more information to sustain their interest.

Many studies have reported positive association between intraspousal communication and family planning adoption

(Mahadevan, 1979; Shivaraju, 1987 and Saisujatha and Murthy, 1993).

Table—4.82

The percentage distribution of respondents by interspouse communication about family size limitation and family planning adoption

Interspousal communication about family size limitation	*Kurnool District*			*Mahabubnagar District*			*Total*		
	Non-Adopted	*Adopted*	*Total*	*Non-Adopted*	*Adopted*	*Total*	*Non-Adopted*	*Adopted*	*Total*
Not discussing	62.63 (176)	37.37 (105)	100.00 (281)	80.43 (222)	19.57 (54)	100.00 (276)	72.18 (454)	27.82 (175)	100.00 (629)
Discussing	60.50 (72)	39.50 (47)	100.00 (119)	79.03 (98)	20.97 (26)	100.00 (124)	66.67 (114)	33.33 (57)	100.00 (171)
Total	**62.00 (248)**	**38.00 (152)**	**100.00 (400)**	**80.00 (320)**	**20.00 (80)**	**100.00 (400)**	**71.00 (568)**	**29.00 (232)**	**100.00 (800)**

P. Chi 2(1) 0.1609, Pr = 0.688 0.0221, Pr = 0.882 4.3468, Pr = 0.037

(vi) Sex Preference and Family Planning Adoption

The sex preference is an age old cultural phenomenon. The cultural values attached to the son have a definite say in adoption of small family norm, which has been found to be true in many studies. Thus the present study also concur with these findings as seen from the Table. The data in the Table—4.83 *(See the table in page 206)* shows the association between sex preference by family planning adoption.

The couple who did not have any sex preference, adopted family planning methods immediately after they attained the desired family size, hence higher family planning adoption (30%) is observed among these couples against the couples who adopted family planning with sex preference (25%).

The data in Kurnool district also represents the similar trend. The couple who does not have any sex preference adopted family planning in a higher rate (38%) as against the couples who had sex preference (35%) whereas in Mahabubnagar district no difference was observed in adoption status based on sex preference.

Table—4.83
The percentage distribution of respondents by sex preference and family planning adoption

Caste	*Kurnool District*			*Mahabubnagar District*			*Total*		
	Non-Adopted	*Adopted*	*Total*	*Non-Adopted*	*Adop-ted*	*Total*	*Non-Adopted*	*Adop-ted*	*Total*
Having sex preference	65.31 (32)	34.69 (17)	100.00 (49)	80.00 (72)	20.00 (18)	100.00 (90)	74.82 (104)	25.18 (35)	100.00 (139)
No sex preference	61.54 (216)	38.46 (135)	100.00 (351)	80.00 (248)	20.00 (62)	100.00 (310)	70.20 (464)	29.80 (197)	100.00 (661)
Total	62.00 (248)	38.00 (152)	100.00 (400)	80.00 (320)	20.00 (80)	100.00 (400)	71.00 (568)	29.00 (232)	100.00 (800)

P. Chi 2(1) 0.2591; Pr = 0.611 0.0000; Pr = 1.000; 1.7587; Pr = 0.185

III. Demographic Characteristics of Respondents and Family Planning Adoption

(i) Current Age of the Respondents and Family Planning Adoption

Women are very fecund in the age group of 15-44. Family building activity and planning for happy family life depends upon several factors like physical and intellectual maturity. Freedom in decision-making in the families specially related to family size limitation and socio-cultural background etc.

The women in the age group of 25 years and above are considered to be in peak fertile period. It is interesting to note that higher percentage of family planning adoption (39%) is observed in this age group, as they felt the importance of family limitation or might have reached the desired family size. Family planning adoption is low, in the younger women aged below 19 years, which increases gradually along with age. The attainment of desired family size of 2 to 3 children is usually completed by 25 years depending on use of spacing methods. Hence it is likely that the adoption also goes up confirming the hypothesis as age increases the level of adoption also increases.

This emphasises the need to approach the eligible couples in these younger age groups in tune by the time they have two children. Both the districts depicts the similar trend.

Higher percentage of family planning adoption was observed in the age group of 25 years and above. In Kurnool district comparatively higher percentage (49%) of respondents adopted family planning against Mahabubnagar district (28%). This may be due to accessibility, availability of health services, exposure to health information and better standards of life.

The higher percentage of family planning adoption is also seen in the women above 20-24 years age group in toto (27%) and in the districts (Kurnool—35%; Mahabubnagar—17%). This is because of the women possessing the desired number of children.

Thus a positive association is observed between current age of the respondents and family planning adoption (Table—4.84).

Table—4.84

The percentage distribution of respondents by current age of respondents and family planning adoption

Current Age of Respondents' (in years)	*Kurnool District*			*Mahabubnagar District*			*Total*		
	Non-Adopted	*Adopted*	*Total*	*Non-Adopted*	*Adopted*	*Total*	*Non-Adopted*	*Adopted*	*Total*
<19	88.46 (46)	11.54 (6)	100.00 (52)	91.14 (72)	8.86 (7)	100.00 (79)	90.08 (118)	9.92 (13)	100.00 (131)
20-24	64.74 (112)	35.26 (61)	100.00 (173)	82.61 (133)	17.39 (28)	100.00 (161)	73.35 (245)	26.65 (89)	100.00 (334)
25 and above	51.43 (90)	48.57 (85)	100.00 (175)	71.88 (115)	28.12 (45)	100.00 (160)	61.19 (205)	38.81 (130)	100.00 (335)
Total	**62.00 (248)**	**38.00 (152)**	**100.00 (400)**	**80.00 (320)**	**20.00 (80)**	**100.00 (400)**	**71.00 (568)**	**29.00 (232)**	**100.00 (800)**

P. Chi 2(3) 25.9161; Pr = 0.000; 16.7641; Pr = 0.001 0.2052; Pr = 0.977

(ii) Age at Marriage and Family Planning Adoption

Age at marriage is a significant variable that influences the family building activity and family size. Lower age at marriage hinders righteous thinking of conceiving immediately following marriage. Higher age at marriage facilitates intraspouse communication. Thus the 'ideas' of family limitation are accepted on time. This trend is evident from the data in Table—4.85.

Table—4.85

The percentage distribution of respondents by age at marriage and family planning adoption

Age at marriage of Respondents' (in years)	Kurnool District			Mahabubnagar District			Total		
	Non-Adopted	Adopted	Total	Non-Adopted	Adopted	Total	Non-Adopted	Adopted	Total
<13	64.71 (77)	35.29 (42)	100.00 (119)	76.74 (198)	23.26 (60)	100.00 (258)	73.47 (275)	27.06 (102)	100.00 (377)
14-15	40.12 (69)	59.88 (103)	100.00 (172)	89.74 (105)	10.26 (12)	100.00 (117)	60.21 (174)	39.79 (115)	100.00 (289)
16-17	40.00 (32)	60.00 (48)	100.00 (80)	81.25 (13)	18.75 (3)	100.00 (16)	46.88 (45)	53.13 (51)	100.00 (96)
>18	68.97 (20)	31.03 (9)	100.00 (29)	44.44 (4)	55.56 (5)	100.00 (9)	63.16 (24)	36.84 (14)	100.00 (38)
Total	**62.00 (248)**	**38.00 (152)**	**100.00 (400)**	**80.00 (320)**	**20.00 (80)**	**100.00 (400)**	**71.00 (568)**	**29.00 (232)**	**100.00 (800)**
P. Chi 2(5)	**1.6640; Pr = 0.893**			**16.7314, Pr = 0.005**			**21.6509 Pr = 0.001**		

The women who married at the age of 16-17 years exhibit high family planning adoption (53%). Thus it is evident that higher age at marriage facilitated higher family planning adoption. This is because of maturity, decision-making, intellectual power, need for the desired family size, exposure to the health information, increased awareness etc. However, in the sample, the respondents who married at 18 years of age and above, show lower adoption (37%) than the proceeding age group (53%). Further, the number of respondents who are in the age group of 18 years and above is too small (38%) to draw generalisation.

The districtwise data shows differential pattern, the women in Kurnool district in all age groups shows higher percentage of family planning adoption against Mahabubnagar district. The percentage of adoption of family planning methods is increasing as age at marriage increased. As shown in the Table—4.85, lesser percentage of family planning adoption was observed among the respondents who married at younger ages (<13 years—35%), it gradually increased to 60 per cent among the women who married between 16-17 years.

Mahabubnagar district is depicting a reverse trend. Higher the age at marriage, the lesser the percentage of family planning adoption. The women who married below 13 years of age show 23 per cent of family planning adoption, whereas 19 per cent of family planning adoption was seen at later age at marriage (16-17 years). This may be due to ignorance, poor decision-making power, influence of traditional practices and low status of women.

(iii) Number of Living Children and Family Planning Adoption

The family planning programme is aimed to provide people with a means to achieve the number of children they desire thus contributing slow population growth, more rapid economic development and improve the health of women and children (Davanzo, 1995). Parity dependent stopping behaviour is a powerful factor in the fertility transition.

The Table—4.86 *(See the table in page 210)* describes the association between number of living children by family planning adoption. It is observed that higher the number of living children, higher the percentage of adoption. Nearly one quarter of sample has one living child. Among them very few percentage (7%) of couple adopted temporary methods. It is appreciable to note that more than one quarter of the women (26%) maintained small family norm by undergoing tubectomy operation. The remaining adopted contraception after reaching their desired family size (3 or more children). The reasons quoted by them for having more number of living children are: more children means more hands to feed the family, add more income to the family, and keep the family strong. They are motivated by satisfied adopters and health personnel, to adopt the contraception.

The district wise data also showed the similar aspect. In Kurnool district, almost double the number of couples adopted family planning against the Mahabubnagar district.

Table—4.86

The percentage distribution of respondents by number of living children and family planning adoption

Number of Living Children	*Kurnool District*			*Mahabubnagar District*			*Total*		
	Non-Adop-ted	*Adop ted*	*Total*	*Non-Adop-ted*	*Adop-ted*	*Total*	*Non-Adop-ted*	*Adop-ted*	*Total*
One	89.69 (87)	10.31 (10)	100.00 (97)	96.77 (90)	3.23 (3)	100.00 (93)	93.16 (177)	6.84 (13)	100.00 (190)
Two	60.48 (75)	39.52 (49)	100.00 (124)	89.52 (94)	10.48 (11)	100.00 (105)	73.80 (169)	26.20 (60)	100.00 (229)
Three	51.04 (49)	48.96 (47)	100.00 (96)	71.43 (60)	28.57 (24)	100.00 (84)	60.56 (109)	39.44 (71)	100.00 (180)
Four+	44.58 (37)	55.42 (46)	100.00 (83)	64.41 (76)	35.59 (42)	100.00 (118)	56.22 (113)	43.78 (88)	100.00 (201)
Total	62.00 (248)	38.00 (152)	100.00 (400)	80.00 (320)	20.00 (80)	100.00 (400)	71.00 (568)	29.00 (232)	100.00 (800)

P. Chi. 2(4) = 50.8353; Pr = 0.0000 45.8530; Pr = 0.0000 81.4262; Pr = 0.0000

(IV) Infrastructural Facilities and Family Planning Adoption

(i) The Visits of Health Personnel and Family Planning Adoption

The frequency of visits by the health providers resulted in good rapport and acceptance of ideas on family planning. The credibility of the health care providers is an important input to influence family planning adoption. The Table—4.87 presents that the contacts are at the minimal, with many health personnel visiting once in a month or beyond one month.

In the study sample, slight improvement in the adoption of family planning was observed, when the frequency of visits are improved, more percentage of adoption (31%) was noticed, (when the health personnel visits them fortnightly) compared to less visits (monthly—29%; or rare visits—27%). This signifies the credibility of service of the health personnel.

Table—4.87

The percentage distribution of respondents by visits of health personnel and family planning adoption

Frequency of visits by health personnel	*Kurnool District*			*Mahabubnagar District*			*Total*		
	Non-Adop-ted	*Adopted*	*Total*	*Non-Adop-ted*	*Adop-ted*	*Total*	*Non-Adop-ted*	*Adop-ted*	*Total*
Rare	60.38 (32)	39.62 (21)	100.00 (53)	81.01 (64)	18.99 (15)	100.00 (79)	72.73 (96)	27.27 (36)	100.00 (132)
Monthly	61.82 (136)	38.18 (84)	100.00 (220)	79.22 (202)	20.78 (33)	100.00 (255)	71.16 (338)	28.84 (137)	100.00 (475)
Fortnightly	62.99 (80)	37.01 (47)	100.00 (127)	81.82 (54)	18.18 (12)	100.00 (66)	69.43 (134)	30.57 (59)	100.00 (193)
Total	62.00 (248)	38.00 (152)	100.00 (400)	80.00 (320)	20.00 (80)	100.00 (400)	71.00 (568)	29.00 (232)	100.00 (800)

P. Chi 2(2) 0.1154; Pr = 0.944 0.2850; Pr = 0.867 5.4232; Pr = 0.066

When the district differentials are considered, Kurnool district shows a reverse trend; lesser the visits (rare—39.62%), higher was the percentage of adoption. It may be due to increased awareness about contraception, accessibility, availability of health personnel and higher literacy levels of respondents irrespective of the visits made by the health personnel.

With regard to Mahabubnagar district, higher percentage of family planning adoption was noticed during monthly visits of health personnel (20.78%)

(ii) Type of Services Provided by the Health Personnel and Family Planning Adoption

The data depicted in the Table—4.88 shows the association between type of services provided by the health personnel and family planning adoption.

Table—4.88

The percentage distribution of respondents by type of services provided by health personnel and family planning adoption

Type of Services Provided	*Kurnool District*			*Mahabubnagar District*			*Total*		
	Non-Adopted	*Adopted*	*Total*	*Non-Adopted*	*Adopted*	*Total*	*Non-Adopted*	*Adopted*	*Total*
Preventive service alone	59.55 (106)	40.45 (72)	100.00 (178)	80.00 (188)	20.00 (47)	100.00 (235)	71.19 (294)	28.81 (119)	100.00 (413)
Preventive promotive and curative services	63.96 (142)	36.04 (80)	100.00 (222)	80.00 (132)	20.00 (33)	100.00 (165)	70.80 (274)	29.20 (113)	100.00 (387)
Total	62.00 (248)	38.00 (152)	100.00 (400)	80.00 (320)	20.00 (80)	100.00 (400)	71.00 (568)	29.00 (232)	100.00 (800)

P. Chi. 2(1) 0.8167; Pt = 0.366 0.0000; 1.000; 5.5178 Pr = 0.019

Not much variation in the adoptive behaviour of the couple by type of services is observed among the total sample and also within the districts. Just 4 per cent of difference in the family planning adoption by the respondents is observed in Kurnool district. People received preventive services in a better manner (40%) against with all types of services (36%). Inaccessibility, non-availability of health personnel, lack of drugs and other factors related to health functionaries were identified as the factors for the above observation.

(iii) Health Education Activities and Family Planning Adoption

The health education activities will influence the modification of behaviour among the women. Higher percentage of family planning adoption (33%) was observed among respondents who are exposed to health education activities. More than one fourth of the respondents (26%) adopted contraception even though they are not exposed to the health education activities. Even in the rural areas, women are aware about the need of family limitation and sharing the fulfilment of responsibilities of their families.

The similar phenomena was observed in the district also. Higher percentage of adoption was observed in Kurnool district among both groups of respondents against Mahabubnagar district. In Kurnool district only a slight variation of 5 per cent was noticed between the women who are exposed and those not expected to health education activities against a small (3%) variation in Mahabubnagar district.

It is clear from the Table—4.89 that health functionaries need to put more efforts to bring behavioural modification specially related to family limitation particularly to the eligible couple in order to enhance the family planning adoption with small family norm.

Table—4.89

The percentage distribution of respondents by health education activities conducted by health personnel and family planning adoption

Health Education activities	*Kurnool District*			*Mahabubnagar District*			*Total*		
	Non-Adopted	*Adopted*	*Total*	*Non-Adopted*	*Adopted*	*Total*	*Non-Adopted*	*Adopted*	*Total*
Carried out	59.73 (132)	40.27 (89)	100.00 (221)	78.50 (157)	21.50 (43)	100.00 (200)	66.98 (282)	33.02 (132)	100.00 (421)
Not carried out	64.80 (116)	35.20 (63)	100.00 (179)	81.50 (163)	18.50 (37)	100.00 (200)	73.61 (279)	26.39 (100)	100.00 (379)
Total	**62.00 (248)**	**38.00 (152)**	**100.00 (400)**	**80.00 (320)**	**20.00 (80)**	**100.00 (400)**	**71.00 (568)**	**29.00 (232)**	**100.00 (800)**
P. Chi 2(1)	**1.0816; Pr = 0.298**			**0.5625, Pr = 0.453;**			**0.1184; Pr = 0.731**		

(iv) Source of Information and Family Planning Adoption

To adopt family limitation, specially by the rural people is a challenge for the health functionaries. Still it needs intensive efforts to accept ideas of contraception particularly the male contraception. The data presented in the Table—4.90 manifests the association between family planning adoption and the sources of information.

Table—4.90

The percentage distribution of respondents by source of information about maternal, child health and family planning services and family planning adoption

Source of information about MCH and family planning	*Kurnool District*			*Mahabubnagar District*			*Total*		
	Non-Adopted	*Adopted*	*Total*	*Non-Adopted*	*Adopted*	*Total*	*Non-Adopted*	*Adopted*	*Total*
Mass-media alone	5.56 (15)	44.44 (12)	100.00 (27)	84.62 (11)	15.38 (2)	100.00 (13)	65.00 (26)	35.00 (14)	100.00 (40)
Community	66.34 (67)	33.66 (34)	100.00 (101)	82.05 (64)	17.95 (14)	100.00 (78)	73.18 (131)	26.82 (48)	100.00 (179)
Health personnel	60.90 (95)	39.10 (61)	100.00 (156)	76.67 (138)	23.33 (42)	100.00 (180)	69.35 (233)	30.65 (103)	100.00 (336)
Combination	60.21 (71)	38.79 (45)	100.00 (116)	82.95 (107)	17.05 (22)	100.00 (129)	72.65 (178)	27.35 (67)	100.00 (245)
Total	62.00 (248)	38.00 (152)	100.00 (400)	80.00 (320)	20.00 (80)	100.00 (400)	71.00 (568)	29.00 (232)	100.00 (800)

Chi (2) = 1.3936; Pr = 0.707 2.3278; Pr = 0.507 2.3183; Pr = 0.509

Mass-media plays a vital role (particularly the contraceptive methods) in motivating the couple and bringing awareness in the total community. Government is spending huge resources for population education programmes. More percentage of adoption (35%) in the total sample is through mass media, followed by health personnel (31%). The combination of all sources also had less weightage (27%) only. Because it is not easy to bring a change within the community. Health personnel have to motivate them by using different resources.

When the district differences are considered, it is observed that in Mahabubnagar district, health personnel influenced the family planning adoption more (23%) followed by satisfied adopters and neighbours (18%) Mass-media influenced few percentage (15%) of respondents. Whereas in Kurnool district, mass-media is the first influencing factor (44%) followed by health personnel (39%) and one third of sample adopted family planning by the influence of satisfied adopters in the community (34%).

It is clear from the data, that the people will be influenced by different sources to have healthy change within their lives by adopting healthy practices. Government has to enrich the people with abundant knowledge so that they can adopt family planning in order to lead a happy family life.

Chapter—5

Multiple Determinants of Utilisation of Maternal, Child Health and Family Planning Services

In this chapter, an attempt is made to examine the independent net effect of the selected background characteristics of the respondents on their utilisation of maternal, child health (MCH) and family planning (FP) services. In the preceding chapters, the influence of various socio-economic, cultural, demographic and infrastructural factors on the utilisation of MCH and FP services have been studied at length through cross-tabular analysis. However, it is a well known fact that the utilisation of maternal, child health and family planning services will be determined by a multiple factors together, rather than isolation. To fulfil this objective, multivariate analysis is carried out here, to assess the extent of influence of the individual factors on dependent variables, controlling for others. Such an analysis is advantageous in manipulating the variables separately for promoting the use of better maternal, child health and family planning services among the eligible couples.

Among the various multivariate techniques, the logistic regression analysis is found to be more appropriate and hence, applied to the data, since all the dependent variables are dichotomous in nature *i.e.* utilisation or non-utilisation of various maternal, child health and family planning services.

Variables Included in the Model

Though several variables are discussed in the earlier chapters, only those variables which have shown significant individual association with the dependent variables as well as of theoretical importance have been chosen to include in the regression models. Further, the earlier cross-tabular analysis has been carried out using the district as a control variable. But, the preliminary logistic analysis did not show any significant independent effect of district background on various aspects of maternal, child health and family planning services and therefore, not included in this analysis. Of course, exclusion of this variable did not affect the outcome of the results anyway.

The following are the variables selected and used for the present analysis.

Dependent Variables

Antenatal Services	:	0—if	not utilised any antenatal services
		1—if	utilised one or the other antenatal services
Natal Services	:	0—if	home delivery and not assisted by untrained personnel.
		1—if	institutional delivery and assisted by trained personal
Postnatal Services	:	0—if	not received any postnatal services
		1—if	received one or the other postnatal services
Child Health Services	:	0—if	not utilised any child health services
		1—if	utilised one or the other child health services.

Adoption of Family Planning method	:	0—if	not adopted any family planning methods.
		1—if	adopted one or the other methods of family planning.

EXPLANATORY (INDEPENDENT) VARIABLES

Socio-economic Variables

Educational level of women	:	illiterate	0
		Primary School	1
		Middle school and above	2
Occupational level of women	:	Not working	0
		Working as Coolies	1
		Working as Cultivators and others	2
Annual family income	:	Rs.10,000 or less	1
		Rs.10,001-14,000	2
		Rs.14,001 and above	3
Type of work performed during antenatal period	:	Both household and outside household work	0
		Household work only	1

Socio-cultural Variables

Caste	:	Schedule Castes/Tribes	0
		Backward Castes	1
		Forward Castes	2
Types of Family	:	Joint Family	1
		Nuclear Family	2
Interspouse communication	:	No discussion	0
		Had discussion	1
Sex preference of children	:	No sex preference	0
		Have sex preference	1

Demographic Variables

Age at marriage of women	:	12 years or less	1
		13-14 years	2
		15 years and above	3

Infrastructural Facilities

Frequency of visits by	:	Rare/Monthly	0
MPHA (F)	:	Fortnightly	1
Type of services extended by MPHA (F)	:	No service/preventive services only received	1
		Preventive, promotive and curative services received	2
Source of MCH and FP information	:	No source/any one source	1
		Two or more sources	2

Besides these three dependent variables *viz.*, the utilisation of antenatal, natal and postnatal services have also been included as explanatory variables in appropriate places (see Table 5.01).

Thus, all variable categorical in nature, are grouped for each variable, one category is being selected as the reference category. Logistic regression analysis estimates the coefficient (with their 't' value) for each of the remaining categories of the variable, which express the magnitude of the net effect of each category on the outcome, in relation to the reference category.

Logistic Regression Result on Utilisation of Antenatal Services

From the first column of Table—5.01, it is evident that the utilisation of antenatal care (ANC) services is significantly higher when the infrastructural variables are good. For instance, utilisation of antenatal care (ANC) services are higher among those respondents who reported that they had received preventive, promotive and curative health services by MPHA (F) visited by MPHA (F) regularly (fornightly) and received information about various aspects of MCH and FP from two or more sources compared to those women who had not received/ received only preventive health services by MPHA (F), visited rarely/monthly by MPHA (F) and not received maternal, child health and family planning services information.

As expected, respondents who had attended household work only during pregnancy and thus less burdened, had utilised ANC services significantly to a large extent. On the other hand, the utilisation of ANC services are significantly at lower side among those respondents who reside in nuclear family and had sex preference (for male), compared to those who reside in joint family and who did not exhibit any sex preference.

The education status and age at marriage of the respondents do not show a consistent effect on the utilisation of antenatal care services. For instance, while the primary level of education had shown a moderate positive effect on utilisation of antenatal care services, middle and above level of education had exhibited a negative (but negligible) effect. On the other hand, the effect of higher age at marriage (15 years and higher) of the respondents is positive (but weak) on the utilisation of antenatal care services. Their younger age at marriage has shown a highly (sig. at.01 level) negative effect.

The socio-economic variables viz, occupational status and annual family income of the respondents, in general, appears to be very weak determinants of antenatal care services utilisation that too in a negative direction. The role of caste background of the respondents also is not clear in influencing the utilisation of antenatal care services.

Logistic Regression Results on Utilisation of Natal Services

On observing the natal care services (column 2 Table 5.01), it can be seen that more women who ever utilised one or the other antenatal care services had a greater tendency to utilise the natal services too. Similarly, the utilisation of natal services is significantly higher when they were visited by MPHA (F) at home, fortnightly as compared to rarely/monthly.

Respondents whoever reported that they had received preventive, promotive and curative health services by MPHA (F) and had discussion with spouses about the number of children they desire to have, had also exhibited a greater chance to utilise natal services, but statistically significant to a lesser extent (.10 level). Likewise, women who ever had participated in household work only during pregnancy and belonging to forward castes, utilised the natal services somewhat higher side (sig. at .10 level) as compared to those who engaged in both household and outside work belonging to Scheduled Castes.

The role of socio-economic variables, by and large, seem to be very weak. This is also is true in the case of respondent's age the marriage, sources of maternal, child health and family planning information and sex preference.

Logistic Regression Results on Utilisation of Postnatal Services

The characteristics associated with utilisation of postnatal care services are shown in column 3 of Table—5.01. As hypothesized, women whoever utilised natal and antenatal care services are much more likely to utilise the postnatal care services (at a highly significant level) than those women who did not utilise. The utilisation of postnatal care services are also found to be higher among those women who received maternal, child health and family planning information from two or more sources (significant at a moderate level) than those who had not received/received information from any one of the sources.

Women whoever reported that they had received preventive, promotive and curative services through MPHA (F) are more likely to utilise postnatal care services (but statistically less significant—.064) than those women who had not. It is rather surprising that women educated upto primary level had utilised postnatal care services to a lesser extent (sig. at .067 level) than those women who are illiterate.

Rest of the variables included in the model, in general, appear to be very weak (and at times contradictory to the expected trend) are predictors of utilisation of postnatal care services.

Logistic Regression Results on Utilisation of Child Health Services

Determinants of utilisation of child health care services by women are assessed in column 4 of Table 5.01. Preventive, promotive and curative services received by women through MPHA (F) is very strongly related to their utilisation of child health care services. Next in that order, is the sex preference. Women whoever exhibited preference for male child(ren) are more likely to seek child health services than those who did not.

Interestingly, occupational status of women had emerged as one of the good predictors (sig. to a lesser extent) of child health care utilisation. While women working as coolies are less (sig. at .071) to utilise the child health services as compared to non-working women, women working as cultivators and others had a greater tendency (sig.at. 069) to sought for child health care services.

None of the other variables included in the model shows any significant influence on the utilisation of child health services.

Logistic Regression Results on Family Planning Adoption

From column 5 of Table—5.01, it is evident that type of services extended by MPHA (F) is the lone variable which has shown a significant (at .070 level) influence on the family planning adoption of women.

Discussion

From the foregoing analysis and results, it may be concluded that the role of MPHA (F) seems to be very crucial for motivating women to utilise all aspects of maternal, child health and family planning services. It is well known fact that MPHA (F) is the only health professional who will have a greater access to all pregnant women and lactating mothers, irrespective of their rural-urban and socio-economic background. It is true also is true that most of the health services like preventive, promotive and curative services are being extended by MPHA (F) and therefore eligible women will have greater belief and confidence on them. MPHA (F) will translate this belief and confidence into action by motivating them to utilise the various maternal and child health services as well as adoption of one or the other family planning methods.

The role of MPHA (F) in influencing the utilisation of maternal, child health and family planning services by eligible women is further increased through the frequency of visits by them. This variable has turned out to be highly significant in the case of utilisation of antenatal and natal care services for which MPHA (F) work hard to visit regularly and impart information and education through which they formulate positive attitude to utilise such services.

The source(s) of maternal, child health and family planning information is strongly associated with the utilisation of antenatal and postnatal care services in a positive direction. Here too, the MPHA (F) have played the key role since they are the one of the major inter-personal sources of information on maternal, child health and family planning, which normally would be more prominent in motivating the women to utilise such services.

As expected, utilisation of antenatal care services has exerted a significant positive effect on both natal and postnatal care service utilisation. Natal care service utilisation as expected has emerged as a significant predictor of postnatal care services utilisation. Thus, it may be concluded that once women are accepted to utilise antenatal care services, there is greater tendency to utilise the natal and postnatal care services. These findings, more or less corroborate with some of the earlier Indian studies (Bhatia and Cleland, 1995; Kavitha and Audinarayana, 1997; Andinarayana and Sheela, 1998; Sivakami and Kulkarni, 1998).

Type of work performed during antenatal period emerged as one of the strong predictors of antenatal and natal care services utilisation. Women whoever performed only household work during pregnancy (antenatal period) are likely to be less burdened and find ample time to visit the service centres to utilise antenatal and natal care services.

Women living in nuclear family, in general, have at a disadvantage in making use of the maternal, child health and family planning services and turned out to be highly significant (in negative direction) in the case antenatal care service utilisation. This implies that women in nuclear family may not have the support of elder female members (who normally) to accompany or look after the young ones at home, which would most likely motivate them not to utilise the antenatal services to a large extent.

Women who belong to forward castes and had discussion with husband on the desired number of children are more likely to utilise the natal care services than those women who belong to Scheduled Castes do not discuss with their spouse. This implies that women belong to higher socio-economic status and had better inter-spouse communication would tend to utilise the natal care services to a large extent.

Socio-economic characteristics of women, in general, have weak and contradictory direction of influences on various dimensions of maternal, child health and family planning service utilisation. For example, it is surprising to not that educational level of women failed to emerge as a strong predictor of use of maternal, child health and family planning services, though its positive role (especially middle and higher level of education) is highlighted in some of the studies conducted in India (Kanitkar, 1989; Bhatia and Cleland, 1995; Kavitha and Audinarayana, 1997; Audinarayana and Sheela, 1998; Sivakami and Kulkarni, 1998). One of the reasons could be that the overall level of education of the sample women is less, besides the sample size, which might have not been sufficient to make a dent in utilisation of maternal, child health and family planning services in presence of other variables.

Occupational status of women though mostly exerted negative effect on all dimensions of maternal, child health and family planning adoption, women working as cultivators and engaged in other occupations had utilised child health care services to a moderate extent. Of course, women working as coolies had utilised such services to a lesser extent than non-working women. Such finding may be expected because women working as coolies may not find time to seek services and economically on the one side they are getting lower wages and on the other side they may not be able to pay for such services since these are mostly charged. More or less, similar finding is also observed by others in Andhra Pradesh (Audinarayana and Sheela 1998) and Tamil Nadu (Kavitha and Audinarayana, 1997; Sivakami and Kulkarni, 1998).

Chapter—6

Case Studies Related to Maternal, Child Care and Contraceptive Adoption

Case Study—I

DANGEROUS PRACTICE OF CONDUCTING DELIVERIES BY SELF

The practice of conducting self delivery is a rare phenomena followed by some of the nomadic communities in the past, however when the health consciousness and health services have percolated to the nook and corners of all the villages, it is surprising to note that still some of the villages, have the same nomadic experiences continuing due to inaccessibility of services. The investigator has witnessed self delivery in Erlapalli, which is an interior village, comes under Gangapur primary health centre of Mahabubnagar district. It was observed at 12:30 p.m.

Mrs. Bharathi, aged 21, wife of Mr. Rajappa, aged 28, married at 11 years had given birth to first child at 17 years. She has three living children. All her deliveries were conducted by herself. She lead a nuclear family. She belongs to scheduled caste community. She and her husband are coolies. Their condition are apathy. They have very less urban contact. The local dai is aged untrained but conducts deliveries. The dai frequently goes to her daughters' place, and so she may not be available all the time to render the health services. The female health assistant post was vacant. The Multi purpose health assistant (M) rarely visits the village.

The day of her delivery Mrs. Bharathi was alone at home and she attended to her household work. Her husband went out for work. Around 11.30 A.M. she had labour pains and was lying on a cloth with no one around, by 12.30 P.M. she delivered a baby without anybody's assistance. She tied umbilicus with a piece of dirty cloth and cut it with a sickle. She was struggling as placenta was not expelled. By that time the investigator had gone to that village for gathering data. At about 1 p.m. the neighbour of Mrs. Bharathi came in running, informed the investigator about the spontaneous delivery of Mrs. Bharathi, half hour ago that placenta was not expelled and there was bleeding. The investigator had gone to the home and examined and expelled. Placenta since it is not adherent, spontaneous delivery of placenta has taken place and she observed the uterine contraction, controlling of bleeding and comfort of the mother. All the parameters were checked. They were within the normal range. Investigator could do all these services because of her nursing background. On enquiry, it has been noticed that mother did not have any antenatal care nor took any immunisation.

Discussion

At an emergency like this, what the woman has acted is quite appropriate, but health hazards regarding umbilicus and infections, bleeding conditions of mother can lead into morbidity and mortality. Since the mother had two normal deliveries at home, she never realised the consequences of self home delivery. The investigator educated the mother to seek the health services during and after pregnancy. Special emphasis was made on prevention of Anaemia and Tetanus, generalised infections, feeding practices, child rearing practices and immunisation. As there is no trained birth attendant. There was no awareness by education for safe delivery, motherhood and child surveillance. Attempts were made to see the village elders to impress the importance of training of birth attendants in Erlapalli village.

Case Study—II

CHILD MARRIAGE

The investigator visited the S. Kottala interior village of Thudicherla sub-centre of Parumanchala primary health centre of Kurnool district and found out a sociological reformation about childhood marriage of girl. It was a custom that the girl should get married by ten years of age and go to in laws' house even before menarache.

The parents of Ms. Madakka settled the marriage for Ms. Madakka, aged 13 years, with a boy of 19 years and made every arrangement for marriage. But Madakka refused to get married and opposed the ideas of parents. When the parents insisted her to marry, she refused very firmly and took up the issue with her peer group girls, who already formed, "Balika sangham" and declared that they are not going to marry before 18 years *i.e.*, the legal age at marriage. They explained to the elders that they can take up some skill oriented work like handicrafts (stitching, painting, basket making, agarbathi making, preparing home foods etc) and stand on their feet. They argued with the leaders about the age at marriage and hazards of early marriage and early adulthood. They also informed the elders in the family and the village that if they insist, they will go to the extent of informing the police. The elders were impressed and convinced with their argument and prevailed upon the parents to postpone the marriage.

Discussion

The growing girls are conscious about their life events, effects of early marriage and consequences of early motherhood. This village is an example, of a strong social reform which would have a future effect on to the social life.

The Balika sangham, which was strong with 25 members was trained up in different trades and also deals the problems of the adolescent girl. This consciousness has modified their ideas. Every village should take this example and follow the steps of these adolescent girls.

A strong education programme for adolescent girls about their changes, health care, hygiene, social responsibilities like age at marriage etc,. will pave the way for behavioural change and for proper personality development. The peer group influence (Balika sangham) will have a strong effect on their ideas, opinions and practices. Proper utilisation of this group definitely helps them to stand on their own feet.

The investigator felt that it is a positive turn of the society towards better society and prosperity. The adolescent girls are educating themselves for a better cause and for a better life. One of these girls have been selected as community health activist in that mandal to bring awareness of health and to render health services for total community in that village.

Case Study—III

MOTIVATION OF THE ELIGIBLE COUPLE FOR SPACING METHODS ADOPTION OF INTRA UTERINE CONTRACEPTIVE DEVICE

Mrs. Nagamma aged 21, wife of Mr. Nagendra, aged 25 are illiterates and are coolies in a joint family with a size of ten members. She got married at the age of 15 years. They have two female children aged 2 years and 4 months. They were not fully immunised. They are from L. Banda, interior village of Bhogulu sub-centre of Veldurthi primary health centre in Kurnool district. The couple has heard of intra uterine contraceptive device and oral pills. The couple were motivated for adoption of spacing methods. But the family members were not willing since they had only daughters, and did not have sons in the total family. But the woman wanted some gap. Similarly there was about 20 couples with one or two children who were willing for spacing with IUD. However the apprehensions were too many particularly complications like profuse bleeding, perforation of uterus, big size of IUD (they felt that along with plunger, it is inserted) etc. Many of them do not know the position of IUD in the body, where it was inserted, besides, the husbands were not willing to discuss them openly. The health care provider has taken it, as a challenge, and conducted intensive health education sessions through group meetings and individual contacts. It was observed that the women preferred the individual contact, wherein they actively discussed about IUD.

Thus Mrs. Nagamma got motivated to go for IUD, but requested the health care provider, not to reveal this to her husband or any other family members. But the health provider made it a point to talk to her husband in the presence of the wife and encouraged intraspousals communication. The health care provider has given the IUD to the couple so that they can feel it by hand, she has also asked them to hold the IUD in a fist and imagine the fist as uterus and how they felt IUD in the fist, whether it is hard or piercing or hurting. The couples said that they did not feel whether, it was in the uterus or in the fist. They said that it was very soft also, thus their apprehensions were cleared. The couple informed that the woman would go for IUD insertion, but they requested that this should not be revealed to any of the people in the family or neighbours. This was accepted and the woman got the IUD inserted. It look about eight individual visits by the health care provider to this couple by using visual aids etc. to convince them.

Discussion

Appealing personally to the needs of the couple, clarifying their doubts, using fist method with IUD and conferring with them in privacy through more number of personal visits by the health provider all have facilitated the acceptance of IUD.

Case Study—IV

NEONATAL DEATH DUE TO POOR UTILISATION OF MATERNAL SERVICES

Mrs. Lingamma, aged 22, wife of Kesava, aged 25. They lived in L. Banda interior village of Bhogulu sub-centre, Veldurthi primary health centre of Kurnool district. They are from low socio-economic strata. Both are coolies from joint family with a family size of 10. They are living in pucca house with two living rooms. Ventilation is poor inspite of the electrification. They reside along with the chattles under the same roof. Mrs. Lingamma is now 4th gravida, 3 para with three living female children. The investigator met the mother on the

3rd day after the delivery. All the members in that family were worried, the investigator noticed pathetic situation in the house. The new born was a male child, severely asphyxiated, cyanosed with a feeble, fast pulse and muscle cramps. The body was bending like a bow and very frequently the child had fits. On enquiry, the mother revealed that she did not take Tetanus Toxoide vaccination in her antenatal period. Her name was registered by the multi-purpose health assistant (F). No other antenatal service was received. The deliveries were conducted by traditional dai, who was untrained. She used sickle to cut the umbilical cord. From first day onwards the child developed problem, and died on 3rd day itself. The investigator has witnessed it. The mother was edemated, legs were swollen and other Preeclamptic Toxaemic symptoms were noticed. The mother was not adopting any contraceptive devices previously. The other three children were 5 years, 4 years and two and half years of age. The mother had no knowledge of a small family norm and contraceptive methods. They are in need of a male child. They did not adopt them and had no mind to adopt also. Her husband and other members in the family are not willing to utilise any type of health service.

Discussion

Even after several years of implementation of family welfare programme, it is very sad note that the focus groups were not properly utilising the needed health services. So they face the tragedies consequently. The interior villages still have the problems of inaccessibility of health services and non-availability of health functionaries. The need was felt to fill all the posts. The health services should be accessible to the community. Efforts should be made to increase the awareness of public about health services to fully utilise the services and to avoid traditional practices.

Chapter—7
Summary and Implications

SUMMARY OF THE FINDINGS OF THE STUDY

Utilisation of Maternal Health Services

An effort was made in the present study, to assess the utilisation of Maternal, Child Health and Family Planning Services with District as a unit, on a contrasting basis by taking deferentially progressed districts in Andhra Pradesh State.

This subsection deals with utilisation of maternal health services (antenatal, natal and postnatal services).

Antenatal Services: Only 54.5 per cent of the respondents utilised antenatal services. In Kurnool district better levels of utilisation was seen (60%) as against to Mahabubnagar district (49%). About 29 per cent of respondents received antenatal services for first pregnancy. One fourth of the women received antenatal services for all pregnancies and among them only 26 per cent utilised services from government facility, the rest from private sector. It is surprising to note 42 per cent of women were not aware of clinical manifestations of pregnancy, however 55 per cent consider amenorrhoea as the only one symptom of pregnancy. During antenatal check up, fundal height, weight, blood pressure was checked and lab investigations were utilised by 42 per cent of respondents. Only 15 per cent of mothers have received health education regarding antenatal care. Whereas 41 per cent of respondents consumed Iron and Folic acid tablets and 42 per cent of women did not take T.T. vaccination.

Natal Services: A low percentage of utilisation of natal services (35%) was observed. In Kurnool district the level of natal services utilisation was higher (38%), against to their counterparts in Mahabubnagar district (32%). In the study area, 82 per cent of deliveries occurred at home. About one fifth of the respondents utilised institutional deliveries whereas 50 per cent of deliveries were conducted by trained persons. In Mahabubnagar district majority of deliveries (75%) were conducted by untrained persons.

Postnatal Services: The present study finds a decline in utilisation of postnatal services (30%) from antenatal period (54.5%) through natal period (35%). It may be, because the women feel, antenatal period is precious and they will be very anxious about child birth and child bearing period, if it went on smoothly they will not bother to utilise health services anymore after childbirth leading to poor utilisation of health services during postnatal period.

The health assistant (female) visited 30 per cent of postnatal mothers and registered births, out of them only 9 per cent of mothers received the health services *i.e.* checking fundal height, vital signs, health education etc. This clearly point to a big gap between the services expected from health personnel and the percentage of services delivered by them. Of the 17 per cent of women who had problems during postnatal period (reproductive problems—8%, Medical problem—9%), majority of them (14%) sought remedial measures.

Determinants of Maternal Health Services

Various intervening factors influence in the utilisation of maternal health services.

(a) ***Education:*** Shows positive association with utilisation of maternal health services. Higher percentage of utilisation of antenatal services was observed among the literates (75%) as against to illiterates (51%). It is also observed that the women, who have studied upto primary school utilised more (75%) than the women who have studied middle school and above (68%). In Mahabubnagar district, a significant variation was not observed with levels of schooling. A similar pattern was noticed with regard to natal services utilisation among the literates (54%) than illiterates (31%). With regards to postnatal services, better level of utilisation was observed with the mothers who had more years of schooling (46%) than low levels of schooling or illiterates (28%).

(b) ***Occupation:*** The nature of occupation influences health service utilisation pattern. Housewives show higher utilisation of maternal health services (Antenatal— 67%, Natal—50%, Postnatal—42%) than cultivators (Antenatal—57%, Natal—40%, Postnatal—33%) and coolies (Antenatal—51%, Natal—31%, Postnatal—27%). Better level of antenatal service utilisation has observed by the women who perform household activity alone (67%) than the women who were engaged in both activities (51%). The Housewives have greater exposure to information perhaps this facilitates higher utilisation of antenatal services. Besides house wives have enough time, to consult health personnel than the working women.

(c) ***Caste:*** The respondents from forward caste have shown higher utilisation of maternal health services (Antenatal—63%, Natal—47%, Postnatal—37%) than the lower castes (B.C.—Antenatal—53%, Natal—35%, Postnatal—31; S.C.—Antenatal—54%, Natal—29%, Postnatal—26%). Thus a positive association was observed between caste and utilisation of maternal health care services.

(d) ***Family Type:*** The respondents from joint families have shown higher utilisation of maternal health services (Antenatal—61.5%, Natal—37.7%, Postnatal—34.5%) than nuclear families (Antenatal—51%, Natal—34%, Postnatal—28%).

(e) ***Interspouse Communication:*** Higher percentage of utilisation of maternal health services was noticed, among the couple who had interaction (Antenatal—65%, Natal—47%, Postnatal—33%) in contrary to the other group of couples who are not discussing about sexual matters and family welfare matters (Antenatal—52%, Natal—47%, Postnatal—33%). Thus a positive association was observed between interspouce communication and utilisation of maternal health services.

(f) ***Consanguinity:*** Non-consanguineous couple (57%) utilised more antenatal services than consanguineous couples (52%).

(g) ***Sex Preference:*** The women who had sex preference utilised maternal services more (Antenatal—65%, Natal—35%, Postnatal—38%) as against to those who had no sex preference, (Antenatal—52%, Natal—35%, Postnatal—30%).

(h) ***Current Age of Women:*** The highest utilisation was observed in the younger age group (<19 years) of women (63%), 53 per cent utilisation was observed among the women between 20-24 years and higher age group.

(i) ***Age of Marriage:*** Better level of utilisation of antenatal services was observed among the women who were married at higher ages (76%) than the women who were married at younger ages (49%).

(j) ***Frequency of Visits of Health Personnel:*** Positive association was observed between the frequency of visits and utilisation of antenatal service. Higher percentage of utilisation of antenatal services was observed with fortnightly visit (68%) followed by monthly visits (51%) and rare visits (47%) of health personnel. Higher percentage of utilisation of natal services was observed, when the health personnel made visits of fortnightly (51%) followed by monthly visits (31%) ad rare visits (27%). Thus positive association was observed between frequency of visits and utilisation of natal services. Kurnool district exhibits higher percentage of utilisation during fortnight visit (58%) as against to Mahabubnagar district (51%) whereas during monthly and rare visits of health personnel the respondents of Mahabubnagar district shows a better percentage of utilisation as against to Kurnool district, however it is marginal variation only (rare visits—Kurnool 25%, Mahabubnagar—27%, Monthly visits Kurnool—30%, Mahabubnagar—31%).

(k) ***Type of Services Provided by Health Personnel:*** Higher utilisation of maternal services was observed when all types of services provided by health personnel (Antenatal—64%, Natal—42%, Postnatal—36%) as against to the provision of preventive service alone (Antenatal—46%, Natal—29%, Postnatal—25%).

(l) ***Health Education Activities Carried Out by Health Personnel:*** The impact of health education over the utilisation of maternal services in the study area, shows a higher level of utilisation among the respondents who were exposed to health education (Antenatal—61%, Natal—38%, Postnatal—34%) activities than those women who were not exposed to health activities (Antenatal—49%, Natal—33%, Postnatal—26%).

(m) ***Source of Information About Maternal Health Services:*** Health personnel were the primary source of health information about antenatal services (58%) followed by mass-media (48%) and the community (40%). Whereas for natal services utilisation, it was observed that community played primary source (50%) followed by health personnel (39%) and mass-media (24%). The similar trend was observed in the pattern of utilisation of postnatal services also *i.e.*, community acts as a primary source (50%) followed by health personnel (39%) and mass-media (24%).

The respondents of Mahabubnagar district exhibit lower levels of utilisation of maternal services as against to the respondents to the respondents belonging to Kurnool district based on several intervening variables, signifying the backwardness of Mahabubnagar district.

THE PRACTICES OBSERVED IN THE STUDY AREA RELATED TO MATERNAL CARE

Practices During Antenatal Period: More than one third of women (34%) stayed in mother's house. In Mahabubnagar district more percentage (72%) of women did not go to natal home for delivery.

Newborn Practices: About 63 per cent of women applied turmeric powder, 8 per cent used oil to the umbilical cord, whereas 8 per cent of respondents applied cow dung also, which is a hazardous practice still noticed. 60 per cent of respondents gave bath to the babies twice a day. 98 per cent of women gave breast feeding and warmth for the newborn. Rooming in is commonly observed. 88 per cent of women initiated breast feeding after 24 hours only. The prelaeteal feeds given were: sugar-water, honey, cow's milk, goat and buffalow's milk.

Hygienic Practices During Postnatal Period: Nearly one fourth of women took bath immediately after delivery or on the first day of delivery (28%), a good sign was noticed in the study area. But only 18 per cent of women had taken perennial and breast hygiene.

Utilisation of Child Health Services

The involvement in child health is a direct entry to improve socio-economic development and quality of the nation. The people think that having a child is an asset for their family. Hence the parents are more concerned about the health and survival of the children everborn. The same trend was noticed in the study area also. Higher percentage of utilisation of child health services was observed (64%) in contrast to maternal health services *i.e.*, antenatal (55%), natal (35%) and postnatal services (30%).

Immunisation Services: More than half of the mothers (57%) are aware of the diseases, *viz.*, Polio myelitis and Tetanus. Only four per cent of women are able to list all vaccine preventable diseases. Major source of information for immunisation and vcaccines are the health personnel (64%) followed by family members (14%) and neighbours (10%). More than three fourths of women (77%) immunised their children either fully (32%) or partially (45%) children not immunised were 23 per cent. The reasons for not immunising the children were: they were healthy (10%) busy in occupational activities (8%) and they do not have time to take their children to the health centre (12%).

Child Morbidity: Children below five years are at greater risk than the rest of the population. The common causes for child morbidity are: acute respiratory tract infections, Diarrhoeal diseases, vaccine preventable diseases and malnutrition. In the study area, 71 per cent of children suffered with diarrhoea, 8 per cent had multiple problems like acute respiratory tract infections (3%). Polilo (2%) and Measles (3%) and 48 per cent of children have taken treatment during illness.

More than half of the respondents (52%) were unware of treating diarrhoea with ORS solution. Surprisingly 59 per cent of mothers did not give any liquids for replacement during dehydration due to diarrhoea.

Child Mortality: Only 10 per cent of women experienced child deaths. Asphyxia and Diarrhoea appears to be the major causes of deaths in the study area, which would have been avoided with utilisation of child health services in time.

Feeding Practices: *(a) Breast Feeding:* Nearly 40 per cent of women fed their babies for 18-24 months, 22 per cent for 9-12 months of duration and nearly one fourth of mothers breast fed their babies for more than 30 months. *(b) Weaning:* Only 11 per cent of women have started liquids other than breast milk from 3rd month onwards. 46 per cent of women gave semi-solids from 5th month onwards. 63 per cent of mothers gave solid foods after 9th month only.

Determinants of Child Health Services

(a) ***Education:*** Higher percentage of utilisation of child services was observed among the respondents who studied upto middle school and above, followed by mother's with primary school education (69%) and illiterates (63%). Thus positive association was observed between education and utilisation of child health services.

(*b*) ***Occupation:*** Mothers, who were cultivators exhibit highest percentage of utilisation (73%) followed by housewives (69%) and coolies (61%).

(*c*) ***Annual Income:*** Nearly two thirds of women in all categories of income utilised child health services.

(*d*) ***Caste:*** Positive association was observed between caste and utilisation of child health services. The women belonging to forward caste utilised more (73%) than backward community (Scheduled Caste—65%, Backward castes—63%).

(*e*) ***Family Type:*** A marginal variation in utilisation pattern based on family type was noticed (Nuclear families—65%, Joint families—63%). In Kurnool district similar percentage of utilisation was noticed (68%) in both types of families.

(*f*) ***Sex Preference:*** Higher percentage of utilisation was noticed by the couples who do not have sex preference (66%) against the couple who have sex preference (57%).

(*g*) ***Frequency of Visits and Type of Services Provided by Health Personnel:*** Nearly two thirds of respondents utilised child health services irrespective of frequency of visits, in the total sample as well as district sample, shows the concern of the parents for their children. A better level in utilisation pattern was observed, when all types of health services are provided (69%) as against to preventive services alone (60%). Better level of utilisation was seen (67%) among the respondents who were exposed to health education activities, as against to their counterparts (62%). Health personnel (64%) and mass-media activities (63%) were the major source of information about child health services followed by the community (62%).

Utilisation of Family Planning Services

An overwhelming percentage of women (91%) were aware of contraceptive methods. Higher percentage (94%) of respondents in Kurnool district were aware of contraceptives than the respondents of Mahabubnagar district. The knowledge of permanent methods was high (88%) among the respondent in Kurnool district contrary to Mahabubnagar district (63%).

Decision-making: The decision-making in relation to family size limitation and contraceptive adaptation still wrests with the husbands alone (77%). About 13 per cent of the couples were discussing among themselves to decide the contraceptive adoption. In mahabubnagar district, dominance is greater for men (86%) than in Kurnool district (69%).

Contraceptive Adoption

Very low adoption of contraceptive methods was observed in the study area (29%). Even among them 26 per cent of the couples have undergone tubectomy operation and the remaining 3 per cent of couples adopted intrauterine contraceptive device (2%) and oral pills (0.38%). Vasectomy cases were nil.

Reasons for Non-adoption: As perceived by the respondents the reasons of non-adoption were: the fear of side effect (23%), need of more children (20%) and unwillingness of husband (20%) were the major reasons quoted by respondents. In Mahabubnagar district, the major reasons quoted were: they are waiting for male child (26%) ad desiring for more children (14%).

Determinants of Utilisation of Contraceptive Services

(a) ***Education:*** Positive association was found between education and family planning adoption. Better adoption status was noticed among the couple who had middle school and above education (41%) than illiterates (29%).

(b) ***Occupation:*** Housewives show higher acceptance (37%) followed by coolies (28%) and cultivators (25%).

(c) ***Annual Family Income:*** Negative association was observed between the income and family planning adoption. Low income group exhibits better adoption status (33%) than middle income group (29%) and high income groups (27%).

(d) ***Religion:*** Hindus adopted more (29%) than Christians (24%) and Muslims (22%). However the sample is inadequate to draw generalisation.

(e) ***Caste:*** As expected the forward caste women was adopted more (37%) followed by backward caste (29%) and scheduled community (25%). In Kurnool district also similar finding was noticed. Whereas in Mahabubnagar district, no difference in the family planning adoption was observed between forward and backward castes (22%) and low percentage of adoption (15%) was observed in scheduled community.

(f) ***Type of Family:*** The couples from nuclear families manifest a higher percentage of family planning adoption (31%) than joint families (24%).

(g) ***Interspouse Communication:*** The adoption of contraception is higher (33%) when the couple interact with each other, as against the couple, who do not interact (28%).

(h) ***Sex Preference:*** The couple who did not have any sex preference adopted better (30%) than the couple who had sex preference (25%). The data in Kurnool district represents the similar pattern. Whereas Mahabubnagar district did not show any difference based on sex preference.

(i) ***Current Age of Respondents:*** Higher percentage of family planning adoption (39%) was observed among the women who were in peak fertile period *i.e.*, 25 years and above.

(j) ***Age at Marriage:*** The women who married after 15 years exhibit higher adoption (53%) than the women who married at early ages (27%). The respondents of Kurnool district exhibits the similar trend whereas Mahabubnagar district is exhibiting a reverse trend, the women who married below 13 years manifests a better percentage of adoption (23%) when compared to women who married between 14-17 years (11%), but the percentage of adoption shoots up among the women who married after 28 years (56%).

(k) ***Frequency of Visits:*** More percentage of contraceptive adoption was noticed during forthnights visits of health personnel (31%) than less visits by the health personnel (monthly—29% and rare visits 27%). This signifies the credibility of service of the health personnel. Marginal variation in the adoption status was observed based on type of services provided. Positive association was observed *i.e.*, better adoption was observed when the women exposed to health education activities (33%) than the other group (26%). Mass-media activities (35%) and health personnel (31%) exhibits primary source of information about family planning adoption.

Thus the study exhibits differences in the utilisation pattern on a contrasting basis and the influence of selected independent variables over the utilisation pattern of Maternal, Child Health and Family Planning services was also studied.

SUMMARY OF MULTIPLE DETERMINANTS OF UTILISATION OF MATERNAL, CHILD HEALTH AND FAMILY PLANNING SERVICES

Multivariate analysis is carried out to assess the extent of influence of the individual factors on dependent variables, controlling for others. It is advantageous in manipulating separately for promoting the utilisation of maternal, child health and family planning services. Logistic regression analysis is found to be more appropriate, as all the dependent variables are dichotomous in nature.

Those variables, which have shown significant individual association with the dependent variables as well as of theoretical importance have been chosen.

LOGISTIC REGRESSION RESULT

Once women are accepted to utilise antenatal services, there is greater tendency to utilise the natal and postnatal care services. It exerted a significant positive effect on both natal and postnatal services utilisation. The role of multi-purpose health assistant (F) in influencing the utilisation of Maternal, Child Health and Family Planning services is further increased through the frequency of visits by them. This is highly significant in the case of utilisation of antenatal and natal care services. The sources of Maternal, Child Health and Family Planning information is strongly associated with the utilisation of antenatal and postnatal care services in a positive direction. Type of work performed during antenatal period emerged as one of the strong predictors of antenatal and natal care service utilisation. Women lining in nuclear family turned out to be highly significant (in negative direction). Women belong to higher socio-economic status and had better interspousal communication would tend to utilise the Maternal, Child Health and Family Planning services to a large extent. Socio-economic characteristics of women, in general, have weak and contradictory direction of influences on various dimensions of Maternal, Child Health and Family Planning service utilisation. Type of services extended by MPHA (F) is the lone variable which has shown a significant influence on the Family Planning adoption.

IMPLICATIONS

Maternal and Child Health Services

The findings of the present study may become the basis for building stronger health services in the remote areas in future, in order to achieve the goals of "Health For All by the year 2000 A.D." and to ensure safe motherhood and child survival, the following suggestions are made:

- Ensure an efficient administration, monitoring and evaluation system to generate the necessary momentum for successful implementation of safe motherhood programme at grass root level in order to improve the qualitative services;
- The inputs may be modified to enhance qualitative services like lab facilities such as urine analysis, Haemoglobin estimation etc. at the sub-centre level;
- Enhance the accessibility, availability and quality of services as the sincerity, commitment and involvement

of health personnel can generate confidence of people and it paves the way to utilise the services properly and the required results will be obtained;

- Utilise "satisfied acceptors" as role model to promote the utilisation of services;
- Referral system for primary health centres has to be streamlined and strengthened;
- Intensive efforts particularly through personal contacts by the health providers has to be strengthened to modify the behaviour of mothers;
- Mobilising new cadres of maternal health workers for a "woman-to-woman" approach to the delivery and utilisation of maternal and child care;
- Stay of Multipurpose health assistants (F) at the sub-centres may ensure better services of antenatal check up, immunization treatment of common ailments etc. This will also increase the credibility of the Multipurpose health assistants (F) as well as promote greater utilisation of services;
- To reflect growing recognition for the need to heightened awareness and mobilisation for active community participation "Information, Education, Communication and Mobilisation activities" should be carried out with innovativeness;
- The rigid enforcement of legal measures must be followed strictly to raise the age at marriage of women.
- All the pregnant women who fall below poverty line must be given maternity benefit funds by government in order to avoid excessive work during later weeks of pregnancy;
- Increase the awareness of pregnant women about maternity benefit funds through different resources such as health personnel, voluntary organisations and mass-media activities etc. So that pregnant woman can avoid excessive work during later weeks of pregnancy;

- Encourage the community to avoid consanguineous marriages to make them to aware about consequences of consanguineous marriages.

Family Planning Services

- Extensive use of mass-media and interpersonal communication has to be made for highlighting the benefits of small family norm and removal of socio-cultural barriers for contraceptive adoption.
- The active involvement of local leaders, religious heads and voluntary organisations in family planning campaigns should be enhanced.
- A satisfied adopter is the best propagator. An association of satisfied acceptors of family planning may be formed in each Panchayat to discuss and clear their doubts.
- Encourage the couple to take decisions regarding family size limitation as most rational and conscious phenomenon. This provides the possibility for them to plan their family size intentionally and choose the most suitable means to achieve that rationally perceived goal.
- The family welfare programme should place greater emphasis on use of spacing methods which improve family planning performance, and the health of mothers and children.
- Strong political and community commitment for small family norm is needed.
- Emphasis should be shifted from the female contraception to male. Presently, the use of contraceptives is highest by females. Hence encourage the male contraceptive methods.
- Strengthen the population education programmes especially for the younger age groups for an attitudinal change towards better utilisation of services.

Bibliography

Abdellah, F.G. and Eugene Levine. 1987. *Better Patient Care Through Research*. New York: Macmillan Company.

Agarwala, S.N. 1982. *A Demographic Survey of Six Urbanising Villages*. Bombay: Asian Publishing House.

Aleyamma, Mammen. 1974. *A Study of the Knowledge, Attitude and Practices of Selected Mothers Regarding Maternal and Child Health Care in Ramanaikenpalayam*. North Arcot District. Unpublished Master's thesis, Madras University.

Al-Mazrou, *et al*, 1993, *Gulf Child Health Survey Executive Board, Riyadh:* Ministry of Health, Saudi Arabia, pp. 125-156.

Amna, M. Swar-Eldahab, 1993. *"Constraints on Effective Family Planning in Urban Slum"*. Studies in Family Planning. New York.

Anderson, J.B.H. Durston and M. Poole, 1991, *Thesis and Assignment Writing*. New Delhi: Willey Eastern Limited.

Arnold, Fred, 1985. *Measuring the Effect of Sex Preference on Fertility*. 22(2): 280-88.

Arrora. 1989. *A Study on Fertility Variation in Rural Women of Ludhiana*. Punjab Agricultural Journal of Research. Ludhiana Vol. 26(2), June 311-314.

Ashok Kumar, 1996, *Knowledge and Use of Health Services in a City of U.P.* Indian Journal of Public Health. Calcutta.

Ashok Kumar, 1994, *"Research and Effectiveness of Maternal Health Services in the Context of Control of Infant Mortality Rate"*, Lucknow Population Centre, Vol. 9:3. 3-6.

Ashok Kumar, 1996. *Knowledge and Use of Health Services in a City of Uttar Pradesh.* Indian Journal of Public Health. Calcutta: Volume 30. No. 2. April-June, 1986. 66-76.

Audinarayana, N. 1985. *Inter Relationships between Socio-economic Variables and Age at Marriage.* The Journal of Family Welfare. Bombay: Vol. 31(4), April. 39-45.

Audinarayana, N. and Rajasree, R. 1995. "*Cultural Determinants of Age at Marriage—an Urban Experience*". The Journal of Family Welfare. Bombay: Vol. 41 No. 1, March, 8-12.

Audinarayana, N. and Sheela, J. 1998. "*Determinants of Maternal Health Care Services Utilisation of Andhra Pradesh,* an analysis of NFHS data." Paper presented in the international Conference on "Reproductive Health, AIDS prevention and Development of Women", at S.V. University, Tirupathi, Jan. 9-10.

Avabai, B. Wadia, 1997. *Special Issue on Safe Motherhood.* The Journal of Family Welfare. Bombay: Vol. 43. No. 2; June, 1-3.

Azuh, E. Dominic. 1994. *Child Survival Under Threat.* New Delhi: B.R. Publishing Corporation.

Badari, V.S. and others. 1993. *Infant Mortality, its Components and Correlates: Findings from a Longitudinal Study in Rural Karnataka.* Genus, Bangalore: XLVII (1 & 2): 89-108.

Balachandra Kurup, 1992, "*Socio-cultural Determinants of Child Survival in Two Southern States*". Thesis submitted to Mohanlal Sukhadia University, Udaipur.

Balakrishna, S. 1971. *Family Planning: Knowledge, Attitude and Practice, a Sample Survey in Andhra Pradesh.* National Institute of Community Development, Hyderabad.

Balakrishna Nair, 1987. *Socio-economic Determinants of Differential Fertility in Kerala.* Unpublished thesis. Department of Population Studies, S.V. University. Tirupathi:

Backer Stain, *et al.* 1993. *The Determinants of Use of Maternal and Child Health Services in Metro Cebu,* Philippines. Health Transition Review. Australia: No. 1: 77-90.

Bhatia, Jagdish, C. and John Cleland, 1995. *Determinants of Maternal Care,* Health Transition Review. Australia: 5, No. 2: 127-142.

Bhatia, J.C. and Cleland, J. 1995. *"Determinants of Use of Maternal Care in a Region of South India"*. The Journal of Family Welfare. Bombay: Vol. 5(2): 127-142.

Bhandari, *et al*. 1989: *"Utilization of Child Health Care Services"* Indian Paediatrics. Vol. 26. March. p. 229-241.

Bhuyan, K.C. 1996. *"Differential Fertility Among Adopters and Non-adopter Couples of Differing Social Status and Mobility Pattern in Rural Bangladesh"*. A case study". The Journal of Family Welfare. Bombay: Vol. 41, No. 2. March, 8-12.

Bloom, D.E. and Reddy, P.H. 1986. *"Age Patterns of Women at Marriage, Cohabitation and First Birth in India"*. New Delhi: Nov. 23(4). p. 509-523.

Bongaarts, J. 1987. *"Does Family Planning Reduce Infant Mortality Rate?"*, Population and Development Review. 13:2: 323-334.

Bangaarts and Potter. 1983. *Fertility Biology and Behaviour—an Analysis of the Proximate Determinants.* New York: Academic Press.

Caldwell, J.C. and Donald, p.Mc. 1991. *Influence of Maternal Education on Infant and Child Mortality, Level and Causes in IVSSP* International Conference at Manila. Liege.

Caldwell, J.C. 1979. *Education as a Factor in Mortality Decline an Examination of Nigerian Data*. Population Studies. Liege: 33(3). 395-413.

Carla Mukhalouf Obermeyer and Joseph, E. Potter 1991. *Maternal Health Care Utilisation in Jordan—A Study of Patterns and Determinants.* Studies in Family Planning. New York: 177-185.

Charles. W, Warren, *et al*, 1996. *"Survey of Fisher Folk in Chidambaram District"*. Social welfare. New Delhi: Vol. 43. No. 1. April.

Charles. W. Warren *et al*. 1990. *"Fertility and F.P. in Jordan Results from the 1985 Jordan Husband's Fertility Survey"* Studies in Family Planning. New York: Vol. 21. No. 1. Jan-Feb. 33-39.

Chaudhary Rafiqul Huda. 1979. *"Socio-cultural Factors Affecting Practice of Contraception in a Metropolitan Urban Area of Bangladesh"*. Studies in Family Planning. New York: Vol. 8, 1-2 p. 127-153.64.

Chander Kishore Joshi *et al*. 1996. *Evaluation of MCH Services in Bikaner District*. Vol. 84. No. 1, Jan. Indian Journal of Medical Association. New Delhi.

Chipoma, R.B. 1986. *"Differential Fertility Behaviour and Attitudes of Rural and Urban Dwellers in Zambia"*. Studies in Family Planning. New York: Vol. XXI. April-June. 54-58.

Chuttani and Nayak, 1986. *A Qualitative and Quantitative Assessment of Maternal and Child Health Services at a P.H.C. and Sub-centre*. Indian Journal of Preventive and Social Medicine. Rothak: Issue No. 0907-151. 15-19.

Cynthia, B. Loy. 1991. *The Contribution of the World Fertility Survey to an Understanding of the Relationship Between Women's Work and Fertility*. Vol. 22. No. 3. May/June, 144-159.

Damodar Bachni Singh *et al*. 1993. *"An Analysis of Birth Interval in India'*. The journal of Bio Social Sciences. Vol. 1, 19-23.

Datta Gupta, H. 1994. *Lacunae of Mother and Child Health Services in India*. Indian Journal of Gynaecology and Obstetrics. Bombay: Volume 44. 86-92.

Davanzo, J. 1986. *'Infant Mortality Decline in Malaysia 1946-1975 the Roles of Changes in Variables and Changes in the Structure of Relationships'*. Demography New Delhi: Vol. 23(2). May,. 143-160.

Deepali Das. 1990. *"A Study to Identify and Analyse the Learning Needs of the Mothers Regarding Feeding of their Infants of 0-12 Months Age and to Evaluate the Effect of a Planned Teaching Programme on Infant Feeding to a Rural Community of Assam"*. Unpublished Master of Nursing thesis. Delhi University.

Deodar, N.S. and Srivastava, N.S. 1990. *Health Conditions of Mothers and Children*. Calcutta: All India Institute of Hygiene and Public Health, 60-67.

Devivanayagam *et al*. 1992. *Reasons for Partial Utilization of Child Health Services*. Indian Paediatrics. Volume 29. 1397-48.

De Silva, W.I. 1995. *'Towards Safe Motherhood KAP During the Period of Maternity'*. The Journal of Family Welfare. Bombay: Vol. 41. No. 3. 18-75.

Dhanalakshmi, N. and Murthy, M.S.R. 1989. *Child Survival and Development Strategies*. Paper presented at National seminar on child survival and development strategies (15th-17th March). Department of population studies. S.V. University. Tirupathi:

Driver, E.D. 1963. *Differential Fertility in Cultural India*. Friendton: Princeton. Unipress.

Dyson, Tim and Mick Morre. 1983. *"On Kinship Structure, Female Autonomy and Demographic Behaviour in India"*. Population and Development Review. 9(1).

Epstein, T. Scarlett. 1978: *South India, Yesterday, Today and Tomorrow*. London: The Macmillan Press Limited.

Fernandez, L. 1988. *"A Comparative Study of Knowledge, Beliefs and Practice of Rural and Urban Mothers in Weaning Children Between 3 Months and 14 Months"*. Unpublished Masters' thesis. Delhi University.

Gandhigram researchers. 1991. *"An Evaluation of Immunization of Children Between 12-24 Months and Expectant Mothers in a Rural Area of Tamil Nadu"*. Unpublished study. Affiliated to rural university, Gandhigram.

Goldman, Noreen and Pebley, A.R. 1994. *"Childhood Immunization and Pregnancy Related Services in Guatemala"*. Health Transition Review. Australia: Vol. 4(1). 29-44.

Government of India. 1991, *Family Welfare Programme—Year Book*. 1989-90. New Delhi: Ministry of Health & Family Welfare.

Government of India, 1991, *Health Information India*. Central Bureau of Health Intelligence, Directorate General of Health Services, New Delhi.

Gurumurthy. G. and Prabhakar Rao, E. 1987. *A Study of Socio-cultural and Health Variables in Relation to Child Survival Among ICDS and Non-ICDS in Chittoor District*. Paper presented at Seminar in Department of Population studies, S.V. University. Tirupathi.

Gupta, U. and others. 1996. *"Changing Trends in the Demographic Profile and Attitudes of Female Sterilisation Acceptors"*. The Journal of Family Welfare. Bombay.

Haga, C. John, 1989. *Mechanism for the Association of Maternal Age, Parity and Birth Spacing with Infant Health from Contraceptive use and Controlled Fertility*. Health issue for mother and children. Allan. W. Parneld (ed) 96-139. New Delhi.

Hasalkar, J.B. and Ganiger, S.B. 1990. New Delhi. *Evaluation of Family Welfare and MCH Programme in India*. NIH-IFW.

Health For All by 2000 A.D. 1981, *Report of the Working Group. GOI. Ministry of Health and Family Welfare*. New Delhi.

Hema Nalini B.E. 1989 *'Health Care Practices Related to 'Maternal Care'* M. Phill Thesis submitted to R.A.K. College of Nursing, New Delhi.

Health for All by 2000 A.D. *Problems, Approaches and Challenges*. 1983. New Delhi: GOI, Ministry of Health and Family Welfare.

Houstan, M.J. 1986. *"Breast Feeding, Fertility and Child Health, a Review of International Issues"*. The Journal of Advanced Nursing. Jan. 11(1) 35-40.

I.C.M.R. Bulletin. 1994. *"Contraception During Lactation"*. New Delhi Vol. 24. No. 6-7; June-July.

I.C.M.R. Bulletin. 1995. *Lactation Current Concepts and Concerns*. New Delhi.

India's Family Welfare Programme Towards a Reproductive and Child Health Appraoch (June 23, 1995). Population and Human Resources Operations Division. South Asia country department II (Bhutan, India, Nepal).

International Institute for Population Sciences (IIPS). 1995. *National Family Health Survey*, India, 1992-93 (MCH and F.P.). Bombay.

Irman, T. Elo. 1992. *Utilization of Maternal Health Care Services in Peru*. The Cultural, Social and Behavioural

Determinants of Health. The role of women's education. Health Transition Review. Australia: Volume, 2. No. 1. April 24-29.

James Allman. 1991. *"Fertility and Family Planning in Vietnam."* Studies in Family Planning. New York: Vol. 22. No. 5. Sept/Oct. 308-318.

Jaswal, S. *et al*. 1992 *"Situation Analysis of Antenatal Care Practices in Rural Punjab"*. Indian Journal of Maternal and Child health. New Delhi: 3:1, 16-18.

Jayalakshmi, Y.V. 1996. *Reproductive Health Status of Rural Women, an Empirical Analysis,* M. Phill Thesis submitted to Sri Padmavathi Mahila Viswavidyalayam. Tirupathi.

Jayasree, R. 1989. *Religion, Social Change and Fertility Behaviour*. A study of Kerala. The Journal of Family Welfare. Bombay: Vol. 3, Jan-Mar. 173-176.

Jolly, K.G. 1986. *A District Level Study, F.P. in India*. New Delhi: Hindustan Publishing Corporation.

Kanitkar, Tara and Sinha, R.K. 1989. *"Antenatal Care Services in Five States of India."* Population Transition in India. New Delhi: Vol. 2. B.R. Publishing Corporation, 201-212.

Kanitkar, T. 1979. *Development of Maternal and Child Health Services in India*. Bombay: Himalaya Publishing House. 301-328.

Kasarda, J.D. 1971. *"Economic Structure and Fertility"*, Demography India. New Delhi. Vol. 26, 307-309.

Kavita, N. 1996. *Utilisation of Maternal and Child Health Care Services in Two Villages of Coimbatore District''*. Thesis submitted to department of Population studies. Bharatiyar University, Coimbatore.

Kavitha, N. and Audinarayana. N. 1997. *"Utilisation of Maternal, Child Health Care Services and its Determinants in Rural Areas of Tamil Nadu"*, Paper presented at XX Annual Conference of IASP. Bharatiyar University, Coimbatore.

Kaur and Kaur, 1996. *Breast Feeding Practice in Varanasi District (U.P.)*. Indian Journal of Public Health. Calcutta: Issue No. 0019-557, Vol. XXXX. No. 2. April-June 52.

Kaushal Kishore Siddu. 1986. *"Infant Mortality: A Strategy for Survival"*. The Journal of Family Weflare. Bombay: Vol. 30(5) September, 34.

Kiran Singh and Purnima Srivastava, 1992. *"The Effect of Colostrum of Infant Mortality Rural and Urban Differentials"*. Health and Population perspectives and issues. New Delhi: 15(3&4): 94-100.

Kucera, M. 1985. *Difference in Levels of Fertility.* Studies in Family Planning. New York: Volume 27. 106-114.

Madhunitkar and Ratna De. 1991. *"Breast Feed and Practices"*. The Indian Journal of Public Health. Calcutta: Vol. XXXV. No. 4. Oct-Dec. 1-3.

Mahadevan, K. and Namboothri, D.N. 1972. *Caste and Fertility in Rural Area of Tamil Nadu*. Bulletin of GIRH & F.P. Gandhigram: VII (1).

Mahadevan, K. 1979.: *"Sociology of Fertility, Determinants of Fertility, Differentials in South India"*. New Delhi: Sterling Publishers Private Ltd.

Mahadevan, K. and Sumangala, M. 1984. *"Social Development, Cultural Change and Fertility Decline"*. New Delhi: Sage Publications.

Mahadevan, K. *et al*. 1984. *"Status of Women and Population Dynamics: A Conceptual Model in Momen and Population Dynamics, Perspectives from Asian Countries"*. New Delhi: Sage Publications.

Mahadevan, K. 1985. *"Infant and Childhood Mortality in India.* New Delhi: Mittal Publications.

Mahadevan, K. 1989. *Women and Population Dynamics*. New Delhi: Sage Publications.

Maya Chansoria, R.K. *et al*, 1989. *"A Study of Immunisation Status of Children in a Defined Urban Population"*. Indian Paediatrics. Volume. XII. No. 9. 878-87.

Maya Natu and Others. 1990. *"Immunisation Coverage Assessment Survey of Nasik District"*. Department of Preventive and Social Medicine. B.J. Medical College.

Maya Natu *et al.* 1995. *"KAP Study of Antenatal Services at Sarsoon General Hospital, Poona"*. Indian Journal of Social and Preventive Medicine. Rothak: Vol. 6. 197-199.

Md. Omer Bajkhaif and Murthy, M.S.R. 1987. *"Socio-economic Differentials in Childhood Mortality"*. National study conducted in three states A.P. U.P. and Kerala.

Meera Shekar. *et al.* 1984. *"Health Practices in Relation to Child Health and Infant Care"*. New Delhi: NPCID, 23-60.

Mosley, H. and Chen, L.C. 1984. *"Child Survival Strategies for Research'*. Population and Development Review. **Supplement.** New Delh: 25-45.

Michael. T. Mbizo and Donald. 1991. *"Perceptions and Practices Relating to Condom Use Among Men in Haiti"*. Studies in Family Planning. New York.

Mothers and Children. 1994. *"Women's Health, Promoting Safer Motherhood: A Checklist for Communications and Training"*, Bulletin on Infant Feeding and Maternal Nutrition. New Delhi: Vol. 13. No. ISS No. 272-6917.

Mukhopadhya, J. and Achar. D.P. 1992. *"Infant Feeding Practices Among Educated Mothers in an Air Force Community"*. Health and population perspevtices and issues. New Delhi: Vol. 3 & 4 Jul-Dec. 889-93.

Mukhopadhyay, S.K. and S.P. Mehta, 1984. *"A Morbidity Study in a Rural Area of Delhi"*. Indian Journal of Preventive and Social Medicine. Rothak: Vol. 15, Nov. 3-4. Sept-Dec.

Nagmoni, 1980. *"Modernisation and Its Impact on Fertility, the Indian Scene"*. New York: Population council. U.S.A.

Nagmoni, 1991. *"Sex Preference in Bangladesh, India and Pakistan and its Effect on Fertility"*. Research Division Working Paper, New York: No. 27. Population council.

Nair, P.S.L.V. and Rajaratnam, T. 1988. Dharward. *"Evaluation of F.W. and MCH Programme (1983-86) in Bellary District"*, Karnataka, Population Research Centre.

National Tuberculosis Institute. 1994. *Report on the Base Line Survey Danida-Health Care Project*. Tamil Nadu, Bangalore: 59-82.

Neeraja, K.P. 1992. *A Study to Assess the Utilisation of Immunisation Services Among Under Five Children in a Selected Sugali Tribal Area of Ananthapur District*. The Nursing Journal of India. New Delhi: Vol. 3.

Obermyer, C. and Potter, J.E. 1991. *"Maternal Health Care Utilisation in Jordan: A Case Study of Patterns and Determinants"*. Studies in Family Planning. New York: 22(3). 177-187.

Obermeyer, Carla Mackhlouf. 1993. *"Culture, Maternal Health Care and Women's Status: A Comparison of Morocco and Tunisia"*, Studies in Family Planning. New York: 24(6). 354-365.

Office of the Chief Planning Officer. Mahabubnagar district: 1993-94. *"Hand Book of Statistics"*.

Office of the Chief Planning Officer. Kurnool district. 1993-94. *"Hand Book of Statistics"*.

Office of the Director of Health, A.P., 1993-94. *"Hand Book on Health and Family Welfare Statistics of A.P."* Hyderabad.

Okafor, C.B. 1991. *"Availability and Use of Services for Maternal and Child Health Care in Rural Nigeria"*. Indian Journal of Gynaecology and Obstetrics. Bombay: Vol. 34; 331-346.

Pachouri, S. and Marwah, S.M. 1990: *"Socio-economic Factors in Relation to Birth Weight"*. Indian Paediatrics. Vol. 7. 462.

Pandey, A. and Chakraborthy, A.K. 1996. *"Under Nutrition, Vitamin-A Deficiency and Acute Respiratory Tract Infections Morbidity in Under-fives"*. Indian Journal of Public Health. Calcutta: Vol. XXXX. No. 1. Jan-March. 13-15.

Park, K. and Park, J.E. 1998. *Text Book of Preventive and Social Medicine*. Jabalpur: Banarsidas Bhanot Publishers.

Population Research Centre. and International Institute for Population Sciences. 1995, Bombay: *National Family Health Survey, Andhra Pradesh 1992 (MCH and F.P.)*. PRC Visakhapatnam. IIPS.

Radhakumari, 1997. *A Study on the Impact of Child Survival and Safe Motherhood Programme*. Unpublished Thesis Submitted to S.K. University of Rural Development and Social Work. Anantapur.

Rafiqul Huda Coudhary, 1982. *Social Aspects of Fertility*. New Delhi: B.R. Publishing company.

Rajaratnam, T. 1994. "*Components of Fertility Change in India and in its Major States During 1972-1992*". Studies in Family Planning. New York: Vol. 42 and No. 3. Sept. 61-66.

Rajaratnam, T. 1995, "*Family Size, Desire, Sex Preference, Socio-economic Condition and Contraception use in Rural Karnataka*". Demography India. New Delhi. Vol. 24(2). 270-290.

Rajeswari, V.V. 1987, "*Evaluation of Family Welfare and MCH Programme in Uttar Kannada, Karnataka*. 1985-86. Population Research Centre. Dharwad:

Rajeswari, N.V. and Hasalkar, J.B. 1994. "*Influence of Socio-economic and Demographic Factors on Utilisation of MCH Services in Rural Karnataka*. Dharwad: Population Research Centre.

Rajguru, K.K. 1989. "*Study of Knowledge and Practice of Immunisation in Sample of 1000 Families in Urban and Rural Areas of Ahmedabad city and District During 1988-89*. The Journal of Family Welfare. Bombay: issue No. 11. August.

Raju, K.N.M. 1989. *Family Functions: Dynamics of Households in a Village of Coastal Andhra Pradesh*. Ph.D. Dissertation Australian National University, Canberra.

Raju, K.N.M. *et al*. 1994. *Differential Acceptance of Family Planning Methods in a High Performance District in Karnataka*. The Journal of Family Welfare. Bombay: Vol. 40(2), April. 30.

Rajaratnam, T. and Patil, R.C. 1989. *Evaluation of F.W. and MCH Programme in Bijapur District, Karnataka*, 1986-87. Dharwad: Population Research Centre.

Rao, N.B. and others, 1994. *Karnataka NFHS Survey, 1992-93*, Bombay: IIPS.

Rao, I.S. *et al*. 1995. "*Socio-economic Determinants of F.P. Acceptance in Orissa*. Bombay: Vol. 41. No. 3 Sept. 39-46.

Rao, K.N.K. 1990. *Religion and Intensity in Breeding in Tamil Naidu, South India*. Social Biology. Madras: Vol. 30-413-421.

Ratna Dhar, 1989. *Factors Affecting the Utilisation of Maternity Bed in Selected Hospitals of Delhi*, Ph.D. Thesis Submitted to University of Delhi.

Rao, I.S. *et al.* 1995, *Socio-economic Determinants of Family Planning Acceptance in Orissa.* The Journal of Family Welfare. Bombay: Vol. 41(3), Sept. 39-46.

Ramana Rao, G.V. and Sitarama Rao, Ch. 1994. *A Report on "Coverage and Evaluation Survey in Mahabubnagar District (Rural).* Hyderbad. IIHFW.

Reddy, R. 1984, *"Population Structure and Family Planning in Sugalis—A Tribal Population of A.P.* M. Phil. Dissertation, S.V. University. Tirupathi.

Rele. T.R. and Kanitkar, T 1980. *Fertility and F.P. in Greater Bombay. Population Studies.* Bombay: 28(2). 299-300.

Reproductive and Child Health Project Proposal. 1996. Hyderabad: IIHFW.

Report of Director of Family Welfare. Article Published in The Hindu paper on 20th April, 1997.

Rita Sapru. 1994. *"Appraisal of Maternal, Child Health and Family Planning Services Rendered Through an Urban Centre and Urban Maternity Homes"*. Unpublished M.D. Thesis. University of Delhi.

Ray, N.C. *et al*, 1988, *"Immunisation Knowledge of Acceptors and Practice of Family Planning"*. The Journal of Family Welfare. Bombay: Vol. 35(2): 23-29.

Sai Sujatha, D. and Murthy, M.S.R. 1993. *"The Journal of Family Welfare"*, Bombay: Vol. 39. No. 1. 13-17.

Sai Sujatha, D. 1991. *Socio-cultural Determinants of Fertility Among Brahmins,* Unpublished Ph.D. Thesis Submitted to S.V. University. Tirupathi.

Sai Sujatha and Murthy. M.S.R. 1993. *Husband-wife Communication and Fertility Among Two Sections of Brahmins.* The Journal of Family Welfare. Bombay: Vol. 39(4) Dec. 27-30.

Sai Sujatha, D. and Murthy, M.S.R. 1993. *Interspouse Communication and Fertility Behaviour.* The Journal of Family Welfare. Bombay: Vol. 43(1), May 13-17.

Sahu and Others. 1989: *Immunization of Children Below Five Years in Defined Rural Population*. Indian Journal of Paediatrics. Volume 41. No. 2.421-246.

Sandhya Rao and Bilia, C. Patel 1994. *Utilisation of Health Services*. The Nursing Journal of India. New Delhi: Issue No. 019-214. November. Page 14-17.

Sarkar, B.N. 1990. *Family Welfare Planning Among Pregnancy Females Based on Calcutta Fertility Survey, Calcutta*. Indian Statistical Institute Research and Training School 68.

Satishkumar *et al*. 1990. *"Follow up Assessment of Maternal and Child Health Care in Chiraigaon Block"* (Varanasi). Indian Journal of Social and Preventive Medicine. Rothak: 11:1 (March, 31-36).

Scultz, T.P. 1994. *Fertility Determinants: A Theory, Evidence and an Application to Policy Evaluation in Rand*.

Sharma, M.L. 1986. *Child Morbidity and Mortality in Rural Community*. Journal of Social Welfare. New Delhi: 23(4). 4-5.

Sharma, S. *et al* 1992. *"Evaluation of Maternal Care Services in a Semi-urban Community of Pondicherry"*. Health and Population Perspectives and Issues. New Delhi: July-Sept. 259-265.

Shrivastav, J.B. 1975. *Health Services and Medical Education—a Programme for Immediate Action*. New Delhi: Allied Publishers (Pvt.) Ltd.

Sharma *et al* 1987.: *"Health Status of Women in Rural Karnataka"* Indian Paediatrics Vol. 41. No. 127.

Sharma, S. *et al* 1995. Swasth Hind. *Family Welfare Programme in India, a close look*. New Delhi: 132-137.

Shah, K.P. and Shah, P.M. 1992. *"Relationship of Weight During Pregnancy and Low Birth Weight"*. Indian Paediatrics. 526-528.

Sivakami, M. and Kulkarni, P.M. 1998—*Rural-urban Differences in Levels and Determinants of Antenatal and Delivery Care in Tamil Nadu: An Analysis of NFHS Data*. Paper presented at the International Conference on Population issues on the eve of 21st

Century and XXI Annual Conference on IASP held at BHU, Varanasi; Feb. 9-12.

Sudha, C. Patel, 1993. *"Maternal and Child Health Services Rendered by the Primary Health Centre,* Bavla in Gujarat. Unpublished Masters' thesis. University of Delhi.

Somayajulu. U.V. 1992. *"Child Survival and Family Planning"*. The Journal of Family Welfare. Bombay: Vol. 32. No. 4. 146.

Somnath Roy *et al.* 1987. *"Management Training Modules for Medical Officer"*. NIHFW. New Delhi: 16-78.

Sivaraju, S. 1987. *Husband-wife Communication and Contraceptive Behaviour*. The Journal of Family Welfare. Bombay; Vol 33(4). 44-48.

Singh, C.M. Badole and Singh, M.P. 1994. *"Immunisation Coverage and the Knowledge and Practice of Mothers Regarding Immunisation in Rural Area"*. Indian Journal of Public Health. Calcutta: Vol. XXXVIII. No. 3.

Singhania, U.R. and others 1990. *"Infant Feeding Practices in Educated Mothers from Upper Socio-economic Status"*. Indian Paediatrics. 27, June, 591-593.

Sreenivasa Reddy, K. 1997. *"Health Care Services for Maternal Child Health Through Primary Health Centre an Innovative Approach"*. Health population perspective and issues. New Delhi: July-Sept.

Sreenivasa Reddy, K. 1998. *"Determinants of Differential Fertility Behaviour in Two Districts of Andhra Pradesh.* Ph.D. thesis submitted to Department of Population studies at S.V. University, Tirupathi.

Srinivas, M.N. 1986. *"The Changing Position of Indian Women"*. New Delhi: Oxford Uni. Press.

Sreevastava, J.N. and Saxena. D.N. 1990 *"Immunisation of Children and its Correlates in Rural Uttar Pradesh"*. The Journal of Family Welfare. Bombay; Vol. 35(1). 22-28.

Swarnalatha. 1992. *"The Contribution of the World Fertility Surveys to an Understanding of the Relationship Between Womens'*

Work and Fertility". Studies in Family Planning. New York: Vol. 22. No. 3 May/June. p. 144-159.

Syamala. T.S. and Roy. T.K. 1994. *A Few Empirical Evidences from Goa,* India Demography India. New Delhi: Vol. 23 (1 & 2) 117-126.

Swing, P. and Swain, P. 1992. *Evaluation of Field Immunisation Programme in an Urban.* Indian Journal of Preventive and Social Medicine. Rothak: Vol. 17(2). 52-55.

Taluja, R.K. *et al.* 1995.: *"A Study of Immunisation Status of Children in a Defined Urban Population"*. Indian Paediatrics. 12:9. 879-888.

Talwar, P.P. and Bhatia *et al* 1985. *Demographic Situation and Utilisation of Health Services in Rajasthan a Baseline Survey.* NIHFW. New Delhi: 82-90.

Talwar, P.P. *et al* 1990. *Demographic Situation and Utilisation of Health and Family Welfare Services in Madhya Pradesh.* NIHFW. New Delhi: p. 132-155.

Teresa Castro Martin. 1995. *"Women's Education and Fertility: Results from 26 Demographic and Health Surveys.* Studies in Family Planning. New York: July/Aug. p. 187-202.

UNICEF, 1990. *Immunizing More Children.* New Delhi: Unicef House.

Usha *et al.* 1990, *Utilisation of Maternal and Child Health Services. Mother and Children.* New Delhi: Volume 2. No. 4, 12 and 13.

Vijayalakshmi Groover. 1994. *"Primary Health Care Needs and Utilisation Pattern of Health and Medical Care Facilities in a Selected Slum of New Delhi"*. Unpublished M.D. Thesis University of Delhi.

Vijayakumar, S. and Chakrapani, C. 1995. *"Availability, Accessibility and Utilisation of Rural Health Services"*. The Journal of Family Welfare. Bombay: Vol. 41, No. 3. Sept. 53-60.

Viswanathan, J. Desai. B. Avalavita. 1996, *Text Book of Paediatrics, 3rd Edition* Madras: Orient Longman.

Vimala, V. and Ratnaprabha, C. 1986. *Infant Feeding Practices Among Tribal Communities of Andhra Pradesh"*. Indian Paediatrics. 24 October, 907-910.

Yadav, N.K. and others. 1984. *Characteristics of Female Sterilization Acceptors*. Indian Journal of Preventive and Social Medicine. Rothak: Volume 15, No. 1-2, March-June, 35-37.

Yesudian, C.A.K. 1991. *Differential Utilisation of Health Services in a Metropolitan City*. The Indian Journal of Social Work. New Delhi: 6:4 January. 381-392.

W.H.O. 1985. New Delhi: *Health Manpower Requirements for the Achievement of Health For All by the Year 2000 Through Primary Health Care:* Geneva Technical report series in W.H.O. Division of Family Welfare.

Index